FORTRESS PRESS
PHILADELPHIA

DIRT
GREED
and
SEX

SEXUAL ETHICS IN THE NEW TESTAMENT
AND THEIR IMPLICATIONS FOR TODAY

L. WILLIAM COUNTRYMAN

First paperback edition 1990

Library of Congress Cataloging-in-Publication Data

Countryman, L. William.
  Dirt, greed, and sex.

  Bibliography: p.
  1. Sex in the Bible.   2. Sexual ethics—History.
3. Sex customs—History.   4. Bible.   N.T.—Criticism,
interpretation, etc.   I. Title.
BS2545.S36C68   1988   241.66'09015   88-45235
ISBN 0-8006-0887-9 (cloth)
ISBN 0-8006-2476-9 (paper)

Printed in the United States of America 1-2476

94   93   92   91   2   3   4   5   6   7   8   9   10

For GHM

Contents

vii

Preface

It was very far from my mind to write a book on sexual ethics until the autumn of 1985, when I was asked to give some lectures on the topic. It has been, of course, very much in the air for some time both in the churches and among the larger public, and one frequently hears claims that the Bible says this or that about sexual ethics. I had reason to suspect that some of those claims needed reexamining, for I had begun to wrestle in my own mind with the question of early Christian attitudes toward sexual property a good many years ago, largely as a result of my study of the rich in early Christianity. I had also begun to include discussion of New Testament teachings on sex in my courses, but I did not immediately recognize that the various insights I had garnered actually formed a coherent picture.

The picture that emerged was of a twofold sexual ethic inherited and transformed by the New Testament authors. One part of it was a property ethic; its cardinal sin was greed, leading one to trespass on one's neighbor's property. The other part was a purity ethic, against which the fundamental offense was—well, it is difficult to say in modern English. We are accustomed to refer to it in academic language as "impurity" or "uncleanness." Yet, these terms, indispensable as they are, have an air of academic remoteness about them; they do not convey a sense of the visceral impact, the repugnance felt toward those things a given society has defined as "dirty." Hence, I have written somewhat indiscriminately here of "impurity," "uncleanness," and "dirt"—varying manifestations of the same phenomenon. Modern American definitions of what is "dirty" lack the precision or coherence of those still to be found in

Leviticus, but only by using the common term can we form some impression—even a pallid one—of the emotional force of ancient purity codes.

The present book owes a great deal to the opportunity I was given of putting my reflections in order when I was asked to lecture on the subject, first to the college chaplains of Province VIII (the Pacific province) of the Episcopal Church at San Francisco in January, 1986, and then to the national convention of Integrity, in Minneapolis in the following summer. Thanks to a sabbatical leave from the Church Divinity School of the Pacific, I was able to devote the fall semester of 1986 to writing the first draft of this book. I owe great thanks to the school and its trustees for that opportunity. I owe thanks also to all those in Austin, Texas, who made me welcome there during that time, including the rector and people of All Saints parish and the faculty and staff of the Episcopal Theological Seminary of the Southwest, particularly those connected with its library and the library of Christ Seminary Seminex, sojourning there. Without the encouragement and support of these groups, I could not have proceeded so rapidly to completion of this project.

I also owe a great debt of thanks to the friends and colleagues who read all or parts of the manuscript and whose critiques have improved it substantially: Linda Clader, Howard Miller, Donn Morgan, Paul Strid, and Penelope Warren. Their varied expertise and careful reading have saved me from pitfalls I was unprepared to see and, I hope, ensured that the book will be intelligible to an audience including but spreading beyond the New Testament scholarly community. I must also thank John A. Hollar of Fortress Press and those who read portions of the manuscript for the press, Jacob Neusner as well as the other, anonymous readers. They all gave both encouragement and many helpful suggestions about clarifying the book's scope and argument. Finally, I owe an incalculable debt to many partners in dialogue over the years whom I could not even begin to name, who have challenged me to explore and clarify the matters discussed here. Needless to say, only I can be held responsible for whatever faults the reader may still find in my treatment of the subject. My responsibility extends to the translations of biblical texts, as well, which are my own except where otherwise indicated.

My great goal throughout has been to present a faithful reading of the pertinent biblical texts, even if that should at times prove uncongenial to one or another group today—or quite different from what I myself expected. If I have succeeded in that, I believe that I shall have offered a useful addition to the ongoing discussion of sexual ethics in our time. If not, I trust that I shall at least have stimulated the kind of careful and dispassionate study by others that will carry the investigation further.

L. WILLIAM COUNTRYMAN

The Church Divinity School of the Pacific
  Graduate Theological Union
  Berkeley, California
12th Sunday after Pentecost, 1987

Introduction

Controversies over sexual ethics have pervaded the Western world in our century, and the Bible has been an important factor in them. Some voices invoke its authority; others attack it as a baleful influence. Some hold that it lays down a clear-cut sexual ethic; others hear in it a multiplicity of messages not always in agreement with one another. Whichever may ultimately be right, we have at least learned that interpreters of Scripture do not all agree with one another and that people can invoke the Bible on behalf of a variety of contemporary ethical positions. Such a situation calls for fresh and careful reading of the Scriptures. We should read afresh, in the sense of not assuming that the Bible has to agree with our presuppositions. We should read carefully, in the sense of attending closely to the details of the text, particularly those that seem odd or alien to our way of thinking.

This volume arises out of an ongoing endeavor to read in these ways. I began looking at the biblical texts on this subject with several quite definite presuppositions. One was a presupposition that the New Testament authors regarded the whole subject as peripheral and would therefore be unlikely to share with one another any coherent ethical stance. I expected to find no more than scattered and independent moral pronouncements on sexual issues. Another presupposition of mine was that the biblical authors as a whole were negative toward sex and regarded it as something to be avoided in general and indulged, reluctantly, only under narrowly defined circumstances. In both cases, I have found that close study of these texts has modified my understanding of the matter sharply and in directions that I could not have predicted.

Two things, I think, have been particularly responsible for this outcome. The first was that I made every effort to read the texts as literally as possible. If a text seemed to be expressing a familiar idea in a clumsy or awkward way, I began to consider whether the awkwardness might really be the result of misinterpretation, whether the text were not in fact expressing some rather different idea which only attention to the precise language could reveal. In many cases, this process forced me to reevaluate familiar passages in unfamiliar ways. The second was that, in studying a variety of texts from different biblical authors, I found a certain commonality of language, presuppositions, and concerns emerging among them that was significantly different from those which frame our own modern discussions of these same topics. The result is a book in which I hope not only to direct attention to neglected features of individual texts, but also to place the whole topic in a different historical, religious, and cultural context and thereby shed an unexpected light on the materials.

What I write here is in the tradition of biblical theology; and since this imposes a certain character, with accompanying limitations, on the book, it seems wise to say a few words in explanation. To begin, let me distinguish it from systematic and dogmatic theology. Systematic theology begins with issues and questions contemporary with the theologian and justifies its answers in terms of the theologian's philosophical presuppositions as well as by their continuity with the Christian tradition. Dogmatic theology begins with various schemata of Christian orthodoxy enunciated from the second century on up through the Reformation and, though it is far from indifferent to philosophical issues, tends to claim authenticity from its coherence with those authoritative statements. Biblical theology, on the other hand, begins with the biblical texts themselves, before the clarification of Christian dogma that began with the Gnostic controversies of the second century and apart from questions of philosophical coherence that later became so dominant. It seeks rather to understand how the biblical authors expressed themselves in terms of the ongoing religious tradition in which they lived and worked. If we understand this, we shall also begin to understand something of what their utterances meant in terms of their own time. Biblical theology thus differs from systematics and dogmatics in seeking not a final answer to theological questions, but rather the historical foundations of theological discourse.[1]

This is not a purely historical exercise, however, either in terms of its method and scope or in terms of its implications. A purely historical method would be equally interested in all possible influences on the biblical authors and in the complete story of the development of their ideas. The influence of Greco-Roman philosophy, for example, has become an important area of research for those studying New Testament ethics in a more strictly historical vein.[2] Or again, ever since the late eighteenth century, one of the great historical projects in New Testament studies has been to reconstruct the life and teachings of the historical Jesus on the basis of the fragmentary and sometimes conflicting records available to us in the Gospels and elsewhere. Biblical theology, however, as I understand it, deals with the biblical writings themselves and the ways in which their authors have expressed, taken up, responded to, and developed the religious tradition of Israel. Other historical questions and inquiries are often pertinent in studying these topics, but they are not part of the central, focal business of biblical theology. This book, accordingly, concentrates on the ways in which the New Testament authors, in their ancient Jewish context, have responded to and developed the themes of sexual ethics that we find witnessed in the Sriptures of Israel.[3]

If biblical theology is, in a sense, narrower than history in its scope and method, it may be broader than history in its implications. It is a function of history to show us the "differentness and irretrievability of the past."[4] This in itself is a worthy goal in the degree that it frees us from the tendency to impose our limited perceptions of reality on other

1. See the brief but lucid remarks of Houlden (*Ethics and the New Testament,* 1–24). For a recent, detailed exploration of the issues involved in bringing New Testament texts into modern ethical discussions, see Verhey, *Great Reversal,* 153–97.

2. I am convinced that Hellenistic philosophy contributed not principles but only details to New Testament sexual ethics. This is not to deny its historical importance or to exclude from consideration whatever derives from it, but to reaffirm that earliest Christian theology is primarily a development of the religion of Israel. Compare Malherbe's observation ("Paul: Hellenistic Philosopher or Christian Pastor?" 3–13) that Paul shows its influence more in the manner of his ministry than in the central issues of his thinking.

3. For a specifically historical approach to the issues of ethics in the New Testament, see Meeks, "Understanding Early Christian Ethics," 3–11, or at greater length, idem, *The Moral World of the First Christians.* I see Meeks's concern for "social world" as pertinent to biblical theology, as I trust the following pages will show.

4. I owe the phrase to Howard Miller of the University of Texas at Austin.

people, places, and times. Biblical theology, however, has the further goal of showing how the inevitably alien past that is canonized in the Bible breaks our present open and directs us to new opportunities of faithfulness in the future.[5] This means, I believe, that the task of the biblical theologian is not done when one has simply elucidated the world of the biblical texts and thereby called attention to its distance from our own. It is also important to offer some reflections on what the Scriptures imply for human life in the present and future.

This is not to say that biblical theologians can settle such issues on their own. Immediate, practical authority for Christian life and belief is located in the ongoing Christian community rather than the Bible.[6] What biblical theology offers is a questioning, even disruptive, intervention in the self-assurance of the present so as to call Christians to new faithfulness and new understanding of what faithfulness means. While biblical theology does not predetermine the results of the church's resulting reflection, it makes an important contribution by identifying the principles which the biblical authors have assumed and by describing the distance between their world and the present. The final chapter of this book is my own effort to contribute some insights drawn from my theological study, in the expectation that they can be useful in an ensuing, more extensive conversation on Christian sexual ethics that must draw in people of the most varied experience and expertise.

The main body of the book is divided into two parts, one on purity ethic, the other on property ethic. My study of the New Testament has convinced me that all the significant texts dealing with sexual morality are expressions of these two principles. Each part begins with discussion of the nature of the ethic in question and its use in the Scriptures of Israel. The remaining chapters then trace the New Testament writers' treatment of the ethical principle in relation to sexual issues. Here I have followed, for the most part, the familiar canonical order of Gospels—Paul—other writings. My choice of this order (over, for example, one based on the relative age of the New Testament documents) arises from a conviction that the traditions about Jesus and his teaching were the major source and venue for theological reflection in earliest Christianity and that other authors are best understood in their context.

5. This, I have suggested, is the principal importance of the authority of the Bible for Christians. See my *Biblical Authority,* 70–75.
6. Ibid., 54–58.

The readers of this book, I suspect, will come to it with varied backgrounds. The book itself aims to be a scholarly presentation of a new way of understanding the sexual ethics of biblical, particularly New Testament writers. The normal course of events in biblical scholarship is that such ideas should first be threshed out and criticized by experts and only then be presented in a form more accessible to nonspecialist readers—whether those who, like the seminary-educated, have some background in biblical scholarship or those who may have little or no formal preparation. In view of the widespread public interest in the topic of the present work, however, I have sought to write in a way intelligible to educated readers generally and to confine topics of more specialized concern to the notes. The nonspecialist reader will still have to reckon, however, with the fact that the book involves close reading of biblical texts and that it could not make its points in any other way. I assume that the reader who is not already familiar with the texts in question will read this book with a Bible translation at hand—preferably a relatively literal translation such as the Revised Standard Version.

There will be a temptation, I realize, for the nonspecialist reader to jump to the last chapter—perhaps before reading this paragraph! If you have persevered this far, I urge you to continue. The final chapter is in no way intended to stand on its own. Indeed, it may seem bizarre to the reader who has not absorbed the argument about New Testament sexual ethics on which it is based. I trust that the interpretive work set forth in the intervening chapters will make the recommendations of the final chapter intelligible as a serious extrapolation of my reading of the New Testament itself.

Finally, it should prove helpful to all readers for me to clarify here the way I am using two key elements in the vocabulary of this book—the terms "morality" and "ethics" and their related adjectives. By "morality" (or "morals" or "mores"), I mean "important norms of behavior accepted in a given community, society, or culture." They tell a person how to behave in order to be thought a respectable and worthy person in that community. These rules may be of a miscellaneous character; they are authoritative not so much because they express any particular principle as because they are accepted custom. They are likely to vary widely from culture to culture: for example, in one society it is perfectly moral for a woman to have several husbands and she would never be criticized for it, while in another it would be proof of depravity.

By "ethics," I mean a systematic presentation of morals, either the actual morals of a particular society or an idealized set of morals, showing their internal coherence. Whereas morals are a set of rules, ethics involve principles which explain why these rules are valid, even beyond or apart from the fact that a given society prescribes them. If one particular set of morals is closely tied together by their dependence on a single principle, one can speak of them as an "ethic"; for example, a purity ethic is a set of rules, all of which depend on and express the principle of purity. Other important ethical principles include justice, love, equality, property, privacy. A justice ethic would not necessarily give rise to the same moral rules as a purity ethic or a love ethic.

An illustration may help make the basic terms clearer: Suppose that a certain family in going to the grocery always spends an exceptionally large percentage of its food budget on fresh produce and would feel that it had done something irregular or unsettling if it did the same on meat. This is a "morality," a rule to which the society (in this case, the family) feels itself committed. There might be several possible "ethics" which would explain or ground this morality. The family might, for example, be vegetarian; and an ethic of meat avoidance (which in turn might be the expression of various other ethical principles such as concern for the poor or for our planetary ecology or reverence for life) would here find expression in its purchasing morality. On the other hand, if the family lives in an area where produce is plentiful and cheap, its moral rule might be an expression of convictions about responsible use of income—an ethic concerned with stewardship of funds. There are other possibilities, too, of course, but these may suffice for illustration.

The moral rule by itself is not self-explanatory, since the same action can arise from diverse ethics. On the other hand, the phrasing of a moral rule will often reveal the ethical principle on which it is based; and the associations of moral rules with one another or the ways in which we change them in new circumstances will often do the same. Our vegetarian family, for example, will probably also have a moral rule against eating fast-food hamburgers, whereas the other family may seek them out as an inexpensive way to eat away from home. Again, if our vegetarian family were to move to a region where produce is expensive, its ethic would demand that it increase its food budget rather than buy meat, while the other family might eat more meat instead. Possibly we could have identified the vegetarian family even before its move; it would tend to express its moral rule by saying, "We don't *eat* meat." The other family would tend to say, "We don't *buy* meat."

In studying the biblical documents, we shall often find that we are dealing with morality, with what is permitted or forbidden; the biblical authors, like all people, conducted most of the business of ethics on the level of moral rules. But we must also ask of these texts, "Why?" The why is critical, for it alone will enable us to understand the precise language of the texts, to perceive the reasons for changes in biblical morality, and to interpret the sexual ethics of the New Testament in terms that will have comparable meaning in our own very different world. We shall be looking for this ethical "why" in the specific language in which moral rules are expressed, in the organization or grouping of moral rules, and in the variability of these rules within the Bible itself.

1

DIRT
Greed
Sex

1   What Is Purity?

One dominant theme in biblical treatments of sexual morality is that of purity. Purity means avoidance of dirt; and this avoidance shapes much popular morality, in our own and other cultures. In particular, all rules that govern the boundaries of the human body tend at least to be *presented* as purity rules. Everything that touches us carries with it the potential of rendering us dirty, and societies are concerned, in varying degrees, to keep dirt at bay. All regulations dealing with human sexual activity, then, are related to purity ethics, since they deal with the body's boundaries. Not all originate, however, from that source. As we shall see, some sexual rules are simply and solely purity rules while others, even if they are sometimes presented as purity rules, have other rationales as well. To take an example from our own culture, we are likely to feel revulsion toward rape as dirty, but our more serious objection to it is that it violates its victim's freedom.

I begin this book with an examination of the principle of purity, precisely because it is so pervasive, both in the biblical world and in our own, and because its particular affinity for sexual rules tends to mislead us in our reading of other aspects of sexual ethics. Problems arise from the fact that our society teaches us its purity rules at such an early age that we tend to regard them, ever after, as self-evident. We may have learned all sexual morality in childhood as a distinction between clean and dirty; and, as a result, we are only half-aware that there are other ethical principles, such as respect for persons, at work. Moreover, since we see the sexual morals of our society as self-evident, those of other societies are apt to seem bizarre and inexplicable to us where they do not correspond with our own. To some degree, that will be because different societies do not identify clean and dirty in the same way. Thus, it is important to begin by identifying the purity aspects of sexual ethics, partly for their intrinsic importance and partly, too, as a necessary first step in disentangling purity from other ethical principles that have been at work.

It may come as a surprise to some readers to hear that modern Western society has purity rules. We are more apt to think of them as an anthropological category or as a concern of specific religious groups such as orthodox Jews or Hindus. While our society does not, in fact, have a highly sophisticated, coherent, or articulated system of purity rules, nor does it display a particularly high level of anxiety about purity issues (at least, not on a sustained basis), it does inculcate in its children a sense of what is dirty. This is in part a matter of rational hygiene, as when children are warned against putting coins in their mouths; it is also, in part, something quite different, as when children are warned not to masturbate, even though it has long been recognized that this is not harmful to health, physical or emotional. What is this "dirt" which children are told to avoid but which is neither literal dirt nor anything threatening to health? Since anthropologists are used to examining such questions in a cross-cultural way, an anthropologist is probably the best person to help us gain perspective on it in our own culture. Such help is necessary, since it is of the nature of dirt in any culture that we do not ask what makes it dirty. We simply know what is dirty and what is not, having learned it so early in life that we were not yet asking the question "Why?" In other words, we have no perspective or objectivity in relation to it; we cannot readily get back from it far enough to see what it is.

Mary Douglas, the cultural anthropologist, has argued that dirt can be understood only in relation to a system that excludes it. "As we know it," she says, "dirt is essentially disorder"; and she also invokes "the old definition of dirt as matter out of place."[1] We might add (what is implied in Douglas's treatment of the matter) that dirt is matter out of place in relation to human beings. We do not care whether animals behave in ways that are clean or unclean except insofar as they subsequently come into touch with human beings. A system that divides clean from dirty is a way of understanding and defining what it is to be human—or, more

---

1. Douglas, *Purity and Danger*, 2, 35.

specifically, what it is to belong to a particular human group that so defines purity. Purity is thus a system with the human being at or near its center. Dirt is what lies outside the system, what is perceived as not belonging in association with people of this particular society, whether as unfamiliar, irregular, unhealthy, or otherwise objectionable.

The enormous differences in purity systems from one culture to another show that humanity does not automatically attach the labels "clean" and "dirty" to the same objects or actions. What is clean in one culture is dirty in another, for instance, pork (Lev. 11:7). This is not merely a matter of greater fastidiousness on the part of the culture that forbids pork; it may well accept other foods (e.g., grasshoppers, Lev. 11:22) that some pork-eating cultures would reject. What is consistent from one culture to another is that purity rules relate to the boundaries of the human body, especially to its orifices. This means that whatever passes these boundaries has particular importance for purity law: foods, waste products, shed blood, menstrual blood, sexual emissions, sexual acts, birth, death. On these topics purity rules issue their directives, but always in terms dictated by the specific system accepted in the local culture and by the history of its development.

Every culture's purity law must be understood as expressing the culture's uniqueness as well as our common human interest in purity.[2] Modern Western prejudices will not be a useful key to understanding the purity rules of ancient Israel, any more than they would be with those of Hinduism or of the Zuni people. This means that we should become aware, in a preliminary way, of some of the main outlines of purity as manifest in modern Western culture and also of the ways in which our use of purity differs from that of ancient Israel.

It is difficult to give any coherent account of purity in the modern West for a variety of reasons. Purity is no longer of the highest importance in our culture. It is subsumed under a variety of headings, such as hygiene and aesthetics, instead of being wholly an aspect of religion. In those societies such as the United States which are made up of immigrant groups, there is no single tradition in the matter; and there is substantial variation along class lines as well. Perhaps it is easiest to see our purity rules at work in connection with food. "Dirt is matter out of place." Thus, the coffee in the cup is clean, but the pair of pants I just spilled it on is dirty. The very young child has no sense of food on clothes

2. Ibid., 76–93.

as constituting dirt; it is something learned. Even if the rule is never expressed to the child verbally, it becomes available through other channels, particularly the observed example of others.

Our distinctions between clean and unclean foods are handed on in a similar way, through direct instruction, through example—and also through a kind of negative example which suggests that what is unknown in our particular cultural setting is in fact unacceptable in it. Most Americans, for example, grow up without encountering snails as an item of human food and are apt to feel some repugnance toward them on first encounter. New food items, unless they are easily approximated to familiar ones, are likely to evoke some discomfort, and the act of eating unusual cuisine for the first time is often, for Americans, a kind of door into adult sophistication. What changes, however, is our list of clean and unclean foods, not the fact of making such a distinction. Those who have passed the threshold represented by their first serving of escargot will probably still gag at the thought of eating that snail's near relative, the garden slug. This is not an issue of abstract edibility, for no one in fact inquires whether slugs might or might not be edible. It is a revulsion dictated by our scarcely conscious laws of clean and unclean foods.[3]

On the other hand, what is clean is apt to seem as self-evident to the average American as what is dirty, perhaps partly as a result of our living in a society of such vast geographic extent that we may seldom encounter radically different codes of food purity. The Gentile American who is repelled by the notion of eating dogs or cats or slugs considers it bizarre that orthodox Jews will not eat pork or lobster. As a result, when such a person reads the dietary laws of Leviticus, these laws are likely to appear pointless and inexplicable, though they are simply food taboos like ours and, for that matter, a good deal more coherent and reasoned than the ones commonly accepted in the United States.[4]

The relative lack of coherence in Western culture's treatment of purity also entails that food purity seems to us unrelated to other kinds of purity. Although slugs and pornography can both be described as "dirty," we don't at first think of the two judgments as belonging to the

3. The California town of Monte Rio, to be sure, is reported to host an annual slug recipe contest, complete with tastings; but it appears that the outrageousness of the exercise is also its point.

4. By "reasoned" here, I do not mean that they are based on health concerns as has sometimes been claimed, but simply that they have been carefully thought through and their consistency ensured.

same world of discourse. Other areas of purity law (e.g., birth, death, and menstruation) are less clearly articulated than food and sex, leaving us without a coherent, overall purity system. Of the two areas where rules are fairly well articulated, we consign food to the purely secular realm and sex, often, to a moral or religious one. In the process, we lose sight of the fundamental relationship among all areas of purity which is manifest in other cultures, including that of ancient Israel.

In the area of sexual activity, American purity law is a powerful force; yet it is, if anything, more fragmented than in the matter of foods. Common observation has it that American society became much more tolerant of sexual activity during the 1960s and 1970s and that it has turned in a more puritan direction in the present decade. Throughout the period since the 1950s, of course, various groups have differed sharply on exactly these issues. Perhaps the most important shift that has taken place is the transition from relative unanimity in the culture to the prevailing multiplicity of voices.

The strong emphasis on sexual purity which characterized the churches' address to the young in the 1950s was highly restrictive. Almost no physical contact between the sexes was approved. Sexual purity allowed physical intimacy within marriage, culminating in vaginal intercourse. Young couples who were engaged might be allowed some forms of physical contact short of such intercourse, but the more conservative teachers might forbid even kissing to any who were not yet engaged. All actual intercourse outside marriage was condemned, as were all nonvaginal forms of intercourse, even within marriage. This purity code was not just that of the churches in the United States of the 1950s; it was the officially acknowledged code of the society as a whole, however much it may have been ignored in practice.

The change in American sexual codes in the last two and a half decades has been the result of many factors: a change in intellectual leadership, where the churches lost ground; a change in popular culture, which was permanently altered by the era of the "flower children"; a change in women's control of their fertility with the invention of more reliable methods of birth control; the rise of movements demanding equality for women and for gay and lesbian people; the increasing respect for the diversity of ethnic traditions; and perhaps most important, a vast demographic change which greatly accelerated the individualization of American society as manifest in the large numbers of "singles" who are now so decisive a part of every American city. One result is that the code of sexual purity has also become individualized. There is a widespread sense at present that everyone has the right to an individual opinion in the matter, provided that no clear harm is done to another person.[5] As in the matter of food, however, this is not so much an abolition of purity considerations as a change in the way that they are expressed. Instead of standards universal to the entire nation, there is the assumption that everyone has to identify personal limits.

Purity codes are very much alive among us, and some groups advocate national acceptance of their particular codes. When one compares the 1980s, however, with the 1950s, one of the remarkable differences is the number of states and cities which have decided that it is not appropriate for them to try to "legislate morality." (That, at least, is the common expression; "legislate purity" would be more in accord with the language of the present study.) This is most evident in the legal treatment of homosexuality, perhaps the greatest purity bugbear of the 1950s. There has been increasing reluctance to impose a single purity code on the community, but not because the legislators in question or other backers of particular legislation regard homosexual acts as "pure" or entirely acceptable. Most such people are undoubtedly heterosexual and many of them are church people who may even regard homosexual acts as sinful (presumably because impure) but do not wish to deny civil rights to homosexual persons. What is new here is a sense that the whole issue of purity does not deserve a major expenditure of public attention.

The shift in American society from a single code of sexual purity to a sense that such purity is a matter for individuals to determine exemplifies yet another important aspect of purity. Mary Douglas has suggested that purity systems function in society by making of the human body a kind of symbol for the society in which the person lives, with body boundaries standing for social boundaries.[6] Since the Second World War, American society has undergone an enormous opening up to the larger world, not only through increased world travel, both to and

5. The appearance of AIDS has rendered the issue of sexual morality newly critical. It does not appear to me, as of this writing, that most people interpret it as calling for an ethic as confining as that of the 1950s. AIDS itself, however, has evoked a deep and irrational purity reaction in many people, who have convinced themselves, despite good evidence to the contrary, that they can catch the disease by casual association and who therefore seek to shun even those who they imagine might be infected. For a preliminary assessment of theological and ethical issues, see my article "The AIDS Crisis."

6. Douglas, *Purity and Danger*, 114–15.

from the United States, but also through increasing internal mobility and urbanization. Moreover, the United States has become the principal world power, without serious rival except the Soviet Union, thus forcing upon its people a greatly enlarged worldview. This new reality was greeted in the 1950s with a kind of siege mentality, intensely concerned with boundaries. The counterpart of such a mentality in the area of purity is an intense stress on avoidance of dirt, such as was manifest in the anxiety about sexuality of the 1950s.

The new reality could not be permanently denied, however, and the succeeding decades were open both to the world and to dirt in a degree that could only be astounding to anyone who lived through the 1950s. Even the militant resistance to the Vietnam War was scarcely a rejection of the new world reality, but rather an amazingly confident popular participation in it in a way that sought to bypass the existing leadership. A generation which resisted the imposition and defense of artificial boundaries in politics would hardly be friendly toward them in the realm of bodily purity.

The current American situation is in flux and cannot be read as yet with any confidence. There are signs that some segments of the society would like to restore a stricter kind of purity code. Even on the religious Right, however, there are also signs—in the form of marital manuals emphasizing the pleasures of sex—that the purity code is not to be restored in exactly the form of the 1950s, when sexual pleasure was deemed virtually unmentionable. In the population at large, the substantial percentage of adults who are single, whether as never married or as widowed or divorced, means that it would be hard to revive a purity code that forbids all sexual activity outside marriage. Finally, women in general and gay and lesbian people will presumably not surrender their new freedoms easily.

In any case, it would be a mistake to imagine a society totally dedicated to purity, whatever its definition, for purity is never an unambiguous value. If the purity code is a manifestation of order and coherence, the dirt that lies outside it is both a residue and also a reservoir of power, whether destructive or creative.[7] The long-standing assumption in Western society that artists are indifferent to purity values (leading "bohemian" lives) shows our culture's awareness of the value of dirt. Dirt also represents the individual's liberation from the sometimes op-

7. Ibid., 94–113.

pressive control of society: children making a deliberate mess of their plates, using dirty words, "grossing" each other out; adults eating suspicious foods such as snails or slugs, refusing to shave on holiday, watching dirty movies. Consequently, one cannot readily predict whether purity or dirt will be symbolically more significant in the near future. A living society never comes to a final resolution of the issue, for perfect purity would create a deathlike immobility and complete dirtiness would be equivalent to catastrophic chaos. The life of a society depends on finding a sustainable balance.

It is likely, then, that the average reader of this work will acknowledge some purity rules in the area of sex, quite probably derived from the society of one's childhood and possibly modified by exposure to others, whether more conservative or more liberal. In some cases, the reader will not have learned to distinguish between purity ethics and other kinds of sexual ethics, but will simply think of all sexual wrongs as "dirty." It may not be easy, at first, for such a reader to separate purity from other considerations. For present purposes, it is enough to say that what marks particular sexual acts as violations of purity rather than of some other ethic is that the acts are deemed repellent in and of themselves, like snails or slugs on a dinner plate. One rejects them because they seem self-evidently unacceptable, not because of any identifiable, concrete harm which they threaten to a society or to a person participating in them. It is possible for an act to be rejected, of course, both as dirty and as harmful, but it should be possible to analyze the principles at work, even where the distinction is blurred to begin with.

Because of the complexity and incoherence of modern Western purity values, the reader of this book has to perform several difficult tasks in order to understand the topic at hand. One is to discover that what has long seemed self-evident with regard to sexual ethics—that certain acts were right in and of themselves—is in fact the reflection of purity values we have drawn from our culture. The equivalent values of other cultures will often be significantly different. Another is to accept that purity systems change and that we cannot assume even that ours is identical with that of our ancestral cultures, Israel and Greece. Yet another is to see that purity systems not only differ in detail from culture to culture, but also differ in the coherence with which they are organized and the intensity with which they are held. Some cultures (e.g., ancient Israel) simply take the whole matter more seriously than others.

Purity and impurity (or "dirt," as we tend to call it) are thus culturally and emotionally powerful for us. They are also difficult topics to grasp and understand, all the more so for the fact that they first presented themselves to us, in our assimilating of the purity rules of our own society, as things self-evident, permanent, and largely beyond question. As we turn now to examine the role of purity considerations in the sexual ethics of the New Testament, we shall find it equally important both to understand the official purity system of ancient Israel and to see how it was actually being appropriated among Jewish groups in the first century of the Common Era. Only then can we begin to comprehend the significance of purity in the New Testament writings.

2

Israel's Basic
Purity Law

THE DISTINCTIVENESS OF ISRAEL

Israel, at the beginning of the Common Era, placed a very high value on its distinctive traditions, that is, on all that distinguished it from the Nations (i.e., the Gentiles). The Jewish people were distinctive in many respects: their rejection of images in worship, their insistence on one God, their observance of a weekly day of rest, their concern for food purity, their practice of circumcision, and their reluctance to intermarry with Gentiles, to name a few of the more obvious. To be sure, every ancient nation had its distinctive traditions, but Israel stood out because of the degree to which it kept itself separate from other ethnic groups and perpetuated its identity from generation to generation. Most ethnic groups in the Eastern Mediterranean world became heavily Hellenized during the last few centuries B.C.E., to the extent of merging their gods with those of the Greeks and, often, of adopting Greek as their principal language, at least among the elite. While the Jews, too, took much from Hellenistic culture, they kept their distance from it in matters of religion, in a way that was virtually unexampled at the time.

Israel recorded its distinctive faith and culture in the writings we now call by the technical term "Scriptures." In antiquity, this technical term did not yet exist, but the importance attached to these writings and the reverence shown them already clearly marked them as of special status. These writings included not only those known to Christians as the Old Testament and Apocrypha (or deuterocanonical books), but also other writings now lost or accorded relatively little esteem. Different Jewish groups in antiquity often held to somewhat different canons (official collections of writings), but one group of books was fundamental for them all: the first five books of modern Bibles, called in Hebrew Torah, or "Instruction." In English, they are traditionally called "the law"; and though that is not an ideal translation of *torah*, it does acknowledge the fact that these writings constituted, among other things, the basic law of Israel, criminal, civil, and religious.

In antiquity, religion was not yet separable from other forms of public life. One's worship was dictated mainly by one's nationality and by other forms of social identification such as the household to which one belonged or the city in which one lived. The family, including slaves as well as the immediate kin group, honored its own household gods. The great holidays in any city were the festivals of its gods, celebrated with religious rites, feasting, and various entertainments. In the Roman world, some religious respect must also be paid to the genius or divinity of the ruling city and, later on, of the emperor who embodies its rule. To be sure, there were unofficial cults as well, often imported by resident aliens from their original country, and these sometimes offered initiation to other interested individuals. Philosophical groups, too, sometimes organized themselves as voluntary communities of worship, as did social clubs. Even so, for most people, religion remained a part of their familial or ethnic identity; and since the individual as such had no place in society (a topic to be explored further in part 2 of this study), one scarcely thought of changing one's worship except as part of a larger social unit.

To be a Jew, then, did not mean primarily to confess a certain faith, but rather to belong to a certain people. As a consequence of that belonging, one was obliged (and no doubt happy) to participate fully in its life, including its faith and worship. The alternative, in most cases, was to become a nonperson. One could not convert to another "denomination" or become a "secular" person. Since one's whole identity arose largely from belonging to a family and to its nation, tribe, or city, there was little possibility of entertaining such an idea. The modern reader who thinks of Torah, then, strictly in terms of a religious document is apt to have a misconception of its importance in late antiquity. It was a religious document, but it was also the basic law of Israel in all respects, no distinction being made between religious and nonreligious elements.

PURITY CODES IN THE TORAH

One highly significant aspect of this basic law of Israel was its intense concern with purity. Indeed, this concern was one of the principal forces keeping Israel separate from the Nations. I have already noted that food purity and the reluctance of Israel to intermarry with Gentiles were important distinctives of the people. The foundations of these and other purity rules lay far back in the past, but the rules themselves were kept before people's attention both by their constant use within the day-to-day life of the society and by their written presence in the Torah. To study Torah was esteemed a high vocation in the society (e.g., Psalm 119; Sirach 39); but even for those who could not read, it was familiar from its being read and expounded in the synagogues. The Torah contains a great deal besides purity rules, but it would be difficult to overstate their importance among its contents.

Though individual rules are scattered through most of the five books, the two most substantial collections of purity law are found in Leviticus (chaps. 11–16 and 17–26). These two codes form the best place for us to begin, since they provide enough examples, treated from a sufficiently coordinated point of view, to give an overall impression of the content and nature of Israel's purity law. Though they are difficult to date, these two codes probably existed prior to their incorporation into the Torah as we now have it. Their written form is not likely to be later than the period just before the exile (587 B.C.E.), and many of the individual laws are no doubt older.[1] This suggests that they were written down at least partly to preserve Israelite traditions in a new era that threatened dissolution and disappearance, but another motive may have been to lay the blame for the catastrophe of exile at the door of those who had been relatively indifferent to the demands of purity in the preceding era (Lev. 18:24–30).

The two codes are distinguished by rather different interests. The first is concerned primarily with those aspects of uncleanness which call for some rite of purification; the second, usually called the "Holiness Code," deals with the historical consequences of uncleanness for the people at large. Thus, the first code gives directions about discerning when uncleanness exists and also about the kind of purification required, and it concludes with a full description of the rites for the Day of Atonement, when the high priest makes "atonement for the holy place, because of the uncleannesses of the people of Israel, and because of their transgres-

---

1. Noth, *Leviticus,* 9–17; Wenham, *Leviticus,* 6–13.

sions, all their sins" (Lev. 16:16 RSV). (Note that uncleanness is a kind of sin, but a recognizably distinct category of it.) The Holiness Code, on the other hand, is characterized by the frequent reiteration of God's claim on the people (e.g., "I am the Lord your God, who brought you out of the land of Egypt"; "You shall be holy, for I the Lord your God am holy") and by its claim that sins of uncleanness caused the land of Canaan to "vomit out" its former inhabitants and may bring about the same result again. The Holiness Code has little interest in the cleansing of individuals, but calls on the people as a whole to cleanse itself by the removal of offenders. If Israel disregards these demands and becomes polluted, God will punish and exile them (26:21–39); yet their repentance will be enough to restore them to God's favor, without reference to cleansing rites (26:40–45).

The difference between the two codes appears clearly in the few instances where they handle precisely the same topics. In dealing with clean and unclean animals, for example, the first code defines what is clean and unclean and provides means for the purification of people and vessels defiled by contact with unclean animals or their carcasses (chap. 11). The Holiness Code simply emphasizes the importance of the distinction and prohibits violations (20:25–26). Again, in the matter of intercourse during the menstrual period, the first code defines how long the man becomes impure (seven days) and how contagious his impurity is (he communicates it to any bed on which he lies; 15:24). The Holiness Code, on the other hand, simply prohibits intercourse with a menstruating woman (18:19) or provides that the two offenders shall be "cut off from among their people" (20:18).[2] The first code thus shows its relatively mundane character; it recognizes dirt as an inevitable aspect of daily existence, however much the society may seek to avoid it, and offers remedies to restore those polluted to the normal state of cleanness. The Holiness Code holds up the ideal of an absolute separation between Israel and all that is unclean and utters a "No" to uncleanness so absolute that it is often enforced through the execution or the "cutting off" of the polluted.

PRINCIPLES OF TORAH PURITY

Despite these differences, however, the two codes are alike in offering us a glimpse into the inner rationale of the purity system in ancient Israel.

2. The meaning of this last phrase is somewhat uncertain. It may mean that God will punish them with untimely death or that the court is to execute them or perhaps banish them—a very weighty punishment in antiquity (Wenham, *Leviticus*, 241–42).

Over the centuries since the writing of these documents, students have offered a variety of interpretations of this system. Some, to be sure, have despaired of finding any logic to it and have regarded it as purely arbitrary. Others, however, have seen it as an allegory of virtues and vices, others as a kind of primitive hygiene, and still others as a reaction against the cults of Israel's neighbors.[3] The allegorical and hygienic interpretations are efforts to explain a purity system in terms intelligible to cultures in which purity as such (or, at least, this purity system) could no longer stand on its own. While they are interesting in their own right, we may set them aside here as unsupported by the text of Leviticus itself.

On the other hand, the explanation that finds here a reaction against non-Israelite cults has in its favor the testimony of the Holiness Code itself: "Do not defile yourselves by any of these things, for by all these the nations I am casting out before you defiled themselves; and the land became defiled, so that I punished its iniquity, and the land vomited out its inhabitants" (Lev. 18:24–25 RSV). Yet, this is scarcely a disinterested historical analysis. Rather, it is a theological interpretation of the situation contemporary with the writer of the Holiness Code. Exile was an imminent threat to the people of Judah—perhaps even a reality for some, since there was a preliminary deportation of many of the Jerusalem elite in 597 B.C.E. It was easy to draw the parallel between the impending end of Jewish independence and Israel's own destruction of the Canaanites in its ancient conquest of the land; and much of the behavior condemned by the Holiness Code was indeed related to cults shared by the Jews with their pagan neighbors. Still, reaction to pagan cults cannot explain the whole of the purity code. Take, for example, the matter of clean and unclean animals: the use of the pig in Canaanite sacrificial rituals may help explain its rejection in Leviticus; but the ox, which is reckoned clean, was at least equally important to the Canaanites,[4] and the dove, likewise clean, was sacred to the fertility goddess of the region.[5] It thus appears that, even though the Holiness Code itself conceives the purity system as a rejection of alien practices, this is not in fact a full description of it.

The most comprehensive explanation to date of the rationale of Israel's purity system is that of Mary Douglas.[6] According to her inter-

3. Douglas, *Purity and Danger,* 43–49; Wenham, *Leviticus,* 165–69.
4. Pedersen, *Israel,* 1–2:482–83.
5. Cumont, *Oriental Religions,* 117.
6. Douglas, *Purity and Danger,* 41–57; cf. Wenham's appraisal, *Leviticus,* 23–25, 169–71.

pretation, God's holiness, for the authors of Leviticus, means wholeness and completeness, not only in God, but in God's creation. A priest, for example, even though duly entitled to the priesthood by descent, may not officiate in that capacity if he suffers from any "blemish"—"a man blind or lame, or one who has a mutilated face or a limb too long, or a man who has an injured foot or an injured hand, or a hunchback, or a dwarf, or a man with a defect in his sight or an itching disease or scabs or crushed testicles" (Lev. 21:18–20 RSV). There was implicit in the purity system an ideal of what constitutes a whole and complete man— and, equally, of what constitutes a whole and complete woman or land animal or water animal. When a species belonging to the category "land animal," for example, does not match up with the general ideal, it is unclean. The ideal for land animals is that they should be ruminants with cloven hoofs; thus, the ox, sheep, and goat match the ideal, while the pig and camel do not (Lev. 11:3–8). Even among the clean animals, however, aberrant ("blemished") individuals which do not perfectly represent their "kind" are not acceptable for sacrifice (e.g., 3:1, 6).

A vivid illustration of Douglas's thesis may be found in an aspect of the law of leprosy that she does not happen to mention. Leprosy[7] renders its victims unclean, and it is the task of the priests to certify the occurrence or remission of the disease, to ban the sufferers from contact with those who are clean, and to purify them with appropriate rites if the disease should disappear. If a little leprosy renders a person unclean, we might readily assume, using the analogy of modern anxieties about disease, that the person who is totally leprous would be totally unclean. The opposite, however, is the case:

> If the leprosy breaks out in the skin, so that the leprosy covers all the skin of the diseased person from head to foot, so far as the priest can see, then the priest shall make an examination, and if the leprosy has covered all his body, he shall pronounce him clean of the disease; it has all turned white, and he is clean. (Lev. 13:12–13 RSV)

The essence of the impurity occasioned by leprosy is not the disease itself, nor even the peculiar appearance of the skin, but the piebald condition of its victim. The whole and complete human being ought to be of a single hue.

According to Douglas's analysis, the Israelite attention to "wholeness"

7. Not the disease that now goes by that name, but a variety of skin diseases; see Wenham, *Leviticus*, 194–97.

demands two things: first, that every individual should be a complete and self-contained specimen of its kind (hence the limitations placed on the "blemished"), and, second, that there should be no mixing of kinds. The first of these principles works itself out in a variety of ways. If the cloven-hoofed ruminant is defined as clean for eating, it means that its life is part of a process which concludes with its being slaughtered by human beings and its blood being returned to God (Lev. 17:1–6). Any breach of this process will occasion uncleanness, so that the clean animal that dies of itself or is killed by wild animals becomes unclean (17:15), and so, too, the person who consumes the blood, even of an animal duly slaughtered (17:10–14). Again, the normal state of a woman is nonmenstrual, especially in an ancient family-oriented culture where the ideal woman married at puberty and, from then on, remained more or less continually either pregnant or nursing until menopause.[8] Accordingly, a woman is reckoned unclean when menstruating, hemorrhaging, or giving birth (Lev. 12; 15:19–30), for in all these conditions her normal wholeness and completeness is being violated by the loss of something proper to her. Any breach in the ideal wholeness of a being or of its place in ordinary processes thus occasions a diminution of its perfection.

It is equally polluting if things which do not belong together are mixed with each other. Hence, human beings must not have sexual intercourse with animals, because it is "confusion" (not "perversion," as in RSV; Lev. 18:23).[9] But, equally, different species of domestic animals must not be allowed to mate (e.g., to produce mules), or a field to contain two different kinds of seed, or a fabric to be woven of two kinds of fibers (19:19), no doubt for the same reason. Thus, beings which represent two unrelated "kinds" must not be allowed to join in sexual or quasi-sexual unions.[10]

In similar fashion, no one person must seek to combine mutually exclusive perfections. This is the reason for the condemnation of homosexual acts, as the phrasing of the rules makes clear; the offense is described, literally, as a man lying with a male "the lyings of a woman" (18:22; 20:13). The male who fulfills the "female" role is a combination of kinds and therefore unclean, like a cloth composed of both linen and

---

8. Pedersen, *Israel*, 1–2:71–74; Wenham, *Leviticus*, 223–24.
9. Wenham, *Leviticus*, 260.
10. The field is like the womb in "receiving seed"; the shuttle of the loom is analogous to the penis.

wool; and the act that renders him unclean is the joint responsibility of both partners. The same point is made in the prohibition of cross-dressing (Deut. 22:5), and the same reasoning also seems to apply to incest in Leviticus. There are certain social roles which stand in such contradiction to one another that one cannot combine them—as, for example, the role of son and that of sexual rival.

Given that these are the principles which shaped the purity law (wholeness and completeness of the "kind" in its individual exemplar and prohibition of mixing "kinds"), the range of social life to which they were applicable was all-encompassing. A brief sketch of the contents of the two codes in Leviticus makes this clear. They deal with the following: clean and unclean animals (chap. 11); a woman's impurity after giving birth (12); leprosy of persons, houses, and textiles or skins (13—14); genital discharges, including menstruation (15); slaughter of animals and disposition of blood (17); incest and other prohibited sexual acts (18); idolatry, errors in consuming sacrifices, oppression, injustice, hatred, mixture of "kinds," the "foreskin" of fruit trees, blood, haircuts, etc. (19); sacrifice of "seed,"[11] wizardry, adultery, incest, and other sexual acts (20); defilement of priests and members of their households and unsuitability of sacrificial animals (21—22); the festival calendar (23); obligations of resident aliens to keep the Torah (24); sabbath years and jubilees (25); idolatry and sabbath-keeping, along with blessings and curses related to the keeping of the laws (26).

The multifarious nature of this "table of contents" (which represents some simplification of the codes themselves) illustrates the breadth of the purity system as a way of shaping life. Despite its seemingly chaotic presentation here or elsewhere in the Torah, the purity system was not arbitrary. As Douglas observes, "the laws would have been like signs which at every turn inspired meditation on the oneness, purity and completeness of God."[12]

At the same time, there was a tendency for purity law, strictly so-called, to attract to itself regulations that had other origins and other rationales. As Douglas has observed, pollution rules, while they do not often correspond closely to other kinds of moral rules, may be used to

---

11. This has traditionally been understood as referring to the sacrifice of children, a practice known from ancient Canaan. The phrase itself, however, is ambiguous. Since "seed" can also mean "semen," it could refer to some sexual rite.

12. Douglas, *Purity and Danger,* 57.

reinforce other rules as a kind of "highlighting."[13] In the Holiness Code, one encounters a number of such instances—for example, "You shall love your neighbor as yourself" or "You shall do no wrong in judgment, in measures of length or weight or quantity" (Lev. 19:18, 35 RSV). These are not purity rules themselves, but are set in this context so that they will be reinforced by association with purity rules, taking advantage of the apparently automatic distaste or even disgust that dirt evokes. Deuteronomy explicitly uses purity language to condemn commercial dishonesty: "You shall not have in your bag two kinds of weights, a large and a small. . . . A full and just weight you shall have, a full and just measure you shall have. . . . For all who do such things, all who act dishonestly, are an abomination to the Lord your God" (25:13–16 RSV). Jeremiah and Ezekiel, too, often apply purity language to other kinds of offenses; and Proverbs almost routinely describes liars, scoffers, and other wicked persons as "abominations." This does not mean that the purity system was being "spiritualized" or "moralized" but that it was a ready source of emotional reinforcement for other kinds of moral or ethical concerns.[14]

In matters of sexual ethics, then, one cannot assume that an act treated in the purity codes is simply and solely a purity concern. I shall show that adultery, prostitution, and incest had about them an element of property law as well. Since sexual acts are an area of great concern to any purity system, all sexual offenses are likely to be felt to some degree as purity offenses, and we shall need to pay close attention in order to distinguish between those rules that are prompted entirely by purity considerations and those where other concerns are at work, too. In what follows, I shall attempt to identify the purity elements in the sexual regulations of the Torah.

SEXUAL PURITY

Emissions from the Sexual Organs

One of the easiest purity elements to identify is concern about the menstruating woman. During her menstrual period, she is unclean for seven days, and her uncleanness is so contagious that it can affect others indirectly through their touching any furniture on which she lies or sits.

---

13. Ibid., 129–33.
14. Cf. Neusner, *Idea of Purity,* 11–15.

This uncleanness also extends to any woman who has a hemorrhage and thus appears to be in a kind of ongoing menstrual state. A man is forbidden to have sexual intercourse with such a woman, with no grounds given for this prohibition other than concern for purity. Likewise, the man's emission of semen defiles him (and also the woman, if it occurs in intercourse), though only for one day. If, however, he has an unusual, continuing discharge (perhaps gonorrhea, as the Old Greek version names it), it is approximated to the woman's menstrual or quasi-menstrual impurity. The importance attached to this matter of discharges from the sexual organs is evident not only from the chapter devoted to it in Leviticus (15), but also from isolated individual laws elsewhere prohibiting intercourse with a menstruating woman (Lev. 18:19; 20:18) and prescribing the correct treatment of one who has an ongoing discharge (Num. 5:1–2) or a wet dream (Deut. 23:11–12, ET 10–11).[15]

Even apart from menstruation, women appear to be a more virulent source of the contagion of impurity than men. The mother's purification time is twice as long after the birth of a daughter as after that of a son (eighty days as opposed to forty; Lev. 12). At Mount Sinai, "the people" are to consecrate themselves for the great epiphany and are told not to "go near a woman" (Exod. 19:10–15). No doubt the fear is that the men will proceed to have intercourse with them and thus pollute *themselves;* yet, the text speaks as if the danger lay in the women. Priests, who must take special pains to avoid impurity, are forbidden to marry "used" women: harlots or those who are "defiled," the divorced, or the widowed (Lev. 21:7, 14). What is more, any woman who is divorced from her husband and then married to another becomes "defiled" in relation to her first husband; should she become free again, through divorce or widowhood, it would be an "abomination" for him to remarry her (Deut. 24:1–4). A priest's daughter who commits prostitution is condemned to be burned, an unusual, perhaps sacral mode of execution (Lev. 21:9). And all foreign women are automatically suspected of trying to introduce foreign cults, so that Deuteronomy requires the slaughtering of all women and children taken captive from nearby enemies, though allowing the enjoyment of those captured at a greater distance (20:10–18; cf. 21:10–14 for sexual use of captives). It is not too much to

---

15. The law about a woman's impurity after childbirth may also be based on an analogy with the menstrual flow (Leviticus 12); see Wenham, *Leviticus,* 188.

suggest that the texts demonstrate a general anxiety about the polluting potential of women.

Cross-dressing and Homosexual Acts

The anxiety over the polluting potential of women may well have contributed to the rejection of cross-dressing (Deut. 22:5) and of homosexual acts among men[16] (Lev. 18:22; 20:13), both of which seemed to confuse the purer male with the "dirtier" female.[17] These prohibitions are given as isolated rules, with the violations being described as "abominations," that is, "disgusting things." This is not to suggest that they are exceptionally horrid in terms of the purity system. The term *toebah* and its synonym *shiqquts*, both traditionally translated "abomination" in English, apply in the Torah to things as diverse as unclean foods (e.g., Lev. 11:10, 11, 12; Deut. 14:3), the sacrifice of a blemished animal (Deut. 17:1), remarriage to a former wife (Deut. 24:4), and idols (Deut. 29:16, ET 17). Since the prohibition of cross-dressing is found only once, in Deuteronomy, and the prohibition of homosexual acts only in the Holiness Code, these, unlike the food laws or the regulations about menstruation, must have formed a relatively peripheral aspect of the overall purity system, which concerned itself primarily with the everyday life of the ordinary household.

Some, to be sure, have understood the account of the angels' visit to Sodom (Gen. 19:1–11), along with the similar story of the Levite and his concubine at Gibeah (Judges 19), as implying a condemnation of homosexual acts. (This tradition of interpretation is preserved in the English word "sodomy.") Both stories tell of visitors who receive rude treatment from the men of a town where they seek lodging. The only person willing to take them in is a resident alien, unrelated to the townspeople and lacking in influence. At night, the townsmen gather outside and demand to "know" the wayfarers, and the host seeks to appease them by offering one or more women to be raped instead. In the Sodom story, the wayfarers are actually angels, who blind their would-be attackers and, after sending their host and his family away, destroy the city. In the Gibeah story, the traveler is a Levite. The appalling

---

16. There is no reference to homosexual acts among women in the Jewish Scriptures.

17. Cf. David's curse on the household of Joab—that it should never lack a man with gonorrhea, a leper, a "man who holds the spindle," or a victim of murder or starvation (2 Sam. 3:29).

sacrifice of his concubine saves his own life, but he stirs up a civil war in retaliation for the outrage.

It is improbable that the point of either story, as it stands in Scripture, is to condemn homosexual acts as such. Genesis does not specify the original complaint which drew down God's judgment on Sodom. The demand of the townsmen there and at Gibeah to "know" the strangers is itself ambiguous. Though it could certainly include a sexual meaning, what is clear beyond question is that the mob, in each case, intends violence. In the Gibeah story, the Levite interprets the demand as meaning that "They meant to kill me" (Judges 20:5).

Condemnation of violence, even where it appears likely that it would have included homosexual rape, can hardly be equated with a universal condemnation of homosexuality or even of homosexual acts. At most, the fact that the Torah includes both the Sodom narrative and the Holiness Code might be taken as a foundation for arguing that the audience of the narrative was expected to regard the homosexual elements in the rape as a sin of impurity. Yet, since the Torah itself does not treat the purity code of Leviticus as existing in Lot's time and since the code never applied to Gentiles in general, it is not at all clear that purity is relevant to the interpretation of the Sodom story, though it would be to the incident at Gibeah, where all the participants were Israelites. If one asks whether the punishment visited on Sodom or on Gibeah was occasioned by impurity or by violence against strangers, it is clear in both cases that only the latter is possible.[18]

Elsewhere in the Old Testament, many references to Sodom use its ruins as an example of desolation and divine judgment but, following the Genesis tradition, do not specify what its sin may have been. Isaiah, however, in comparing Jerusalem with Sodom, suggests that the sin was oppression (1:10–17) or partiality (3:9 RSV; the Hebrew is of uncertain meaning). Jeremiah refers to adultery, lies, and the encouragement of the wicked (23:14). Ezekiel says that, although Sodom had pride and abundance, it refused to help the poor and that it committed "abominations" (16:49–50). While abominations could certainly include homo-

18. Cf. the analysis of the horrors and ironies of violence in the Gibeah narrative by Trible (*Texts of Terror,* 70–82). Alter's proposal ("Sodom as Nexus," 33) that the Sodom story is serving mainly as part of a series of narratives dealing with the relationship of righteousness and fertility is ingenious, but he is forced to assume that the author wants us to connect the story with a critique of homosexual acts as necessarily sterile—something that is never mentioned in the text itself.

sexual acts, the word is so little specific that one cannot be sure that Ezekiel had them uniquely in mind. When Zephaniah threatens Moab and Ammon with the fate of Sodom, he is denouncing their taunting of Israel and their paganism (2:8–11). Whether one looks to Leviticus, then, or to the tradition about Sodom, one must assume that the issue of homosexual acts was relatively peripheral to the Scriptures of Israel and that the large place homosexuality assumes in modern purity systems has some origin other than a simple reading of Torah.[19]

The Holiness Code invokes the death penalty for homosexual acts (Lev. 20:13). This is of a piece with its generally Draconian style, which reflects the peculiar purpose of the work. As we have already noted, the author of the Holiness Code threatens that if the people fail to keep themselves pure, the holy land will become defiled through them, God will punish the land, and the land will vomit them out (18:24–30). But what if some individuals do not heed these warnings? Must the whole people suffer for the transgressions of a few? The Holiness Code allows for the people as a whole to purge itself of responsibility for the offenses of the few by separating itself decisively from the offenders. It is not quite clear how this absolves the *land* of impurity, but it does at least separate the people from these specific offenses. Thus, Leviticus 20 largely repeats the list of unclean acts in chapter 18, this time not to prohibit them, but to call for the eradication of offenders from Israel. It demanded the execution of some: those who offer "seed" to Molech, children who curse their parents, adulterers, those who commit certain types of incest, those who engage in homosexual acts, and both the human and the animal involved in cases of bestiality. Other offenses, such as intercourse with a menstruating woman and certain other types of incest, were to be punished by "cutting off" or by childlessness, which would deprive the offender of a continuing name in Israel.

Bestiality, Cult Prostitution, and Masturbation

The Holiness Code places bestiality (18:23; 20:15–16) in fairly close proximity to homosexual acts, which may suggest some association

19. Among later writings, *Testament of Benjamin* 9.1 takes the sin of Sodom as having to do with intercourse with women. The second-century Christian hymn that constitutes Book 6 of the *Sibylline Oracles* understands it as failure to recognize God at his visitation (21–25). Only in Philo (*Abraham* 133–36) do we find a clear statement that the sin of Sodom included (though it was not limited to) homosexual acts.

between the two matters in the mind of its author.[20] They may have been connected only as examples of "confusion" or as relatively rare or unusual violations of purity in contrast to the more everyday problems occasioned by marriage and family life; but they may also have shared another feature, an association with idolatry. This link becomes more visible in materials outside the Holiness Code. Exodus prohibits bestiality in an interesting context: "You shall not permit a sorceress to live. Whoever lies with a beast shall be put to death. Whoever sacrifices to any God save to the Lord only, shall be utterly destroyed" (Exod. 22:18–20 RSV). In this tiny, isolated purity code, the theme that links the three elements is their association with non-Israelite cultus, which may at times have included intercourse with animals and which was often lumped with "sorcery" in Hebrew thinking (e.g., Isa. 8:19).

There is, as noted above, no condemnation of homosexual acts as such in the Torah outside the Holiness Code; but Deuteronomy forbids Israel to allow its children, female or male, to serve as cult prostitutes (literally, "holy people") or to use the wages of such prostitution in payment of vows (23:18–19, ET 17–18). While we do not know much about male cult prostitutes in the Israelite milieu, it is possible that they engaged in intercourse with other men.[21] Such a cultic connection would have reinforced a prohibition of homosexual acts based on more general purity considerations.[22] Returning to Leviticus with this connection in mind, one observes that the chapters condemning homosexual acts and bestiality also prohibit other cultic acts, namely, sacrifice of seed to Molech (18:21; 20:1–5) and sorcery (20:6). While the chapters are too miscellaneous in organization to be quite clear on the point, the author may well have regarded both homosexual acts and bestiality as tainted with idolatry.[23]

The Torah contains no prohibition of masturbation, which is sometimes associated with homosexuality in the modern mind. The death of Onan (Gen. 38:1–10) was at one time taken as expressing a judgment on masturbators, but this interpretation is unlikely at best. Onan was obligated by an ancient Hebrew tradition (levirate marriage) to beget

20. Deut. 27:21, on the other hand, seems to connect bestiality with incest.

21. Driver, *Deuteronomy*, 264–65.

22. The prohibition on cross-dressing may have had a similar background; ibid., 250–51.

23. On the connection of the death penalty with idolatry, see Forkman, *Limits of Religious Community*, 17.

children for his dead brother with the brother's widow. Since any male children born might then take precedence over him as heirs, he sought to avoid conception. The narrative suggests that he practiced *coitus interruptus.* Elsewhere spilled semen is treated merely as a source of temporary uncleanness (Lev. 15:16–17). Onan's sin was not the way in which he performed the sexual act, but rather his refusal to fulfill his obligation to his dead brother.[24] Masturbation to orgasm would have occasioned temporary uncleanness for a man, but it does not otherwise seem to have been an issue for the purity system. Female masturbation would not have violated the purity code at all; but, like female homosexual acts, it could hardly come within the law's purview. Like the rest of Israelite culture, the purity code placed the man at the center and was interested in other beings only as they impinged on him.

Incest

By contrast with the rather incidental handling of homosexual acts or bestiality, the more detailed treatment of incest found in the Holiness Codes and elsewhere suggests it was a problem of more substantial dimensions. Incest is a particularly difficult topic for us to discuss in any dispassionate way. We have the revulsion toward it that marks it as a purity issue for us, but we also argue that it should be prohibited on other grounds, usually those of eugenics (since inbreeding is likely to make inherited disorders that are dependent on recessive genes more prevalent) or of family order (on the grounds that incest involving a child is a form of child abuse). Incest thus calls forth a variety of responses. The strength of our response, however, makes it relatively difficult for us to look calmly at another society's rather different rules in the matter.

The circumstances of family life in ancient Israel and the rules governing it were indeed quite different from ours. Whereas we define incest as intercourse between two persons too closely related in terms of their shared genetic endowment, ancient Israel defined it in terms of the social obligations owed by either a male or a female to immediate kin. A son must not act disrespectfully toward male kindred of his own or a prior generation: father, father's brother, or own brother. This respect demands that he not approach their wives sexually, for the man's wife was an aspect of him. The language of the Holiness Code makes the

---

24. Pedersen, *Israel* 1–2:77–81.

point clear: "You shall not uncover the nakedness of your father's wife; it is your father's nakedness" (Lev. 18:8 RSV). The gravity of the affront implied in "uncovering your father's nakedness" is evident from the account of the drunkenness of Noah, when Ham saw his father naked and was cursed for it (Gen. 9:20–27). The sacredness of the patriarch's genitals was such that, in an early time, one even swore oaths on them (Gen. 24:2–3, Abraham; 47:29–31, Israel), suggesting that any failure of respect toward one's physical progenitor or the head of one's household was sure to be visited with swift retribution.[25] Thus, it is the man's father whom he violates in incest, even though the physical act takes place with his wife.

In a culture that accepted polygyny as normal, a man might very well have more than one wife in his household at the same time. The grown son could readily become interested in a wife who was not his mother. No blood relationship would be transgressed; yet, the offense was not the less serious. There are narrative instances of such incest in Scripture, with suitably disastrous consequences. Reuben had a liaison with his father's concubine, for which he lost his preeminence as firstborn (Gen. 35:22; cf. 49:4); and when Adonijah requested the hand of David's concubine, Abishag the Shunammite, Solomon took it as a claim on the whole household and power of their father David (1 Kings 2:13–25). The gist of the matter seems to be violation of family hierarchy by arrogating to oneself a father's rights. If this were all, it would not make incest a violation of purity law, and I shall suggest in part 2 of this study that we can in fact best understand it as a "property" offense. Yet, incest also implied an intolerable mixture of roles. An ideal son cannot be the father's sexual rival. The mingling of roles makes both person and act impure as well.

Adultery and Prostitution

The same mixture of ethical concerns shows up with reference to two other sexual offenses, which will form the last items we shall investigate under the heading of purity violations: adultery and prostitution. In Hebrew law, adultery is defined as a man's having intercourse with a woman married or betrothed to another. The male who commits adultery does not violate his own marriage, but that of the woman and her

---

25. Similarly, Deut. 25:11–12 provides that if a woman, intervening in a fight between her husband and another man, takes hold of the other man's genitals, her hand is to be cut off.

husband.[26] The Holiness Code treats adultery as defiling (Lev. 18:20) and calls for the execution of both the man and the woman (20:10). As noted above in the discussion of homosexual acts, such executions are a way of purging the people as a whole of uncleanness so that the land will not vomit them out. There are signs, however, even in the Holiness Code to show that adultery was not solely a purity offense.

If adultery were entirely a purity offense, we could not explain the unusual rule about the slave-woman who has been designated as another man's concubine or wife but not yet ransomed and emancipated for the purpose (Lev. 19:20–22). The woman appears to be at least approximately in the state of betrothal, and elsewhere this is held to mean that any violation of her is equivalent to adultery (Deut. 22:25–27). Nonetheless, if a man other than her betrothed has intercourse with her, the Holiness Code specifically provides that the two shall *not* be put to death "because she had not been emancipated." The law demands "damages"[27] and instructs the man to offer a ram as a guilt-offering. The passage is difficult until we recognize that in this case an exception is being made to the purity system itself. Since uncleanness is defiling in and of itself, the objective of the Holiness Code is to purge it from the people and thus prevent it from working its inevitable destruction. In cases of bestiality, for example, the animal is killed as well as the human being, because both have become centers of impurity. In ordinary cases of adultery, Leviticus does not even make an exception to the death penalty for women who may have been raped, as Deut. 22:23–27 does. The object is to expunge the uncleanness as such. In this particular case, however, Leviticus rejects the death penalty for *both* partners on the grounds that the woman had not been emancipated.

Since the ordinance gives her slave status as the reason why they are not to be executed, it may mean simply that slave women are incapable of adultery, that is, that adultery is by definition an offense that can be committed only with a free woman. This, in itself, would make it clear that adultery is a property-related matter. Another explanation, however, would suggest that her slave status is what *links* the two offenders; in other words, the man who has had intercourse with the slave-woman is her master. Hence the difficulty that the Holiness Code feels about this particular case: the relationship between the slave-woman and her

---

26. Pedersen, *Israel* 1–2:70.

27. RSV translates "an enquiry"; but cf. Noth, *Leviticus,* 143; Wenham, *Leviticus,* 270–71.

intended has been violated, but by a man who himself had some rights in relation to her, since a master could make sexual use of his female slaves. The act is a violation of the purity system and therefore demands an act of atonement, but the author of the Holiness Code refrains from invoking the full severity of the system in order to avoid diminishing the rights of sexual property. Since two men's rights were involved, they are then rebalanced by requiring the woman's master to pay damages to her intended.[28]

The inclusion of adultery within the Holiness Code exemplifies the tendency for all sexual rules to be assimilated to the purity ethic, whatever their true ethical origins. Outside Leviticus, we find little to suggest that adultery was a purity violation. The rite of the water of bitterness, used to determine whether a woman accused of adultery was in fact guilty, may be the only clear instance (Num. 5:11–31). There was, perhaps, a sense that the perfect woman was to receive only the semen of her husband and that reception of other semen defiled her in relation to that husband. Thus, the ideal woman was the one who married as a virgin and remained all her life with a single man (and perhaps continued in widowhood if he died before she did). The priest, as the male who must avoid uncleanness most rigorously, was forbidden to contract any other sort of marriage (Lev. 21:7–15); and it was a "disgusting thing" ("abomination") for a man to remarry his divorced wife if she had been married to another in the interim (Deut. 24:1–4, affirmed in Jer. 3:1).[29] Adultery seemed a breach of purity precisely in that it violated this sense that the ideal example of womanhood is consecrated to a single man.

Like adultery, ordinary secular prostitution was treated as both a property and purity offense. The purity element makes itself felt as a link between prostitution and "alien" cults, made easy by the existence of

28. Wenham (*Leviticus*, 271), and Noth (*Leviticus*, 143) both assume that the violator of the slave-woman is a third party and must therefore question whether "damages" were to be paid to the woman's owner or to her intended. If we assume a third party, however, it is no longer apparent why the woman's slave status would protect the *man* from the death penalty. Only if her violator is also her master would her slave status be relevant, for it would require her to submit to his advances and would authorize him to make sexual use of her.

29. *Jubilees* 33.7 confirms this interpretation; Bilhah was polluted in relation to Jacob after Reuben slept with her even though, according to *Jubilees*, she did not participate voluntarily. Philo, however, explains the matter more in terms of property (*Special Laws* 3.30–31); the husband who accepts such a wife back would be suspect of pimping and procurement, i.e., of having connived in her marriage to another. Such a man, says Philo, would also stand condemned of weakness (*malakia*) and "unmanliness" (*anandria*).

cult prostitutes. These persons, whose sexual activities played some role in the worship of the gods, existed within Israel itself before the exile. They were present, for example, in the reigns of Rehoboam (1 Kings 14:24) and Asa (22:46), despite the latter's efforts to abolish them (15:12); and Josiah found chambers set aside for them in the temple at Jerusalem, which he destroyed in his reform (2 Kings 23:7).[30]

Deuteronomy bans cult prostitutes, male and female, and prohibits use of their wages in payment of vows, as a "disgusting thing" (23:18–19, ET 17–18). An equivalent prohibition in Leviticus (19:29) refers only to women and uses different language, which could include secular as well as sacred prostitutes; yet it is placed in the context of a series of prohibitions on various cultic acts, from eating blood to tattooing to the consulting of mediums and wizards. Both passages are actually concerned to prohibit Israelite men from making their children prostitutes; the danger envisioned was probably the dedication of children to such cultic use, not so very different, in principle, from sacrificing seed to Molech (Lev. 20:1–5). Precisely speaking, condemnation falls upon the parent who prostituted the child rather than the prostitute herself or himself or even the person who might visit them.

It remained possible, to be sure, that a child might exercise his or her own volition in choosing a life of prostitution. Such a child would disgrace the parent, for cult prostitutes were considered the dregs of society (Job 36:14); but the Torah has nothing to say about this except where a female prostitute might compromise the holiness of a priest. A priest may not marry a prostitute (Lev. 21:7), and if his daughter becomes a prostitute, she is to be burned because her action has profaned her father (21:9). The daughter of a priest, before she married or if she returned to him as a divorcée or a childless widow, was reckoned a part of his family and given the right to eat of the sacred dues he received for the part he played in sacrifices (22:10–13); hence her purity was more critical than that of other Israelite women.

The Torah does not explicitly condemn men who visit prostitutes. In the story of Tamar, Judah exhibits no particular shame about his own behavior in stopping with the wayside prostitute (Gen. 38). Still, a partial condemnation is implied in the prohibition of idolatry. Some of

---

30. One may even speculate about the functions of the "ministering women who ministered at the door of the tent of meeting" in the wilderness years (Exod. 38:8). The only thing told of them is that they dedicated their bronze mirrors for the making of the laver of bronze in which the priests were to wash (cf. Pedersen, *Israel*, 3–4:468–72).

the prophets make this connection explicit. Hosea, for example, says that God will not punish Israel's daughters for prostitution or their wives for adultery, since the men themselves, in their pursuit of idolatrous rites, visit prostitutes and sacrifice with "holy women" (4:12–14). "Playing the harlot," as the English translations tend to put it, became a common idiom for worshiping other gods, both in the Torah (e.g., Exod. 34:16) and in the prophetic literature, so that both sacred and secular prostitution were under a religious cloud.

Summary

We can summarize the purity system of the Torah as it touches on sexual matters thus: All sexual and quasi-sexual emissions defile, and the rules which govern these matters belong entirely to the sphere of purity concerns. The prohibitions against homosexual acts, cross-dressing, and bestiality also belong entirely to the sphere of purity ethics. Prostitution is a purity offense only insofar as it is an aspect of rejected cults. What is particularly condemned under this head is the dedication of one's children to cult prostitution or anything that might bring prostitutes into close association with the priesthood. Males do not otherwise appear to be defiled by associating with prostitutes. Incest, which Israel understood or defined differently from the modern West, is partly a purity offense, but there are also aspects of family hierarchy involved which we must consider more fully in part 2 of this book. Adultery is primarily an offense against sexual property, but there is a certain purity element in the Torah's treatment of it, partly because the purity system has a certain affinity for all sexual rules and partly because adultery was a breach in the perfection of the ideal woman. This code was the scriptural basis of the purity system in force among Jews at the time of the origins of Christianity, as far as sexual matters are concerned.

PURITY AND THE GENTILES

Israel did not regard its purity system as a universal law, applicable to all of humanity; it was a gift to Israel specifically, affirming its separation from other nations and its unique relationship to God.[31] Other nations might have purity laws, too, and these might be sharply at variance with those of Israel. The Egyptians thought it a "disgusting thing" to eat with

---

31. As Riches notes, "the sociological sense of . . . purity regulations was fully acknowledged and understood" (*Jesus and the Transformation of Judaism,* 116).

Hebrews (Gen. 43:32), and abominated shepherds (46:34) and the kinds of sacrifices that the Israelites offered to their God (Exod. 8:22, ET 26). Israel, on the other hand, must avoid doing "as they do in the land of Egypt where you dwelt" and "as they do in the land of Canaan, to which I am bringing you" (Lev. 18:3 RSV). Gentiles who lived among the people of Israel in Canaan were liable to keep a high level of purity (see, e.g., Lev. 18:26). Yet, even in Canaan, the carrion which Israelites must not eat because of its impurity is permissible for resident aliens (Deut. 14:21). In other words, the Torah understands purity systems to be specific to each nation.

The purity codes contained within the Torah itself belong not only to the specific nation of Israel, but to a certain stage in its life which began with the exodus and the revelation at Sinai. Not only did they not bind other nations, but even the patriarchs of Israel were free of them. Thus, two of the patriarchs were guilty of incest: Abraham by reason of having married his half-sister (Gen. 20:12; cf. Lev. 18:11) and Jacob because his two principal wives were sisters to one another (Gen. 29:21–30; cf. Lev. 18:18). Even Amram, the father of Moses and Aaron, married his father's sister (Exod. 6:20; cf. Lev. 18:12). If this were to be held against them, there would have been no need to report the information in the first place; but the Sinai covenant and its purity rules simply did not apply to those who were outside it.[32]

There is a partial exception in the case of the pre-Israelite inhabitants of Canaan, for the Holiness Code maintains that their uncleannesses caused the land to vomit them out and threatens that it will do the same with Israel unless they purge their impurity from among them (e.g., Lev. 18:24–30). This is a special case, however, because Canaan is a special case. It is the Lord's own land, which he will give to his own people. No other land is pure, and therefore capable of defilement, in the same sense. The purity system, therefore, is simply not relevant to the Gentile world at large, the pre-Israelite population of Canaan excepted.[33]

Though the Gentiles are not required—or even, for the most part, given the opportunity—to embrace the purity system of the Torah, they are not thereby rendered "clean."[34] Just the contrary, since they neither

32. *Jubilees* 33.15–17 gives exactly this reason to explain why Reuben could be forgiven his act of incest with Bilhah—not that it was not impure, but that it was not yet truly culpable before the giving of the Torah.

33. Cf. Wenham, *Leviticus*, 161–62.

34. Thus, *Joseph and Aseneth*, even though it does not speak of Gentiles as immoral in comparison with Jews, still insists on complete separation from them with regard to food and sex (7–8). Cf. C. Burchard in *Pseudepigrapha*, edited by Charlesworth, 2:194.

know how dirty they are nor have means of cleansing available to them, they are irremediably filthy. Those Gentiles who have the status of resident aliens in Israel and are therefore expected, according to Lev. 18:26, to abide by certain Israelite purity laws are partial exceptions. There was some historic uncertainty, however, even about them.[35] Numbers 9:14, for example, might appear to grant all resident aliens the right to participate in the Passover, but Exod. 12:43–49 makes this right dependent on their males' receiving circumcision. Ultimately, circumcision formed the decisive boundary.

It was an apt boundary marker. For one thing, the practice distinguished ancient Israel from most of its neighbors, the Egyptians, it seems, being the major exception. For another, the foreskin seems to have symboled, for Israel, excess and closure. To be a whole and complete man, therefore, as in Douglas's definition of purity, one had to surrender it. Gentiles, accordingly, were not fit marriage partners (Gen. 34:14)—not even their women, since they were committed to their ancestral culture (Exod. 34:16). The decisiveness of this boundary between Israel and the uncircumcised lost nothing with time. Ezekiel, approximately contemporary with the Holiness Code, regards it as an abomination for a Gentile to enter the Temple. After the destruction of the Temple, the Second Isaiah promised that Zion, once revived, would be forever free of "the uncircumcised and the unclean" (Isa. 52:1). After the return from exile, Nehemiah found that Tobiah the Ammonite actually had a suite of rooms in the Temple, and he expelled him and cleansed the chambers (Neh. 13:4–9). Nehemiah and Ezra both acted to halt mixed marriages and dissolve those already contracted (Neh. 13:23–31; Ezra 9:1—10:44).

Biblical writings of the Hellenistic period make the same points.[36] In the Rest of Esther, which is found in the Old Greek version but not in the Hebrew, Esther gives vent to her loathing for "the marriage bed of uncircumcised men and of every foreigner" and declares that even the crown on her head (a sign, of course, of her marriage to the Gentile king) is as disgusting to her as "a rag used during menstruation" (Rest of

35. See Pedersen, *Israel* 3–4:273–74. Deuteronomy draws a distinction between what is permitted to Israel and what is permitted to the resident alien in the matter of carrion (14:21). In this particular respect, if in no others, such aliens must have served as a kind of purity sink, into which unclean but still valuable property might be diverted. Compare the function of untouchables in India in Gokhale's "Castaways of Caste," 32.

36. See also *Jubilees*, which speaks of circumcision as what separates Israel from both Gentiles and apostates (15.25–32), forbids intermarriage with Gentiles (30.7–17), and holds that the evil of sexual defilement lies in the fact that it violates Israel's special relationship to God (33.18–20).

Esth. 14:15–16 = Esth. 4:17u–w LXX). The author of 3 Maccabees speaks, as a matter of course, of the "abominable lawless Gentiles" (6:9). Gentiles, in turn, perceived circumcision, along with the observance of Sabbath and the refusal to eat pork, as the distinctive signs of Jewishness.[37] Over the long history of Jewish-Gentile relations in antiquity, the degree of animosity varied with the degree of provocation on either side,[38] but Jews seem to have retained, on the whole, a sense that the uncircumcised represent the opposite of all that is pure.

So clear was the dichotomy that it could be used metaphorically in ways that are sometimes surprising to the modern reader. The Holiness Code directs that the fruit of a newly planted tree shall be treated as its "foreskin" for three years. The fruit of the fourth year is holy to God, rather like the act of circumcision, and only in the fifth year does the fruit become available for human use (Lev. 19:23–25). In another context, Moses speaks of himself as a man of "uncircumcised lips," meaning that he is a poor public speaker and incompetent to represent God (Exod. 6:12, 30). Again, authors who wish to reproach Israel itself are apt to address the people as being uncircumcised of heart (Lev. 26:41; Deut. 10:16; Jer. 4:4; 9:25–26) or ears (Jer. 6:10), implying that they are, to that extent, not fully Israel. Israel may become unclean by falling short of what the purity system demands, but Gentiles are unclean because they are entirely outside the purity system. Circumcision is the boundary of that system.[39]

UNITY OF THE PURITY SYSTEM

The purity system of ancient Israel is difficult for most modern readers to grasp for a variety of reasons: it is complex, intricate, and historically remote. Most important, however, many of us lack any analogue in our own experience, since our own culture's purity rules are relatively fragmented and incoherent. Perhaps the most difficult thing for us to grasp is that the ancient purity system of Israel was more or less of a single piece. The modern Western reader is apt to distinguish sharply between different aspects of the system, discarding those that have no real equivalent in our experience, such as the food laws and the laws

37. Whittaker, *Jews and Christians,* 63–85.
38. Sanders, *Paul and Palestinian Judaism,* 206–12, 374–75, 400–402. See also *Jubilees* 22.14–20; 30.10–14.
39. Greeks had their own interests in purity, but these were not as organized nor as pervasive as the Levitical system among Israelites. See Burkert, *Greek Religion,* 75–82. As a result, no specifically Greek system of purification ever became a part of Greek identity.

about the menstruating woman, while retaining those that have a more familiar quality—usually a selection of other sexual rules. The former seem self-evidently unimportant to us, while the latter seem self-evidently relevant.[40] The self-evident quality of such responses lies chiefly in the eye of the beholder.

This is not to say that the purity system we have been examining is a seamless web. Like all cultural systems, it is not the logical, context-free working out of a few abstract principles. We have noted from time to time how Israel's reaction against the religion of its neighbors has helped to shape specifics of the codes and how purity considerations interpenetrate with other important factors, such as property and hierarchy. What is more, it was possible for individual rules to drop out of active use, even after they were committed to writing and the writings themselves achieved scriptural status. For example, the Holiness Code forbade the slaughtering of domestic animals for food without a presentation of their blood at the sanctuary of the Lord (Lev. 17:3–6). Yet, Deuteronomy specifically commanded that such animals should be slaughtered, with certain safeguards, in a nonsacral manner (12:20–28), and the provisions of Deuteronomy in this matter triumphed. Again, the author of Judith, who was punctilious enough in most matters of purity, makes the conversion of Achior the Ammonite one of the crowning points of the book (Jth. 14:10) despite the fact that Deuteronomy absolutely forbids an Ammonite to "enter the assembly" (23:3).

Nonetheless, the Torah, in principle, stood or fell as a whole; one did not ascribe greater authority to one class of laws or to another. Even though one could distinguish between purity and other concerns (as in the law for the Day of Atonement, Lev. 16:16), they were of equal weight and of a single piece. Anyone who doubts, for example, the seriousness with which the food laws were regarded need only read 4 Maccabees, an oration in celebration of some martyrs of the second century B.C.E. The dramatic exchange between the emperor Antiochus and the Jewish sage Eleazar in chapter 5 is no doubt a creation of the orator's art, but it expresses persuasively the significance the purity law had come to have for observant Jews. Antiochus challenges Eleazar to show his moderation and good sense by taking a single small bite of pork and thus saving his life. Eleazar refuses, saying, "Do not suppose that it is a small sin if we should eat what is polluted, for to transgress the laws in small

40. See, e.g., Wenham, *Leviticus*, 161–62, 260.

matters or in great comes to the same thing, since either way the Law is still being scorned" (4 Macc. 5:19–21). The language borrows heavily from contemporary Stoicism, but the substance is nonetheless an authentic interpretation of purity ethics.[41]

The reverse of Eleazar's position was equally possible. If eating a single bite of pork was equivalent to idolatry, idolatry was in some sense equivalent to eating a bite of pork. When one faction of the Jewish elite in Palestine decided, early in the second century B.C.E., that it would be a good thing to assimilate more closely to the Gentile environment, they did not adopt a policy of trimming at the edges, as if food laws were less critical than prohibitions of idolatry. Their program seems to have included the building of a gymnasium (which implied nude athletic exercises in the Greek fashion[42] and perhaps Greek customs of pederasty), operations to reproduce the appearance of a foreskin, violation of the Sabbath, introduction of sacred images with their altars and cultus, sacrifice of unclean animals such as pigs, and prohibition of circumcision (1 Macc. 1:14–15, 44–49). It is not clear that these "reformers" thought that they were abandoning the worship of the Lord or their own identity as Jews. They may have been simply "modernizing." What stands out, however, is that for them as for Eleazar, the purity law was of a piece. There was no reason to retain one bit of it and ignore another; it was all or nothing. The significance of purity law for the New Testament will become clear only if we keep this point firmly in mind.

41. It was a Stoic axiom that "All sins are equal." See Rist, *Stoic Philosophy,* 81–96. Though the Stoics understood the principle differently from the author of 4 Maccabees, the latter probably derived it from them.
42. Cf. the antagonism toward Gentile nudity in *Jubilees* 3.30–31.

3

Purity in First-Century Judaism

The purity code of Israel as found in the Torah had probably reached its final form by the fifth century B.C.E., while the New Testament documents date from half a millennium later. We cannot expect that any societal code will remain absolutely unchanged over so long a time. Changes of political and social circumstances can easily make "ancient good uncouth," and, even where ancient customs are preserved, people may do so without full understanding of their original meaning. In antiquity as today, there was an ongoing process of reappropriating the past for contemporary use; and for this reason, the student of the New Testament needs to ask not only, "What did the Scriptures of Israel say about a given subject?" but also, "How was their witness being understood and put into practice in Israel at the time of Jesus and his disciples?" The latter question is the more difficult of the two to answer, for Jewish life and thought at the turn of the eras were rich and complex— and not always well documented.

The reader who is not familiar with early Judaism will need to know a few basic points by way of introduction. Membership in the nation of Israel was primarily by birth (though there were also Gentiles who became full converts to Judaism). The center of national life lay in the territories of Judaea and Galilee, which were subject to the Roman Empire, but the majority of Jews lived elsewhere, in what was called the Diaspora ("Scattering"). Some of these Jews lived to the east in Mesopotamia, outside the Roman Empire; others lived to the west and north, especially in the large, Greek-speaking cities of the Empire. Judaism was not a religion of the modern type, representing a personal choice of community and beliefs, but was rather an integral aspect of national identity. At the turn of the eras, this was a people which had been politically subject to others for the better part of the preceding six centuries; and for the last century and a half of this period, the Jewish community in Palestine had been through a bewildering period of historical flux, taking them from near-dissolution to revived independence and then into new subjugation.

During this difficult period, intensely religious Jews began to band together into like-minded groups whose way of practicing the national religion distinguished them from one another and from their less devout compatriots. There were four such groups or "sects" of particular importance in the years before the destruction of the temple in 70 c.e.: Sadducees, Essenes, Pharisees, and what one ancient writer called the "Fourth Philosophy." The first two were mainly priestly groups; but the Sadducees were wealthy and powerful because of their control of the Jerusalem temple, while the Essenes were dispossessed, alienated from the temple, and leading a withdrawn kind of life. The Pharisees were mainly laymen committed to a very high standard in observing the Torah and highly regarded by the populace as legal experts. The Fourth Philosophy was an assortment of revolutionary groups including the Zealots which aimed to restore the independence of Israel.

Of these sects, we know very little about the Sadducees except that they were literalists and strict constructionists in the interpretation of the Torah. Probably, their attitude toward purity was still close to that of the Torah itself. There was one law for all of Israel, but it bore on them, the Sadducees, with particular stringency—not because they were Sadducees, but because they were priests. Since priestly families received special portions from the sacrifices, which had to be eaten in cleanness, they were compelled to keep a higher standard than others.

ESSENES

By an archaeological accident, we have come to know the Essenes much better. The discovery of the Dead Sea Scrolls, beginning in the late 1940s, revealed to us something of the life of a Jewish group which had a settlement, between about 150 b.c.e. and 68 c.e., at a place in the Judaean desert called Qumran.[1] The writings did not prove altogether

---

1. Vermes, *Dead Sea Scrolls: Qumran in Perspective,* 32–35.

easy to interpret, but there is now broad agreement that they come from the group described by several ancient writers under the name "Essenes." This sect thus became the only first-century Jewish group other than the Christians for which we have contemporary documentation in the form of their own writings. The works in their library spanned a long period of time, and not all were uniquely theirs, for they included fragments of almost all the books of Jewish Scripture and of the many quasi-biblical documents which we call Pseudepigrapha. There were also books more particular to their sect, however, ranging in time of origin from the *Temple Scroll*, which may reflect a time before the sect reached its classic form,[2] to the *Commentary on Habakkuk*, which can hardly be earlier than the reign of Augustus (27 B.C.E.–14 C.E.).[3]

The sect probably included two distinct orders of adherents. A plausible reconstruction holds that the majority of the members lived in the towns and villages of Judaea but kept themselves rather apart from their neighbors. These people married, had children, held private property, and worked at ordinary occupations. The inner circle of the group, on the other hand, lived at Qumran itself, were celibate, merged their property into a single communal purse, worked the land surrounding their settlement, and devoted a significant amount of time to study of Scripture. In all the life of the community, priests took the lead, and one of them was probably the head of the whole community.[4]

The complex organization thus established drew its sense of unity and significance from conceiving itself as the only true Israel or as the real temple (in contrast to the building in Jerusalem). To their mind, the rest of the Jewish people had forsaken the right way, and the priests who had been in command of the Jerusalem temple since the mid-second century B.C.E. had defiled it and made it useless. In place of chosen Israel, then, was the membership of the sect, and in place of the temple with its sacrificial worship were the "men of perfect holiness," who made atonement for sins through prayer and "perfection of way" (*CR* VIII,20—IX,5).[5]

The sect's writings treat the issue of purity in a highly consistent way. That it was a matter of central importance to the Essenes is clear from the process of initiation into the inner circle: only after instruction,

---

2. Maier, *Temple Scroll*, 118.
3. Vermes, *Dead Sea Scrolls: Qumran in Perspective*, 149.
4. Ibid., 87–109.
5. Ibid., 170–72, 180–82.

examination, and a year's probation did the initiate gain the right to "touch the purity of the many." This "purity" has been variously interpreted. Most probably, it signified the solid foods served as part of the group's common meal. (The new initiate had to wait another year before sharing in the community's drink, for liquids, as Lev. 11:29–38 specifies, are more liable to pollution.)[6] More broadly, the "purity" may have included other common property of the community that could receive or transmit impurity and therefore had to be guarded from the careless or uninformed.[7] Purity thus lay at the center of the meaning of the inner group, or Council of the Community.

Very likely, this was connected with the sect's conception of this group as equivalent to the temple. Just as the sanctuary and priesthood, according to Leviticus, had to be kept pure of the people's uncleanness, so, too, must the Council remain undefiled, even more than the lower rank of the sect. Thus the men of the Council were severely admonished against any display of nakedness (*CR* VII,12–14), just as the priestly rules in Torah forbid steps at God's altar so that there will be no exposure of the priests' genitals (Exod. 20:26) and require the priests always to wear underwear when officiating (28:42–43). No equivalent rule survives for the ordinary Essene, though purity was surely important at both levels.

The purity system of the Torah was fully binding on the community, but in accordance with the Essenes' own particular interpretation of it. In the specific area of sexual purity, the *Damascus Rule* (which included rules for ordinary Essenes) reaffirms the Torah's rules on incest (V), but extends them by claiming that the rules are meant to be the same for women as for men; thus a woman may not marry her uncle any more than a man his aunt (V,7–11). The *Temple Scroll,* an idealized picture of the perfect Temple and its environs, also "rationalizes" the incest rules in a similar way (66.12–17).[8] The *Damascus Rule* also forbids "fornication" and defines it to mean polygyny. Since many of the Torah rules assume that a man may have more than one wife, it was necessary to explain such a claim and ground it in terms of Torah, and the Essenes constructed such a grounding by reading into the creation narrative and other passages a requirement of monogamy (IV,19–V,6). Similarly, the

---

6. Ibid., 95–96.
7. Newton, *Concept of Purity,* 21–26.
8. This Essene interpretation was opposite to that of the Mishnah; Vermes, *Dead Sea Scrolls: Qumran in Perspective,* 166.

Temple Scroll forbids polygyny, though, as far as one can tell, only in the case of the king (56.18–19).

The Essenes also added some purity rules of their own, following a general pattern of restricting sexuality further than the Torah did. One program for an ideal community life forbade a man to have intercourse with a woman before he was twenty (*MR* I,9–11). The *Damascus Rule* forbade all sexual intercourse in the "city of the sanctuary" on the grounds that it would defile the city (XII,1–2). The *Temple Scroll* may have assumed the same kind of rule, as it forbade a man who is unclean because he has ejaculated during intercourse with his wife to enter the "city of the sanctuary" for three days (45.11–12). For the *Temple Scroll*, the "city" in question was Jerusalem; but for the practical purpose of the *Damascus Rule*, it may perhaps have been the settlement of Qumran, which was, in many ways, the Essenes' equivalent.[9]

The Essene sect thus saw itself as committed to a level of purity far above that required of ordinary Israelites in the Torah, a purity, in fact, more suitable to priest and sanctuary. In Leviticus (21:16–24), there is a list of deformities that disqualify a priest from officiating in the temple. In the Qumran documents, we find similar lists of people who are excluded from membership in the sect: the mad, the simple, the blind, the maimed, the lame, the deaf, those with a visible blemish, minors, the old and tottery (*DR* XV,15ff.; *MR* II,3–9; *WR* VII,3–6). The community was to be a kind of consummation of purity understood as perfection.[10] (Even more than with the Torah itself, this perfection is assumed to be male; women are alluded to only as dependents of the members of the lower order of the sect.)

It has been suggested recently that this focus on purity is not to be understood as a true purity system and that the Qumran community had, in fact, little interest in or conception of purity as a distinct quality. "It is inappropriate," says one scholar, "to put weight on the distinction between 'moral' and 'ritual' purity at Qumran. If one slanders one's brother or touches a corpse, one has transgressed and is unclean, one's sin pollutes the community, and means have to be taken to cleanse the community and prevent further contamination."[11] This statement is undoubtedly correct in the sense that the Essenes, like Jeremiah, Ezekiel, and the Book of Proverbs, spoke of all kinds of sin as unclean-

9. See Vermes, *Dead Sea Scrolls: Qumran in Perspective*, 106–9.
10. Forkman, *Limits of Religious Community*, 74–77.
11. Newton, *Concept of Purity*, 46–47.

ness (see above, p. 28). Indeed, they went further and required rites of purification from sins originally unrelated to the purity system.[12] It would be a mistake, however, to assume that all kinds of uncleanness were equated with deliberate sin or that one could not distinguish at all, in the context of Qumran, between purity issues and other kinds of ethical concerns. The *Temple Scroll,* for example, distinguishes between the man who has had a wet dream and is therefore excluded from the sanctuary for three days and the man who has ejaculated during intercourse with a woman and is therefore excluded from the whole city of the sanctuary for the same time (45.7–12). The distinction here is whether the defilement was deliberately incurred. Impurity deliberately courted apparently seemed more defiling, though not, in this case, more sinful. If one also refused to restrict one's activities while impure (thus spreading it to others through contagion) and failed to undertake the prescribed methods of purification, no doubt one's impurity crossed over into the realm of sin. The community of the scrolls, however, could not have maintained its existence at all if it had regarded all impurity ipso facto as sin.

It was possible, from the Essene perspective, for life in flesh to be entirely free of impurity. Humanity is a thing kneaded of dust and water, originating in the nakedness of the sexual act; and only God's grace renders one righteous (*H* XIII,14–17). Still, the Essenes saw themselves as unique in Israel in terms of their understanding of and commitment to the purity system, and this led to a significant redefinition of the boundaries which that system marked and defended. The Qumran sect still regarded the Gentiles as the ultimate outsiders and foes. The sectarians were to avoid them as much as possible, not spending Sabbath near them (*DR* XI,14–15), not selling them any clean animal, any grain or wine, or any slave who had become a member of the sect (XII,8–11). In the last days, the members of the sect would participate in a great messianic war which would lead to the defeat and enslavement of the Gentiles (*MR* I,21; *WR passim,* esp. XII,14–15) and would set them permanently at a distance from the "sanctuary of men," that is, the Qumran Community itself (*Midrash on the Last Days* I,3–7).

The Gentiles were not, however, an immediate threat to the Qumran sectarians during most of their existence. Particularly in their formative period, their enemies were to be found in the Jewish establishment and

12. Neusner, *Idea of Purity,* 54.

other Jewish sects. The Wicked Priest who persecuted the Essenes' Teacher of Righteousness was a high priest of the Jerusalem temple, and their subsequent opponents included Sadducees and Pharisees.[13] Since the Essenes made a point of their own devotion to purity, it is not surprising that they accused their opponents of a comparable contempt for it, particularly of having "committed pollution" (*MA* 27) and defiled the temple (*CHab* XII,7–9). One specific complaint against their opponents was that they condoned (and perhaps committed) intercourse with menstruating women (*DR* V,6–7).

Because the Essenes perceived these Jewish opponents as indifferent to the requirement of purity and to pollution of the temple, the Essenes spoke of them in terms borrowed from the tradition about Gentiles. The author of the *Hymns* describes them as having chosen "uncircumcision of lip" and a foreign tongue (II,18–19; cf. IV,16). The *Commentary on Psalm 37* links together "the violent [of the Gentiles and] the wicked of Israel" as the people who are to be "cut off" (III,12–13).[14] The *Commentary on Habakkuk* declares that the Wicked Priest "did not circumcise the foreskin of his heart" (XI,13). The Qumran sect, in other words, understood Jews outside its ranks as quasi Gentiles. Perhaps they saw a poetic justice in the death of the Wicked Priest at Gentile hands (*CPs37* IV,9–10) and in predicting a similar fate for their other enemies (*CNah* II,4–5).

So strong was their sense of the outside world as "uncircumcised" that they even spoke of themselves as having been, figuratively, Gentiles before they became members of the sect. The author of the *Hymns*, speaking of how one recognized the truth of the sect's teaching, described it as a grace granted to the uncircumcised mouth (II,7) and ear (XVIII,20); and every member was exhorted to "circumcise in the Community the foreskin of evil inclination and of stiffness of neck" (*CR* V,5). What is more, they were to shun other Jews as unclean and to avoid sharing anything with them, except through commercial transactions (*CR* V,10–20), as was allowed also with Gentiles. Figurative use of the language of circumcision was not, of course, new; I noted its biblical occurrence above (p. 42). What is new here is that the purity system is being used to draw a line not only between Israel and the Gentiles but

13. Vermes, *Dead Sea Scrolls: Qumran in Perspective*, 150–52.

14. I follow the reconstruction assumed in Vermes's translation (*Dead Sea Scrolls in English*, 245). For an alternative interpretation, with no reference to Gentiles, see Lohse's *Texte aus Qumran*, 272; a comparison with IV,10 suggests, however, that Vermes's restoration is correct.

also between a small group of pious people and the great mass of Israelites, including those other groups of pious people who were at odds with the Essenes. The sect represented "the way of [holiness] where no man goes who is uncircumcised or unclean or violent..." (*H* VI,20–21).[15] The world outside it was now understood to be occupied by Gentiles and quasi Gentiles. Neither had any part in the true Israel; in order to become part of the elect, either kind of outsider must undergo a conversion. The boundary function of purity rules had now been applied to a quite new border.

PHARISEES

If we turn to the sect of the Pharisees, we shall find a related picture; but the lines here are less sharp, because of the nature of the sources and the historical problems they present. Our knowledge of the Pharisees is based on three groups of writings: the New Testament, the works of the first-century Jewish historian Josephus, and the Mishnah. Of these, the first two are close in time to the historical Pharisees, but Josephus stood in an ambiguous political relationship to them while the New Testament authors treat them only incidentally and usually in a hostile fashion. None of these authors could be said to view them with detachment. The Mishnah, on the other hand, includes many traditions about the Pharisees handed down through their own disciples; but since the material was not reduced to writing until about 200 c.e., the choice of what was preserved and the way in which it was recorded and edited must necessarily reflect the interests of later generations. The result is that students of the Pharisees, by reason of their varying evaluations of the data, can sometimes produce surprisingly divergent descriptions of the group.[16]

In what follows, I shall take my cue from what appears to me to be the predominant view, which holds that the Pharisees went through several distinct phases in their existence over a period of centuries. For our present purposes, it will be enough to think of these as three in number. First, from their origins in the second century b.c.e. to the time of Herod the Great in the late first, they were primarily a political party, competing with the Sadducees for influence at the Jewish royal court. By the time of Herod, they had lost this contest and, under their great leader

---

15. Translation from Vermes's *Dead Sea Scrolls in English,* 170.
16. Contrast, for example, Neusner's *From Politics to Piety* with Rivkin's *Hidden Revolution.* Both offer descriptions and evaluations of the sources and of their own methods.

Hillel, entered a second phase in their self-understanding. Withdrawing from the political arena, they became an association of men committed to the precise observance of the Torah, which for them meant not only the written Torah so important to the Sadducees and to all Jews, but also the unwritten traditions of their own sect, the "oral" Torah, to which they accorded an authority at least equal to that of its written counterpart. This phase of their community life lasted until the First Jewish War (66–70 C.E.), after which, in the social and political disarray that followed the Romans' victory and the burning of the temple, they reemerged, in a third phase, as a significant political power, gradually becoming the supreme Jewish authorities. The writing down of their oral traditions at the very end of the second century C.E., signified the completion of this process, and the Rabbinic Judaism of the Mishnah is their enduring legacy to the world.[17]

The second and third of these periods overlap with the writing of the New Testament, and the second (or sectarian) phase is of particular interest, since it is also the period of the origins of Christianity. During this time, the Pharisees seem to have concentrated their attention on issues of table fellowship. They undertook to eat their ordinary meals in the state of purity that Leviticus demanded only of the priestly families who ate the special sacrificial portions reserved to them. This commitment required constant vigilance against contracting uncleanness or, if one had contracted it, against communicating it to utensils and foodstuffs. In this regard, the concerns of the Pharisees were not markedly different from those of the Sadducees, who were obliged to maintain a high degree of purity since most of them were in fact temple priests, or of the Essenes, who undertook a similar obligation when they identified their desert community as a substitute for the temple and its sacrifices. The working out of these concerns, however, had to be quite different, for where the Sadducees and Essenes were surrounded by institutions (the temple, the desert community) which kept the ignorant and careless at a suitable distance, the Pharisees lived among the general population and sought to maintain purity household by household.

The oral Torah which the Pharisees generated and handed on seems

17. I have followed, in the main, the tradition of interpretation represented in Neusner's *From Politics to Piety.* It seems to me, however, that Rivkin's reconstruction of the history is not without merit. If his absolute identification of the Pharisees in their two earlier stages with the scribes (or legal experts) goes too far, it remains true that there must have been a substantial overlap between the two groups, which would have given the Pharisees much authority of an indirect kind, even in their second, or sectarian, phase.

to have been concerned largely with just the issues that would be involved in assuring such a result. They were interested in the correct tithing of produce, since untithed food, though not precisely impure, was nonetheless beyond the bounds of the priestly table. They were also interested in those types of uncleanness which were understood to be particularly contagious and which might therefore result in the pollution of food. Among these, menstruation was particularly important, since women did most preparing of food. Alongside menstruation, of course, went other forms of genital discharge: hemorrhages in women and gonorrhea in men. Corpses were also sources of contagion and particularly virulent, since they could transmit uncleanness through "overshadowing," that is, by being under the same cover (tent, roof, etc.) as a person or object susceptible to being made unclean. By contrast, purity issues raised by the written Torah but having no relation to the issue of table purity received little attention; examples would be wizardry, incest, emissions of semen, homosexual acts, or bestiality, which were not considered to generate contagion.[18]

In the great corpus of Mishnaic law, it is difficult to disentangle the earliest elements, coming from the first or second phase of the history of the Pharisees, from the overlay of later interpretation and elaboration (in its literal sense of the detailed "working out" of principles). Jacob Neusner has argued, however, in his massive work on "Purities" (the sixth major division of the Mishnah) that the authorities of what I have called the third phase were interested not only in the exploration of principles and the spelling out of detail, but also in the theme of personal responsibility and, therefore, in the role which human intention had to play in matters of purity. The purity code of the written Torah had no great interest in intention. Purity and impurity were simply facts: Play with mud and you will get dirty. The later Mishnaic authorities, however, saw in the purity system a grand interchange between nature and human purpose that took it out of the realm of the merely factual.[19]

Whether this theological and anthropological interest existed in the first or second phase is far from clear. It has been argued that the rabbis as a whole "felt" violations of purity as guilt rather than as a quasi-physical contamination, that is to say, that they saw purity and impurity in terms of virtue and vice rather than as simple facts of existence.[20] We

18. Cf. Neusner, *History*, 28, 110–36.
19. Ibid., 21, 293.
20. Sanders, *Paul and Palestinian Judaism*, 116.

have already seen that purity and virtue get mixed up with one another in a variety of ways: feelings associated with purity are used to reinforce virtue, and violations of virtue may be regarded as communicating impurity. Certainly, the earlier Pharisees must have seen their decision to maintain levitical purity at their own tables as something more than irrelevant fastidiousness. They, like the Essenes, probably intended a direct reference to the temple and its altar, though, unlike the Essenes, they wished not to replace that altar but only to claim a related and comparable sacredness for their own life of piety. This does not mean that, for them, purity was subsumed under virtue or that it became a "mere" theological gesture; it still maintained its distinct reality and importance, which interpenetrated with the other aspects of their religious concern.[21]

The Pharisees of the early first century c.e., then, had a strong interest in maintaining a high degree of purity at their own tables.[22] In the absence of tight boundaries around them as a community, they had to devise ways to make this possible. In all probability, they did so by creating a network of "associates" who understood the sect's standards and were pledged to maintain them rigorously. Any Pharisee could eat with confidence what was set before him by a fellow associate; but, conversely, he had to be suspicious of food prepared by other Jews. The Pharisee who bought produce from an outsider, even if the seller claimed to have paid tithe, tithed it anew in order to be sure that all obligations had been met. In matters of food preparation, too, those who were not members of Pharisee households were at least suspect. While one should not overplay the division between Pharisees and *am ha-arets* ("people of the land"; ordinary, nonsectarian Jews), turning it into some sort of deep-rooted and invariable antipathy, it remains true that the Pharisees' interest in purity imposed a barrier between them and less rigorous Jews—a barrier which, at one and the same time, gave a particular identity to the Pharisees and characterized outsiders as habitually unclean.[23]

The Pharisees did not retreat to the desert or hide behind the walls of

21. Neusner notes that ". . . while in 1QS one is unclean who violates the norms of the community, in Mishnaic law, early and late, one is unclean who is made unclean only and solely by those sources of uncleanness specified in Scripture or generated by analogy to those of Scripture" (*History*, 105; cf. 186).
22. Neusner, *From Politics to Piety*, 81–96.
23. On the relation between purity and the boundaries of the Pharisaic groups, see Forkman, *Limits of Religious Community*, 87–98.

the temple; yet, they did separate themselves decisively from the other Jews among whom they lived—by a barrier of purity. If the original purpose of that barrier was to associate their meals with the sanctuary, the inevitable effect of it, nonetheless, was to set them apart. As long as the Pharisees continued primarily as a sect within Judaism, this would have given impetus to the elaboration of purity laws, for these laws, in effect, defined them as a group. By the late second century, the spiritual descendants of the Pharisees were no longer a sect, whose foremost task was to keep themselves distinct, but the acknowledged guides of the whole people. One may guess that this carefully elaborated system then ceased to be useful. In fact, as Neusner has observed, it fell out of use just as it approximated perfection of form and completeness of substance.[24]

The Pharisees, then, used purity for purposes similar to those of the Essenes, though without desiring or producing the drastic measure of separation that Qumran represents.[25] If we accept Josephus' claim (*Antiquities* 18.23) that the advocates of the Fourth Philosophy among the Jews, that is, the Zealots and other revolutionaries, differed from the Pharisees not at all except in their uncompromising devotion to the independence of Israel, then we can say that, of all the first-century Jewish sects known to us, every one made some use of purity as a device to mark itself off from other Jews, whether adherents of rival sects or ordinary "people of the land." It is this which marks the situation of the first century as radically different from that envisioned in Leviticus. The older presupposition was a single people adhering to a single law of purity, although, to be sure, a higher degree of that purity was incumbent upon the priestly families than upon the laity in their daily life. The purity law had always functioned to draw boundaries, but they were primarily boundaries between Israel and the uncircumcised. In the first century c.e., however, purity law was also important in the way it could draw boundaries between Jew and Jew.[26] The sects learned to identify themselves in terms of the interpretation of the law to which they adhered and the structures they created to support them in their practice of it. Outside the boundaries of the sects, the ordinary "people of the

24. Neusner, *History*, 300–303. I would not wish to propose my "post-sectarian" explanation of these events as a substitute for Neusner's better qualified and more profound observations, but only as a supplement to them.
25. Ibid., 38, 101.
26. The distinction between Jew and Gentile, of course, did not cease to be important; see the appraisal by Riches (*Jesus and the Transformation of Judaism*, 119–27).

land," whether by explicit judgment or only by clear implication, were unclean, removed from holiness.[27]

THE DIASPORA AMONG THE GREEKS

The picture I have drawn thus far applies only to Palestine. A great many Jews, as I mentioned earlier, lived outside of Palestine; and those who lived in the great Hellenistic (Greek-speaking) cities of the Roman world are particularly important to any study of the New Testament, for it was among them and through their synagogues that Christianity first began to spread widely. These Jews spoke Greek as their principal or, in most cases, only language. They read their Scriptures in the Old Greek Version, often called the Septuagint. They interacted with the Gentile culture that surrounded them to a degree nearly unthinkable in Palestine itself. The circumstances of their lives made the issue of purity somewhat different for them from what it was to their Palestinian coreligionists.

One important difference is that the Jews of the Diaspora do not seem to have given rise to a rich growth of sects as in Palestine. The only one that we know of was a contemplative group called the Therapeutae. Like the Essenes, they retreated into a kind of monastery in the desert, though, in their case, it was near Alexandria rather than the Dead Sea. They seem to have had only this one center. Philo, our one source of information about them, describes them as ascetics who devoted themselves to the study of Scripture and held periodic common meals marked by teaching, singing, and sacred dance. He says nothing of specialized purity rules surrounding their life together, though it is not impossible that such existed.[28]

The heart of the purity issue, however, for Hellenistic Jews lay not in the self-definition of sects but in that of Israel itself. Surrounded as they were by Gentiles who spoke the same language as they did and with whom they were compelled to deal constantly in matters of trade and politics, the issue of their own identity came to the fore. Jew and Gentile

27. Neusner (*History*, 106) denies that the law was "made to define a sect." It may be that it was not originally intended to do so, but it can scarcely have failed to have that effect.

28. Philo observes that women were part of the group, which might indicate a certain indifference to purity; but in describing the great feast of the fiftieth day, he says that these were mostly aged women who had remained virgins of their own will (*The Contemplative Life* 32–33, 68). Women past menopause presented less of a threat to purity.

alike were conscious of the purity laws and of the related matter of the Sabbath as things which separated Jews and Gentiles from one another. Some even accused Jews of disliking humanity in general because of what seemed to be standoffish behavior. It was important for Jews to respond to this kind of critique, both for their own sake and also to present a more amiable account of themselves to their neighbors.

We find such an account in the *Letter of Aristeas,* an Alexandrian Jewish work of perhaps the second century B.C.E. that tells a somewhat legendary tale of the origins of the Septuagint.[29] A long speech (128–71) ascribed to the high priest explains that the food laws were given to Israel precisely to keep them separate from other peoples. This separation then preserved them from being tempted into idolatry and left them free to focus entirely on the wonderful wisdom given them by God in the Torah. Even the contents of these laws are not merely arbitrary, but they set before the people, as they practice them, an ongoing allegory of just living. The weasel, for example, is forbidden as food because it conceives through the ear and gives birth through the mouth, thereby serving as an allegory of the informer, whose unjust way of life is to be rejected. Here, we see a Jewish thinker accepting the fact that purity laws have an exclusionary effect and seeking to make of that fact an apologetic virtue.

Not all Hellenistic Jews were content with this answer. Some, in fact, wished to abolish the purity laws or at least let them drop out of use. In Jerusalem itself, in the early second century B.C.E., Greek-speaking Jews who had drawn close, politically and culturally, to their Gentile neighbors sought to reform Judaism by eliminating the distinctive purity laws, probably in the name of a return to a more primitive and universal form of their ancestral faith.[30] In the Diaspora, some Jews argued that the allegorical meaning of the purity laws, their hidden teaching about the just life, was in fact their whole significance and that the person who understood this meaning and lived by it need not obey the commands in their literal sense.[31] While the dominant tradition within Judaism insisted on retaining the purity code, Jews were not completely united in the matter. The code itself, therefore, had to be explicated and defended

29. See the summary discussion on dating by R. J. H. Shutt in *Pseudepigrapha,* edited by Charlesworth, 2:8–9.

30. Hengel, *Judaism and Hellenism,* 1:268–70, 292–303.

31. We know these thinkers from Philo's attacks on them, e.g., in *Migration of Abraham* 89–93.

in terms that would make it intelligible both to Gentile outsiders and to those insiders who had come to regard it as an imposition.

Several apologetic tacks were possible. One was to say, "We are just like you only better." This approach would emphasize the areas of overlap between Jewish and Greek morality without making a point of Jewish particularity except where it could be related to some theme in Gentile ethics. Since most Greeks and Jews agreed in disapproving of sexual promiscuity, this could provide the rubric for a presentation of common themes. The *Testaments of the Twelve Patriarchs*, accordingly, presents a series of moral exhortations, in a context redolent of biblical history, that would nonetheless have been generally intelligible to Gentiles, too.[32]

A similar approach is found in the work of a first-century Jewish writer posing as the ancient Greek poet Phocylides. He warns his audience against most transgressions of the Mosaic laws of sexual purity: adultery (3), prostitution (177–78), incest (179–83), bestiality (188), homosexual acts (3, 190–92), and perhaps even intercourse with a menstruating woman, though the language is unclear (189). Yet, he does all this "in character" as Phocylides and therefore never mentions the Torah as an authority. He also forbids a couple of acts not mentioned in Torah but sufficiently common in Greek culture that they served as convenient illustrations of the differences between Jews and Greeks: abortion (184–85) and castration of youths (187). He reproves sensuality, even in a man's relations with his legitimate wife (193–94). The whole work offers a sexual morality far more Jewish than Greek, especially in the matter of homosexual acts; yet, it is presented without reference to its sources and in a thoroughly Greek manner.

The most thorough examination of the Israelite purity ethic from the perspective of the Diaspora comes from one of the greatest thinkers of Late Antiquity—Philo of Alexandria, a contemporary of Paul. He seems to have addressed a significant portion of his massive literary achievement to Gentiles who had a strong interest in Judaism and may even have accepted it as true in principle, but who still found the particularity of Israel, as manifested in its purity code, a barrier to their full identification with it.[33] Philo takes a somewhat different apologetic tack from

32. The work dates from c. 250–150 B.C.E. and probably comes from Syria. In it, the Torah is understood as in some sense a universal law, directly related to "nature." See H. C. Kee in *Pseudepigrapha*, edited by Charlesworth, 1:776–80.

33. Goodenough, *Introduction to Philo*, 30–45.

pseudo-Phocylides or the author of *Testaments of the Twelve Patriachs*. Where they were content to make Judaism speak in the accents of Greek ethics ("We are like you, only better"), Philo prefers to say, "We are intelligible in terms of the best of your own thinking, but we have things to tell you that you could never have arrived at on your own." He thus balances efforts to make Judaism speak Greek with efforts to emphasize its distinctiveness.

The clearest examples of his method come from the third book of the *Special Laws*, an exposition of Torah under headings provided by the Ten Commandments. In discussing the prohibition against intercourse with a menstruating woman, he seeks to show the rationality of this commandment in terms meaningful to any ancient reader and finds his point of departure in a common ancient understanding of conception. Since there was no specific knowledge of the mammalian ovum until the seventeenth century, ancient people were apt to assume that the male's semen constituted the entire germ of the new being, while the mother provided a place for it to grow and the essential nourishment while it was in the womb. This made the ejaculation of semen into the womb precisely analogous to the planting of seed in a field.

Philo agreed with some Greco-Roman philosophers of the time who taught that the only "natural" purpose of sexual intercourse was the begetting of children.[34] To sow seed in a menstruating woman was therefore wrong for the same reason that sowing barley in a swamp would be (3.32–33). The same analogy explains for Philo why the Torah condemns male homosexual intercourse; it is equivalent to sowing seed in a desert (3.39–40).[35] The analogy, however, has implications that go beyond the laws of Moses. If it is wrong to sow seed in a male because it cannot grow, it must be equally wrong to do so in a woman known to be barren, which Torah does not in fact forbid. Philo allows some excuse for the man who stays married to a wife he married as a virgin and who has proven barren in their marriage, for their "long love will have been impressed on their souls by the length of their life together." The man who deliberately contracts a fruitless marriage, however, is acting under the sway of pleasure alone (3.34–36).

Philo has thus shifted the focus and scope of the Torah purity code in the process of making it intelligible to his Gentile contemporaries. Hav-

---

34. So, too, pseudo-Phocylides, 175–76.
35. The basic analogy goes back to Plato (*Laws* 8.838e–39a).

ing made the begetting of children the only justification for sexual intercourse and categorized all other indulgence in it as hedonistic and animalistic (3.113), he finds that this newly imported principle makes marital intercourse with a barren woman as wrong as intercourse with a man. Accordingly, he must then add to the Torah's commandments in order to accommodate this new principle. In this way, Philo approximates the Torah more than he may have understood to the kind of contemporary Gentile ethic which regarded pleasure and passion as the great moral evils to be avoided and therefore exalted self-control and orderliness.[36] In his treatise *The Contemplative Life*, he exalts self-control (*enkrateia*) as the basis of all the virtues (34); and in *Special Laws* 3.8−10, he argues, like pseudo-Phocylides (193−94), that even intercourse with a lawful spouse deserves blame if one indulges in it immoderately and insatiably. In the process of defending the Torah by Hellenistic standards, Philo has actually recreated it in a new form.

The Jews of the Diaspora among the Greeks thus found themselves in the delicate position of interpreting their particularity in terms of a thought-world that bore no original relationship to it. The particularity of Israel was sometimes a burden to them in relationships with Gentiles, but it was also essential to their own sense of national and religious identity. Without it, they could not survive as a people. Yet, they could not survive with it, either, unless they were prepared to explain and defend it in terms intelligible to the larger world; and the very process of explanation and defense tended to alter the character of the thing being explained.

This is most vividly apparent in regard to a subject that comes up repeatedly in Hellenistic Jewish writings: homosexuality. In the earlier history of Israel, as we have already noted, the Holiness Code forbade homosexual acts; but otherwise, the Scriptures paid little attention to the matter. Even the traditions about Sodom had their focus elsewhere. The prohibition of such acts was simply one aspect of the working out of an ideal of holiness as wholeness and distinctness; and it served the basic function of all purity law—that of setting a boundary between one group of people and another.

As long as Jews lived basically to themselves in Palestine, this was a minor issue. Jews of the Hellenistic Diaspora, however, found them-

---

36. Cf. *Special Laws* 3.22−25, where Philo claims that incest was forbidden in order to promote these virtues.

selves living in the day-to-day context of a culture which accepted homosexual relationships, usually of a pederastic type, as quite usual.[37] From being a largely theoretical dimension of the purity code, disapproval of homosexual acts thus became a day-to-day defining characteristic of Jewish culture. Apologetically, such ethnic distinctiveness was both a problem and an opportunity. It was a problem because it made Jews odd, an opportunity because they could claim it as a point of ethical superiority in terms that at least some Gentiles would acknowledge as valid.

Hellenistic Jewish authors, accordingly, made homosexual acts a perennial theme of their ethical discourse and borrowed motifs from those streams of Greek philosophical thought which had come to be critical of homosexual relations. For this purpose, the contemporary Stoic doctrine that sexual intercourse was solely for the purpose of begetting children, with its attendant rejection of homosexual intercourse, was ideally suited.[38] Since the Stoics often described what is morally right as "according to nature," Jewish authors could appeal to "nature," however defined, as a universal criterion which would justify their culture's traditional antagonism toward homosexual acts.

One must understand that the presupposition behind this use of the word "nature" is that procreation is the only "natural" end of sexual acts. If procreation is not in view, as for example, in sexual intercourse during menstruation or after menopause, one must assume that the goal of the act was pleasure or the satisfaction of passion, which are not "natural" in this sense.[39] The "unnaturalness" of homosexual acts, in this sense, is a recurrent theme of Hellenistic Jewish literature. Pseudo-Phocylides condemned both male and female homosexual acts in these terms (190–92). And several of the Jewish authors whose works are

37. The cultural accommodation of homosexual acts among the ancient Greeks and Romans is a very complex topic. Not all possible liaisons were acceptable, and even what was accepted was not always to be made public. On the other hand, there was, for most people, no presumption that intercourse with one's own sex was in any way morally distinct from intercourse with the other. For a good brief survey of Roman attitudes and a helpful analysis of the presuppositions behind them, see Veyne, "Homosexuality in Ancient Rome," 26–35.

38. The early Cynics and Stoics regarded sexual acts as a legitimate expression of the love that draws the wise together and had not therefore seen homosexual acts as wrong; Rist, *Stoic Philosophy*, 60, 65–69, 79.

39. Philo (*Special Laws* 3.32–33) condemned intercourse with a menstruating woman on precisely this basis as a violation of the "law of nature."

collected in the *Sibylline Oracles* make a point of pederasty as a characteristically Roman offense.[40]

Philo himself attacked homosexual acts and those who perform them, not only in *Special Laws*, as we have seen, but also in *The Contemplative Life* 59–62 and *Abraham* 133–41. In all three contexts, he attacked pederastic homosexuality for depopulating cities and wasting semen, and also for what he claimed it did to the characters of the partners. Boys were feminized by it—a grave matter both to Jews and Greeks of the age, for both groups regarded women as intrinsically inferior to men;[41] and the men involved were not only responsible for the corruption of the boys, but also for their own financial and physical ruin as they chased after them. In *Special Laws* 3.41–42, Philo went on (more for rhetorical reasons, it seems, than logical ones) to associate male homosexuals with the unpopular eunuchs who filled offices in the imperial bureaucracy, and he even claimed, wrongly, that Moses required the execution of eunuchs.

In Philo and other Diaspora authors, the usefulness of the subject of homosexuality in both distinguishing and defending Jewish culture gave it a certain prominence. One should not overread the evidence, however, as if all Jewish authors were preoccupied with the subject. Some texts that have been instanced as condemnations of homosexuality seem to me dubious. In Wisd. of Sol. 14:26, one finds the Greek phrase *geneseōs enallagē*, which David Winston translates "interchange of sex roles."[42] As Winston notes, however, the language is odd, and one would expect *genous* rather than *geneseōs*. A more literal translation would be "alteration of generation," or "of procreation," which would designate the whole range of nonprocreative sexual activities rather than homosexual acts specifically.

Another such passage, *Testament of Naphtali* 3.4, warns against becoming "like Sodom, which altered the order of its nature." While this sounds, from a modern perspective, very much like a warning against

40. This is true both of the early materials (second century B.C.E.) in Book 3, which repeatedly contrast Romans and Jews on this score (175–95, 573–600, 762–66), and of later ones (late first century or early second century C.E.) in Books 4 (24–39) and 5 (162–79, 386–96). I follow the datings suggested by J. J. Collins in *Pseudepigrapha*, edited by Charlesworth, 1:354–55, 381–82, 390.

41. Philo had in mind the Greek tradition whereby the beloved was typically a freeborn adolescent; the Romans preferred slaves or freedmen. See Veyne, "Homosexuality in Ancient Rome," 29.

42. Winston, *Wisdom of Solomon*, 280.

homosexuality, the above discussion of Sodom (chapter 2) suggests that one should not leap to such a conclusion with regard to ancient texts without examining the context. In this case, what leads into the statement quoted is a warning against idolatrous practices; a knowledge of God as Creator will serve to keep Naphtali's descendants from becoming like Sodom. And there follows immediately an admonitory reference to the wickedness of the Watchers in Genesis 6, "who altered the order of their nature" and thereby brought on the Flood. The fault of the Watchers was not homosexuality or nonprocreative sex of any kind, but intercourse between angels and human women. It is quite possible that, for this author, "becoming like Sodom" means indulging in any kind of prohibited sex; and this hypothesis is confirmed by the reference to Sodom in *Testament of Benjamin* 9.1, where it serves as a warning against sensual indulgence with women.

The overall picture that emerges of the Hellenistic Diaspora is that of a minority community with a strong need to defend its particularity in terms of the dominant culture. The purity laws which surrounded Israel and preserved its distinct identity also served to characterize it, often in an unflattering way, among outsiders. It was necessary to try to explain these laws in terms intelligible to Gentiles while, at the same time, not allowing Israel to dissolve into the larger culture. The food rules were difficult to handle in this regard; it was easier to stress the sexual restrictiveness of the Mosaic purity code, since one could do so by associating it with those strands of contemporary Greek philosophical thought which were suspicious of passion and of pleasure and which held that sexual intercourse could be justified only as procreation. Philo, by arguments of this kind, may have expected to win sympathetic Gentiles to full conversion. Other writers, too, looked forward to a time when Gentiles would come under the Law of Moses, though they may have thought of it more as a remote and miraculous result of divine intervention in history.[43] In the meantime, the role of Israel was to serve as an island of purity in the midst of the unclean Gentiles.

CONCLUSION

Though the life and faith of all Jews, whether in Palestine or in the Diaspora, rested on the common foundation of Torah, there were significant differences among them in the matter of purity. For the Hellenistic

---

43. *Sibylline Oracles* 3.194–95, 741–95; 5.264–65.

Jew of the Diaspora, purity continued to function almost entirely as a way of distinguishing Jew from Gentile. The social pressures of being a minority group in an alien culture, however, demanded that Jews attempt to justify their separateness and particularity in Gentile terms. The apologetics by which they did so had the effect of skewing the Torah's purity interests to a significant degree by approximating them to Greek philosophical interests. Yet, this shift was the price of preserving the purity code under the circumstances.

In Palestine, by contrast, the purity code was, to a great extent, simply the way of life of the dominant population group. It served, though not to the same degree as in the Diaspora, as a daily reminder of Israelite identity. Of more importance, however, was that particular interpretations of the purity code, especially those of the Essenes and Pharisees, became ways of distinguishing one Jew from another, both in terms of their understanding of the code and in terms of their devotion to the keeping of it. In both cases, the code was still serving its intrinsic function of establishing and keeping boundaries; the boundaries thus guarded, however—ethnic, in the one case, sectarian in the other—were significantly different.

4

Purity and Christianity—
A First-Century Historian's
Interpretation

Given the pervasive importance of purity in their world, any Jewish group of the first century c.e. had to define its position on that issue. The early Christians were no exception to this rule. Indeed, we would expect purity to be a critical subject for them to deal with. They originated as a sect among the Aramaic-speaking people of Palestine, where their founder came into conflict, according to the Gospels, with Pharisees and Sadducees. They soon expanded to include Greek-speaking Jews of Palestine and the Diaspora and eventually even Gentiles. In the course of this development, they would have encountered the purity code in both its boundary roles: distinguishing one Jewish sect from another or from the people of the land, and separating the Jewish people from their Gentile neighbors.

The business of this chapter is to discover and lay out the basic principles by which the Christians (or that stream of Christianity which has left us the New Testament writings) dealt with these boundary issues, with the purity law of Israel and its effects on their mission. I begin this exploration with Acts of the Apostles, a choice which calls for some explanation here. Acts is not the oldest work in the New Testament, nor does it deal with Christianity's first origins in the teaching of Jesus. Moreover, there are ongoing debates about Luke's accuracy and reliability as a historian. The usefulness of Acts to this inquiry, however, lies in the fact that it contains a contemporary observer's interpretation of the single most critical passage in the early Christians' struggle with the issue of purity, the decision to admit Gentiles into their community without requiring circumcision of the males among them.

Whether Luke, in writing Acts, recorded the historical data accurately is not of primary importance for this study.[1] My purpose is not to trace the actual historical developments, but to see how Luke interpreted events in relation to the inherited, biblical motif of purity. Luke has given us, in Acts, an exceptionally clear and sustained treatment of the issues. After taking a close look at what he tells us, we shall be in a better position to look afresh at the more fragmentary and uncertain evidence we find in the other New Testament writings. Although we cannot assume that the other writers necessarily agreed with Luke, we shall have the advantage, when we turn to their works, of having heard one first-century voice speak explicitly to the matter at hand.

ACTS

How, then, from the point of view of Luke, did purity figure in the origins of Christianity? We find an emphatic answer to that question— one made emphatic by Luke himself—in the vision of Peter, narrated first in Acts 10. It is a double vision, actually, with each part confirming the other. The first vision was granted not to Peter, but to a Gentile, a centurion in the Roman army named Cornelius. This man was earnest in giving alms and prayed faithfully to the God of Israel, his household joining him in this; but he had not become a proselyte, that is, a full convert to Judaism. He remained uncircumcised and unclean. An angel appeared to him at the time of the evening sacrifice in the temple,[2] telling him that his prayers and alms had won him a hearing with God and that he should send for one Simon Peter to bring him an important message.

Peter's half of the double vision was timed so that it just preceded the arrival of Cornelius' messengers. He was hungry and was waiting for lunch to be brought when he saw an enormous sheet being let down from the sky, containing all sorts of animals, many if not all of them unclean. A heavenly voice said, "Get up, Peter, slaughter and eat." Peter, perhaps thinking this a test of some kind, answered, "Certainly not, Lord, for I've never eaten anything common and unclean." To this the voice responded, "What God has pronounced clean, you are not to

---

1. One can argue that he reported the circumstances of the apostolic decree on this subject (Acts 15) quite erroneously. See, e.g., Catchpole, "Paul, James, and the Apostolic Decree," 428–44.

2. The allusion, ironically, suggests particular holiness and purity.

regard as common." This conversation was repeated three times, and then the sheet was drawn up into heaven.

According to Luke, Peter did not know what to make of this (10:17). Matthew and Mark represent Jesus as having dismissed the issue of food purity during his ministry (Matt. 15:1–20; Mark 7:1–23); but Luke did not include this tradition or anything quite equivalent to it in his Gospel. To the contrary, Luke represented the early Christians as keeping to a very high standard of purity, as manifest in the fact that they spent much time in the temple from the time of Jesus' ascension onward (Luke 24:53). At times, they even went daily (Acts 2:46; 5:42). Since worshipers were expected to be pure when entering the temple, the implication is that the Christians maintained themselves in such a state constantly.[3]

It did not occur to Peter, then, that he, as a Jew and a disciple of Jesus, might take this vision literally as a simple canceling of the laws of food purity. His reflections were interrupted, however, by the arrival of the messengers from Cornelius, and by the voice of the Spirit commanding him to go with the men without hesitation. At this point, in Luke's narrative, be it noted, there was not a single Gentile in the Christian community. There were other people marginal to Israel, a large number of Samaritan converts and a eunuch who served the Queen of Ethiopia, all noted in Acts 8, but no full-fledged Gentiles.[4]

Peter goes, then, to see Cornelius, taking several other believers with him; and arriving there, he tells the story of his own vision and explains its significance—a significance that is only now clear to him. "*You* know," he says, "how unlawful it is for a Jewish man to associate with or visit a foreigner; and to *me* God has shown that one is to call *no* human being common or unclean" (10:28). Peter preaches to the assembled group, as requested, but in the midst of his speech, the Holy Spirit falls upon this audience of Gentiles. The Jewish Christians accompanying Peter are astonished, but there is no denying the event, since they hear the Gentiles speaking in tongues and glorifying God. Peter

3. By Essene standards, this would have meant sexual abstinence as well as great caution about food. The Pharisees, however, seem to have allowed, contrary to the explicit words of the written Torah (e.g., Lev. 15:16), that a simple immersion purified one of many kinds of uncleanness, without waiting for the following sunset; if the early Christians followed their teaching in the matter, sexual intercourse would not have been a barrier.

4. Samaritans saw themselves as true Israelites, but Jews largely treated them as quasi Gentiles. Luke did not specify whether the eunuch was Jew or Gentile, but he had apparently been on pilgrimage to Jerusalem. In any case, eunuchs were anomalous figures whose lack of family ties made them rather independent of ethnic distinctions.

then says, "Can anyone forbid the water and keep these people from being baptized?" The purpose of this question is to ascertain the consent of the other faithful present, so that this is not an individual decision on his part. Hearing no objection, he orders the baptisms to proceed (10:44–48).[5]

Others did object, however, to the idea that Gentiles could be Christians. More exactly, they objected even to the fact that Peter had visited and shared food with such persons (11:1–3); but, of course, the sharing of food was a basic way of expressing membership in the Christian community, as Luke made clear earlier (2:46). Many of the community, like Essenes or Pharisees, would have been sharing their food in a state of purity, for they were in daily attendance at the temple. Some Christians, in fact, were themselves Pharisees (15:5). Thus, the addition of true Gentiles to the community created a serious problem about the relationship of believers to one another in terms of the purity of their food. Luke acknowledged the seriousness of this issue by having Peter repeat the whole incident of chapter 10 in full detail for his Jerusalem colleagues in chapter 11. Since Luke was not normally given to the use of repetition in his narrative style, his choice of this solemn device shows not only that he wished to be sure his audience heard and absorbed all the details of a most important incident, but also that he wanted to clothe the telling of it in an aura of divine authority. (His own book, of course, was not greeted as Scripture instantly upon publication; it had to acquire that status over generations.)

For Luke, the baptism of Cornelius was pivotal to an understanding of the development of the church. At the time when it happened, to be sure, it appeared to be only an isolated incident. God had specifically chosen a certain Gentile, with his family and friends—one distinguished for his almsgiving and devotion to prayer; it was not taken as precedent for the deliberate missionizing of Gentiles. That mission began quite separately, at Antioch, under the auspices of Greek-speaking Jews who had fled Jerusalem because of a persecution a short while earlier (8:1–3; 11:19–21).[6] The leaders in this new departure were Christians

5. For the significance of this account in relation to issues of Luke's time, see Segal, *Rebecca's Children*, 163–65.

6. There is some uncertainty in the manuscripts as to whether one should understand their audience as "Hellenes" or as "Hellenists." In Luke's usage, "Hellenes" refers to Greek-speaking Gentiles while "Hellenists" means Greek-speaking Jews. While "Hellenists" is perhaps the *lectio difficilior*, it seems to me impossible to make any sense of it, for Luke plainly assumes a little later on that we know there are Gentile converts in Antioch (15:1).

in sympathy with Stephen, who had been stoned for suggesting that the temple at Jerusalem and its sacrifices had no true religious value (6:8— 8:1). The skepticism these "Hellenists" felt toward the temple probably implied a certain lack of interest in purity as well, which in turn made it relatively easy for them to accept Gentiles into their Christian community. Their initiative and the success that attended it, however, caused misgivings in Jerusalem; and the church there sent Barnabas, one of its trusted members, to inspect (11:22–24). His approval was apparently enough to quiet critics for the moment; but in due course the matter had to be dealt with at the highest levels.

This is the significance of the apostolic council in Acts 15. Some visitors from Judaea had told the Gentile Christians at Antioch, "Unless you get circumcised according to the Mosaic custom, you cannot be saved" (15:1). This teaching divided the community there, which sent Paul and Barnabas to Jerusalem to consult with the authorities. At the ensuing council, Peter now claimed his experience with Cornelius as giving divine sanction for the present mission. God, he said, "made no distinction at all between us and them, having pronounced their hearts clean by faith" (15:9). In other words, the church could not require circumcision of Gentiles, nor could it treat them as unclean. Peter went on to say, "So why are you now putting God to the test by laying on the disciples' necks a yoke that neither our fathers nor we have been strong enough to bear?" (15:10).

Of what yoke was Peter speaking? It seems unlikely that he, or Luke, would have thought of circumcision, in and of itself, as an impossible yoke.[7] Greeks frowned on it as an act of personal mutilation; but it did not constitute a true disadvantage for most Jewish men, certainly not for one who, like Peter, lived in a predominantly Jewish environment. The "yoke," rather, was all that went with circumcision—the special relationship of Israel with God expressed both in Israel's special status as the chosen people and in the Torah. This suggests that the Judaeans who started the controversy at Antioch were demanding of Gentile converts not only circumcision, but also observance of the whole Torah.[8] This was by no means an irrational or narrowly partisan demand on their part. No one had yet explained exactly how clean Jews and unclean

7. Contra Haenchen (*Acts*, 459) who declares that the "yoke" was primarily circumcision, but has to add that it included the multiplicity of other laws.

8. Cf. Paul's declaration that every circumcised person "is obliged to practice the whole law" (Gal. 5:3).

Gentiles were to coexist in a single community and share the same table. The problem was both genuine and serious. If the Gentiles were not going to accept responsibility for keeping the whole purity system, those Jewish Christians who were faithful in their observance of it would inevitably be compromised.

At the council, the arguments that won the day, according to Luke, were based on revelation and miracle. Peter recounted his vision and experience with Cornelius, and Barnabas and Paul told of the "signs and wonders that God had done among the Gentiles through them" (15:12). The weight of the evidence and its evident effect on the assembly allowed James, "the Lord's brother," as president of the council to sum up its consensus, which was "not to cause trouble for those of the Gentiles who are turning to God" (15:19). This did not in itself, however, resolve the outstanding question, which was how such Gentiles were to coexist with Jewish Christians who took purity seriously. James suggested that a compromise could be reached, by which the Gentile Christians would be strongly urged to practice a modified purity code, involving abstinence from "pollutions of idols and harlotry and what has been strangled and blood" (15:20).[9]

What, specifically, did these rules entail? Like many compromises, they are not particularly clear. "Pollutions of idols" is a vague expression which could be interpreted in a variety of ways; but it probably had to do specifically with food.[10] At a minimum, avoidance of these would exclude direct and immediate participation in such meals as were part of Gentile worship. Questions, however, would arise about just where to draw the line. Could one supply the sacrificial animal, if one took no part in the sacrifice? (The Essenes forbade all trade in animals with

9. There are substantial variations in the text of the decree among ancient manuscripts and quotations of Acts. "What has been strangled" is missing from some, "harlotry" from others. Omission of "what has been strangled" may have been an early effort to make the decree something other than a purity code; some manuscripts, to the same end, add a negative form of the Golden Rule. For fuller discussions, see Ropes, *Text of Acts*, 265–69; and Metzger, *Textual Commentary*, 429–34. There can be little doubt that the original text, whatever its exact wording, did indeed represent a minimal purity code, though one that was never truly binding. It became progressively less and less intelligible as the church became exclusively Gentile and was therefore altered in the manuscripts.

10. The specific term *alisgēmata* ("pollutions") occurs nowhere else in Scripture, even in the letter of the council (Acts 15:29), where *eidolothuta* ("things sacrificed to idols") takes its place. In the LXX, however, the related verb occurs several times, always with reference to food that is somehow defiled (Dan. 1:8; Mal. 1:7; Sir. 40:29). It would scarcely be possible for most Gentile Christians to avoid absolutely all contact with idols; and, in any case, they could perhaps have pleaded the exemption granted to Naaman the Syrian by Elisha (2 Kings 5:18–19).

Gentiles, lest they use what they bought for sacrifice to their gods.)[11] Could one eat, in a nonsacrificial context, meat from an animal that had been sacrificed? (This would become a difficult problem for Paul.)[12] Nothing in James's language would help in settling such issues.

The other provisions about food purity are somewhat clearer. The prohibition of eating blood (and therefore strangled meats, from which the blood had not been drained) is one of the very few purity laws in the Torah to which a theological rationale is attached: "For the life of the flesh is in the blood; and I have given it for you upon the altar to make atonement for your souls; for it is the blood that makes atonement, by reason of the life" (Lev. 17:11 RSV). What is more, Torah presents the prohibition of eating blood as a law given to all humanity through Noah at the time when God first authorized the eating of meat (Gen. 9:1–7), so that one could argue that this was a universal law, equally applicable to Gentiles. Finally, Leviticus itself directs that this prohibition be equally applicable both to native Israelites and to resident aliens living among them (17:10–13).

Thus, there was a variety of reasons which might have animated the adoption of such a rule; and, compromises being what they are, that may have been exactly what recommended it. Different parties within the church could understand it in quite different ways. Those who were most insistent that Gentile Christians did not have to become in any sense Jewish were free to see it as a command given to Noah or to derive it from the theological principle that blood is for the altar. Even if they were uninterested in the altar at Jerusalem, they might agree with the author of Hebrews that Christians "have an altar from which those who minister in the Tabernacle cannot eat" (13:10) and might therefore avoid animal blood because of its symbolic relationship to the blood of Jesus. Yet, those who wanted Gentile Christians to accept circumcision and become full proselytes could draw encouragement from the fact that Leviticus 17 lays this law specifically on resident aliens and that the Old Greek version called these people *prosēlytoi*. The council's decision thus, in some ways, represented a postponement of any final solution to the problem. It expressed an interest in having Gentile Christians observe a limited degree of purity in relation to foods, but left the nature and extent of that interest vague.

In this context, we must ask about sexual purity. What did the council

11. See above, chapter 3.
12. Romans 14—15; 1 Corinthians 8—10.

mean by its rule against "harlotry"? That question proves very difficult to answer. Even a suitable translation of the Greek word in question *(porneia)* is problematic.[13] I have chosen the rather archaic "harlotry" because it both incorporates the basic meaning of the Greek term, which is "prostitution," and also has other overtones drawn from nonliteral usages commonly found in the Bible. In the Scriptures of Israel, *porneia* (or its Hebrew equivalent, *zenuth*) is sometimes used in an expanded sense to include sexual offenses other than literal prostitution; it also frequently serves as metaphor for Israel's unfaithfulness in abandoning its own God to worship others. Perhaps the commonness of sacred prostitution in the environment of ancient Israel accounts for the ease with which this metaphorical shift was made. Elsewhere in the New Testament, *porneia* usually appears in contexts, such as lists, which give us little help in defining it. When Paul gives specific content to it, he includes incest (1 Cor. 5:1) as well as literal prostitution (6:12–17). But since it appears nowhere in Luke's works except in passages associated with the decision of the Jerusalem council, we cannot be certain how he would have used it.[14]

In James's speech to the council, the term *porneia* appears sandwiched between "pollutions of idols" and "what has been strangled and blood" (Acts 15:20). Given that order of words, we might readily understand "harlotry" as metaphorical for worship of other gods. Interestingly, this same usage is found in the very chapter of Leviticus discussed above in relation to the eating of blood, which describes the people as "playing the harlot" after rural fertility deities ("satyrs" RSV; 17:7). Leviticus, in fact, uses "harlotry" only in the literal sense of prostitution (19:29; 21:7, 9, 14) or in the metaphorical sense of practicing alien cults (20:4–6), not in the expanded sense of "fornication." If the Leviticus reference is dominating James's choice of words, then "harlotry" in the context of the Jerusalem council has no direct reference to sexual ethics, but refers to participation in Gentile cults. It thus supplements the rule against "pollutions of idols" by including other kinds of worship along with the eating of sacrificial foods. It would, for example, rule out magical practices; and it is worth noting that Luke does tell a story about how Gentile Christians gave these up in Ephesus (Acts 19:11–20).[15]

13. In the New Testament, the RSV variously translates it "unchastity," "fornication," and "immorality."

14. *TDNT,* s.v. πόρνη κτλ.

15. Yet another possibility is that "harlotry" in this case equals "mixed marriage," something repeatedly associated with idolatry; e.g., *Jubilees* 20.1–13; Philo *Special Laws* 3.29; pseudo-Philo *Biblical Antiquities* 9.5, 18.13–14, 21.1.

On the other hand, in the actual letter of the council (and in James's later reference to it), the order of the rules is different: they are to abstain from "things sacrificed to idols and blood and things strangled and harlotry" (15:29; cf. 21:25). This arrangement of the list could suggest that the council was following not so much the language as the order of Leviticus 17—18, which begins with regulations about sacrifice, goes on to the prohibition of eating blood and carrion,[16] and then proceeds to a list of sexual offenses, including incest, intercourse with a menstruating woman, adultery, giving "seed" to Molech, homosexual acts, and bestiality. These sexual rules, like the prohibition of blood, are said to be binding on both native Israelite and resident alien or proselyte (Lev. 18:26). On this analysis, "harlotry" might include this whole range of sexual offenses,[17] and the Jerusalem council would have been reenacting the whole of Leviticus 17—18 as a kind of abbreviated purity law for Gentile converts.

If one wished, however, to maintain that the council was specifically reaffirming those two chapters of Leviticus as binding on all Christians, one would be forced to admit that no one paid much attention to its key provision. Among the sexual concerns of Leviticus 18, one stands foremost among all the rest in terms of its relationship to table fellowship and was a key issue for both Essenes and Pharisees. It is the contagious uncleanness of the menstruating woman; and there is no evidence either in the New Testament or in other early Christian literature that Christians retained any concern about this matter. To anyone familiar with the Mishnah, this will seem an inexplicable oversight, unless in fact Gentile Christians regarded themselves as completely free of that concern. That, in turn, implies that they saw themselves as under no obligation to Leviticus 18.[18]

On balance, it seems likely that the council concerned itself with only two matters: idolatry, whether in the form of sacrificial meals or of other rites, and the eating of blood. By the exclusion of these, the Christian leaders hoped to ensure that Jews and Gentiles in the church could continue to enjoy table fellowship with one another without "causing trouble" for the Gentile converts or outraging Jews concerned for purity.

16. It is far from clear, however, that *pniktos* can be equivalent to "carrion."
17. Or perhaps only incest, as the rabbis apparently connected it with *porneia*; Haenchen, *Acts*, 449.
18. E.g., Yarbrough (*Not Like the Gentiles*, 28–29) has noted the conspicuous absence of this motif from Paul's writings.

It is important to note that Luke did not represent the council as having laid down conditions for Gentile membership. Both James's speech and the council's letter are carefully worded to avoid that impression. James says only that they should "write to them to abstain," not "command them" to do so. The letter is more strongly worded, but not in a way that violates what James had suggested: "It has seemed good to the Holy Spirit and to us to lay on you no heavier weight than these necessary things: to abstain from things sacrificed to idols and from blood and from things strangled and from harlotry. If you keep yourselves from these things, you will do well" (Acts 15:28–29). The letter brings strong pressure to bear in such phrases as "these necessary things." (Necessary to what end? To the preservation of table fellowship.) Yet, it stops short of saying "You shall" or "You shall not," and, in the end, says only, "If you do this, you will do well." One might legitimately paraphrase these expressions as saying, "This is a matter of greatest importance in which we need your cooperation; do not fail us."[19]

Peter provided the theological reason for the council's caution at the beginning of its deliberations when he said, "Why are you now putting God to the test by laying on the disciples' necks a yoke that neither our fathers nor we have been strong enough to bear? But through the grace of the Lord Jesus we believe that we are saved in just the same way as they" (15:10–11).[20] Since Luke presents Peter elsewhere as abiding faithfully and uncomplainingly by the Torah, presumably he does not mean him to say here that no one can keep the Torah or that Jews (or Jewish Christians) ought to give it up. He means rather that the history of Israel turns out to be a history of failures in this respect—a teaching with a venerable ancestry in Scripture itself. God gives salvation, accordingly, by grace, not waiting for the perfect fulfillment of the Torah, and

19. Some translate, "you will do right"; cf. Haenchen, *Acts*, 453–54. Even so, the language falls short of establishing an ethical imperative, much less a condition of salvation. Some later Gentile Christians, at least in the West, did avoid eating blood; but we know this only incidentally and have no evidence that they attached any theological importance to it. Note the letter about the martyrdoms at Lyons, preserved in Eusebius' *Ecclesiastical History* 5.1.26. Also see Minucius Felix *Octavius* 30.6; Tertullian *Apology* 9.13–14. As for idolatrous rites, refusal to participate in them quickly became a test of faith and was rejected for quite new reasons, above and beyond the council's decree.

20. Catchpole ("Paul, James, and the Apostolic Decree," 429–32, 438–43) argues that the council intended to impose on the Gentiles a modified purity code on the authority of Torah and that it therefore stood diametrically in opposition to Paul's insistence on grace. If this is correct, Luke's use of Peter's speech is doubly interesting, for he thereby makes such an interpretation of the decree impossible within the context of his own narrative.

this is why salvation is available now to Gentiles in the same free way as to Jews. If any further condition were applied to them, whether circumcision or even abstinence from blood, it would imply that the grace of the Lord Jesus was not sufficient by itself. The council is free to urge certain kinds of purity upon Gentile converts for the sake of unity in the church, but not to set them as conditions of baptism.[21]

The rest of Luke-Acts bears out the interpretation of the apostolic council offered here. The opening of the church to the Gentiles and its problems in adjusting to their impure presence form the main themes of Acts. The work moves from a strong emphasis on the pure Judaism of the earliest Christians, as manifested by their frequent presence in the temple, to Paul's unsatisfactory interview with leaders of the Jewish community at Rome and his final turning to the Gentiles: "Let it be known to you, then, that this salvation from God has been sent to the Gentiles. And *they* will listen" (Acts 28:28). Luke presents the turn to the Gentiles as being the result of divine guidance, not human planning. This is nowhere more obvious than in the two great visions which Luke recites or refers to so often in the book—that granted to Peter, which we have looked at in some detail, and that granted to Paul, which, in every recital, concludes by saying that he will become God's messenger to the Gentiles (9:1–19; 22:6–21; 26:12–18).

At the same time, Acts does not suggest that the gospel abolishes the Torah with respect to Jewish Christians. Quite the contrary, all the Jewish representatives of Christianity are represented as being fully law-abiding. Paul, for example, circumcises Timothy before including him in his ministry (16:1–3). As the son of a Jewish mother and Greek father, Timothy's nationality was ambiguous, and the Jewish communities where Paul worked would take his resolution of that ambiguity as a sign of his commitment to the faith and identity of Israel. Paul also fulfills his own vows (18:18) and assists others in doing so (21:20–26). Wherever possible, he begins his missionary work in the local synagogue. He calls attention to his Pharisaic training and his lifelong faithfulness (22:3; 23:6; 25:8; 26:4–5; 28:17). Luke even presents him as more law-

---

21. Theologically, Peter's position also implies that the purity code is not binding on Jewish Christians either, at least as far as salvation is concerned. It might perhaps be argued that it was still integral to their Jewish identity and that this was a good in itself; Luke, however, avoids the issue by making all his Jewish Christian leaders irreproachably devout observers of Torah. Neither in New Testament nor in rabbinic Judaism is membership in Israel simply equated with salvation; cf. Segal, *Rebecca's Children*, 168–69, 176–79.

abiding than the high priest (23:1–5). Others claimed that Paul had brought a Gentile into the temple (21:27–29), but Luke makes it clear that this was a false charge. Even James, in his speech to the council, does not propose to dismiss or devalue the concern for purity but rather to leave its propagation to the existing network of synagogues (15:21).[22]

For Luke, the major Jewish Christian leaders were distinguished by their zeal for the whole law. He also acknowledges that there were those, like Stephen, who were perhaps less committed to the temple and its sacrifices and who were pivotal figures in the original opening toward the Gentiles. Perhaps Luke has made less of these persons than they in fact merited; but our task here is not so much to reconstruct the actual events as to understand the way in which Luke presents them. For him, the earliest Christian church was composed of Jews who were personally committed to the Torah in all respects, including its purity requirements—people who, like Peter, had never eaten anything common and unclean and, like Paul, practiced their people's faith with great strictness. Only the insistence of the Spirit could lead such people to break the ultimate boundary of purity and accept unclean Gentiles into their community. Yet they did so, under the conviction that any other course of action would violate the fundamental reality of God's grace.

LUKE

Luke's Gospel provides an appropriate introduction, in this respect, to his account of the church's development in Acts. The book begins and ends in the temple—with the annunciation to Zechariah and the rejoicing of the disciples after the ascension. In between, we meet a Jesus who is, in some respects, a model of purity. He was circumcised on the eighth day (2:21) and his parents took him to the temple for his mother's purification and the redemption of the firstborn, obeying, as Luke specifies, the dictates of the Torah (2:24, 27). There he was greeted by Anna, an aged woman so pure as to be virtually a permanent resident of the temple (2:36–38). He exorcised unclean spirits (4:31–37; 9:37–43a). When he healed lepers, he commanded them to do everything the law required (5:12–14; 17:11–14). And, although he allowed a woman with a hemorrhage to touch him and himself voluntarily touched a

22. This verse has proved very difficult to interpret (Haenchen, *Acts*, 450 n. 1), I think because it has been wrongly taken as James's reason for *imposing* a purity law on Gentiles. It is in fact his reason for *not* doing so. The Christian community, he says, does not have to make purity a requisite for membership; its decision not to do so simply leaves the advocacy of purity to the same institution which had always advocated it, the synagogue.

corpse and a corpse's bier (7:11–17; 8:40–56), the results, which were healing and resurrection, perhaps justified his recklessness.[23]

Still, Jesus foreshadows the church's future openness to the unclean in important ways. His own disciples are not all gathered from among the most law-abiding Jews (5:27–28). He is repeatedly shown as associating, of his own volition, with tax collectors and sinners (5:29–32; 7:29–30; 15:1–2; 19:1–10). He rejects the Pharisees' concern for cleanliness of hands and the tithing of herbs—in other words, their concern for table purity (11:37–42); and he flouts their concern for such purity by accepting the ministrations of a "sinful" woman at one Pharisee's own table (7:36–50). He even goes on the attack, comparing the Pharisees to concealed tombs, which render people unclean without their knowing it (11:44), and telling a parable in which a Pharisee's prayer is unfavorably contrasted with that of a tax collector. All in all, the Jesus of Luke's Gospel seems considerably less concerned about purity than Peter is at the time of his vision in Acts.

Jesus also shows an interest in and concern for Gentiles, even though his experience of them is minimal. In his first sermon, a programmatic piece which Luke places at Nazareth, he reminds his hearers that, at a time when there were many widows in Israel, Elijah was· sent only to one who was a Gentile and, at a time when there were many lepers in Israel, Elisha only healed one who was a Gentile (4:24–30). Jesus heals the slave of a centurion and says of this Gentile soldier, "I tell you, not even in Israel have I found so much faith" (7:1–10). He forbids his disciples to attack a village of the quasi-Gentile Samaritans who had refused to receive him (9:51–56). He says more than once that Gentiles will fare better in the judgment than will Israel (10:12–15; 11:29–32), and he himself commands the Gentile mission after his resurrection (24:47).

Luke was not unrealistic about Gentiles. He was well aware that it was Gentiles who killed Jesus (Luke 18:31–34) and destroyed Jerusalem (21:24). He also included them among the antagonists of Paul on his missionary tours (e.g., in Ephesus; Acts 19:23–41). The point about the opening of the church to Gentiles was not that Gentiles were somehow better than Jews or more favored of God or even readier converts; Luke's history did not extend far enough for him to have to deal with a time

23. I have omitted the virginal conception of Jesus from this list of purity motifs, since there is little evidence, if any, that virginity was considered especially pure in ancient Israel.

when Gentiles were the dominant group within Christianity. The point rather is the sufficiency of grace. "Through the grace of the Lord Jesus we believe that we are saved in just the same way as they" (Acts 15:11). For Christians to make such a claim, purity law had to be relativized. For Israel, purity gave access to the temple and the temple to God. For Christians, now a different understanding of the dynamics of the holy took precedence—one which said that grace gives access to Jesus and Jesus to God. By the inclusion of Gentiles, the Spirit forced a choice, according to Luke; and the church responded as it should have. Jewish Christians would continue to keep the purity rules, while Gentile converts were urged to avoid blood and the kinds of idol-connected foods and rites that would render their table fellowship obnoxious to Jews.[24] Even this reduced purity code, however, was not a condition of their being baptized or remaining in the fellowship of the community; and other aspects of purity law were simply irrelevant to them. Salvation itself could come only by the grace of Jesus.

24. If, alternatively, one should be persuaded that *porneia*, for the council, did involve the sexual activities condemned in Leviticus 18, it is still true that the council did not forbid these, but only urged their avoidance.

5

Purity in the Gospels

The teachings of Jesus were the fountainhead of Christianity, but Jesus' followers did not begin writing them down until some decades after his death and resurrection. At first, they were preserved through oral tradition by trusted teachers, who repeated them and, as one second-century source tells us, adapted them to the needs of the moment. Only during the second half of the first century, it seems, did people begin committing the traditions to writing, eventually producing the four New Testament Gospels.

Jesus' teachings were preserved not from historical interest alone, but because they were part of the very fabric of Christian faith. Teachers not only retold them, but applied them, interpreted them, perhaps even added to them. The evangelists (i.e., authors of written gospels) probably continued this tradition. Their books not only report the traditions about what Jesus did and said, but also present them as coherent aspects of their four different portraits of Jesus. It is never easy to identify, on the basis of what the four evangelists tell us, exactly what Jesus actually said; and, from the perspective of biblical theology, it is not of primary importance.[1] We shall be looking here not so much for the Jesus of history as for the Jesus to whom the four evangelists point in their distinctive ways. Each evangelist's portrait of him treats purity differently, but all four are of interest and share some deep-lying principles in common.

---

1. Though I shall sometimes write, "Jesus says," in what follows, I always understand it to be modified by "according to Matthew, Mark, etc."

LUKE

We have already noted how Luke presented the life and teachings of Jesus as a prelude to the vital decisions the church subsequently made about the role of physical purity in determining its community boundaries. While he portrayed Jesus' parents and, to a degree, Jesus himself as remaining within the prescribed limits of purity, he also showed him as foreshadowing later developments by his open treatment of Gentiles and of the impure within Israel itself. A closer look at an important text will help us see how Luke understood this opening to the impure in ethical terms.

The text is an encounter between Jesus and a Pharisee who had invited him to eat with him—an encounter turning on the issue of table fellowship and the kind of legal care which Pharisees took in relation to it:

> As he was talking, a Pharisee asked him to eat with him, and he came in and sat down. And the Pharisee was astonished when he saw that he did not wash first before the meal. But the Lord said to him, "Now you Pharisees cleanse the outside of the cup and the plate, but what's inside of you is full of rapacity and evil. Fools, didn't the one who made the outside make the inside, too? Only give the contents for alms and, behold, all things are clean for you. But woe to you Pharisees, because you tithe mint and rue and every herb and bypass judgment and God's love. You should have done the latter and not omitted the former." (Luke 11:37–42)

The discussion of inside and outside is not immediately clear, for the terms are being used in a condensed metaphorical way that is hard to unravel. The simplest sense would be that the Pharisees cleaned the outside surface of hollow containers, but not the hollow interior. Since it is unlikely, however, that this was so,[2] one must see this not as a factual claim, but as an attention-getting riddle. A second sense would be to take the "outside" as meaning "all surfaces," while the "inside" would mean the body or the fabric from which the vessel was made—clay, for example. This makes little sense in relation to the literal vessel, but is intelligible in terms of the application to the Pharisees, who are thus said to be externally pure, but inwardly rapacious and evil. In a third and final twist, the terms come to refer to the container as the "outside" and

2. Neusner, *Idea of Purity,* 62–63. Matthew's version of the saying (23:25–26), on the other hand, seems to take account of the position of the School of Shammai, namely, that the inside and outside of a vessel contract uncleanness independently of one another; cf. Neusner, "First Cleanse the Inside," 492–95.

its contents as the "inside," so that if the contents are given as alms, both contents and container are assured of being pure.

The point of this curiously compressed saying is that physical purity is radically subordinate to another kind of purity subsisting on the level of intention. Physical purity has a certain facticity about it; when one touches a corpse, one is rendered impure, regardless of whether one intended to touch it or not. Luke's Jesus, however, subordinates that kind of purity concern to another, metaphorical kind of purity or impurity, consisting of the intent to do good or to do harm. Thus, the care one takes to ensure the physical purity of hands or of containers is, for Jesus, wasted if one is impure at the level of intent—not intent to contract or to avoid impurity, but intent to do good or to do harm. Rapacity, that is, the intent to do harm, renders everything in a person's life unclean; conversely, the intent to benefit another, as expressed, for example, in almsgiving, makes everything clean. We are suddenly far removed from the automatic cleanness or dirtiness of acts in a true purity ethic. This is a radical shift in the understanding of purity, one that we shall see expressed in other accounts of Jesus' teaching as well.[3]

Luke is not saying that the sense of physical purity is obliterated for Christians or that it is now illegitimate for Christians to practice purity as an aspect of their religious life. That is clear from what Jesus says about tithing mint and rue. While exactitude in tithing was not strictly a purity issue, it was an aspect of the Pharisees' carefulness about table fellowship, so that they may have tithed, as in the present instance, even those forms of produce which Torah had not specified as subject to the tithe.[4] What Jesus faults, in this situation, is not care about tithing, but failure to be equally attentive to the claims of justice and love. The externals of religion, whether purity law or tithing or public recognition (11:43), have a tendency to displace the interior demands. When this happens, external, physical purity may actually be an evil, if it disguises internal "uncleanness" of intent. Hence, Jesus goes on to say to the Pharisees, "Woe to you, because you are like concealed tombs, and people do not know they are walking over them" (11:44). Inner rapacity and evil are only concealed by outer attention to purity; they do not lose their power to defile.

---

3. As Luke makes explicit, this kind of "deepening" of purity requirements does not abolish them, but adds a dimension to them. A similar development had long been at work in Greek religion; see Burkert, *Greek Religion,* 77.

4. The Mishnah, however, exempts rue from tithe (*Shebiit* 9.1).

The practical consequences of such teaching appear in the story of Zacchaeus, a rich tax collector with whom Jesus stayed in Jericho (19:1–10). The Mishnah suggests that tax collectors were under suspicion of being impure in such a way as to transfer their impurity to whatever they touched (*Tohoroth* 7.6).[5] When Zacchaeus, however, becomes a follower of Jesus, not a word is said about the purity issue. He promises rather to give half of all that he owns to the poor and to compensate anyone he has defrauded four times over. Jesus' response is that "today there has come to be salvation for this household, for he, too, is a son of Abraham" (19:9). This resolution to the story is perfectly in tune with the principle Jesus had already enunciated: "Give the contents for alms and, behold, all things are clean for you" (11:41).

Luke, then, suggests that Jesus had already raised a fundamental objection to any ethic of physical purity. The problem of such an ethic is that conformity to it is a matter of externals. Since it takes no account of motive, it is possible for persons to be pure for the worst of reasons and to combine a high level of physical purity with vicious behavior in other respects. Similar themes are found in Matthew and Mark, but they are developed there more fully.

MARK

Mark is perhaps the most radical of all the Gospel writers on the general subject of purity; he has Jesus dismiss physical purity as a matter of religious concern and replace it with the kind of metaphorical purity of intent which we have already seen hinted at in Luke's Gospel. As in Luke, the occasion was a disagreement with the Pharisees (and "certain of the scribes") about washing before eating. Mark stresses the importance of the matter for contemporary Jews: "[coming] from the marketplace,[6] unless they wash they do not eat; and there are many other things that they have accepted as traditional to keep: washings of cups and jugs and bronze pots and couches" (7:4). Questions have been raised about the accuracy of Mark's report here;[7] but in any case, it shows us what he regarded as being at stake in Jesus' confrontation with his critics. The conversation itself is complex, since there are really two topics under discussion. One topic is tradition: since the specific regula-

5. Cf. Forkman, *Limits of Religious Community,* 90.
6. Or perhaps "[what they bring] from the marketplace." In either case, some words have to be supplied that are not made explicit in the best Greek manuscripts.
7. See Booth, *Jesus and the Laws of Purity,* 189–203.

tions about washing were part of the oral rather than the written law, the authority of the oral law is at issue, and Jesus rejects it (7:5–13). The other topic, more important to us here, is purity itself, and Mark goes out of his way to mark this part of Jesus' response as of great importance.

Mark has Jesus summon "the crowd," thus making his response to the other religious leaders part of his public teaching. Jesus says to the crowd, in his most solemn style, "Listen to me, all of you, and understand. There is nothing outside the human being that, by entering into him, can render him unclean, but the things that come out from a human being are what render the person unclean" (7:14–15). Then, after this public pronouncement, Mark has Jesus explain what he said privately to his disciples, while Mark, speaking in his own voice, provides a crucial element of the interpretation (7:17–23). This explanation is necessary because the public declaration admits of more than one interpretation.

We could understand it entirely in terms of physical purity, meaning that one is rendered impure only by what leaves one's body, not by what enters it. In this case, to choose a sexual example, an ejaculation of semen during intercourse would render the ejaculator unclean, but not the other person involved. This, of course, would represent a substantial revision of the written Torah, but it would not negate the principle of physical purity.[8] In his private explanation, however, Jesus speaks quite differently: "Whatever enters into the human being from without cannot render him common because it does not enter into his heart, but into his belly, and passes out into the latrine." By this, Mark says, Jesus was "declaring all the foods clean" (7:18–19).

At this point, a certain discrepancy has appeared between the original statement and the elucidation of it. The original statement said that *nothing* from without could render one unclean; and, as we have seen, it was easy enough to find a sexual example that would correspond to that language. Does Mark, then, mean to limit its applicability to food in such a way as to exclude its being applied to sexual uncleanness? We need not think so. Mark's language represents not a restriction of the original subject under discussion, but an expansion of it. The original issue was whether one must wash before eating, and Jesus' response

8. Booth gives a thorough exposition of this possible explanation (*Jesus and the Laws of Purity*, 206–10), ultimately rejecting it as unworkable.

could be heard as applying only to that one matter, namely the incidental ingestion of unclean matter adhering to the hands.[9] Mark asserts instead, in his authorial aside, that Jesus set aside not only the purity concerns related to washing, but the whole category of physical purity and impurity. He thus not only rejected provisions of the oral Torah of the Pharisees, but even the plain distinction between clean and unclean animals in Leviticus. Mark's aside, then, should not be understood as restricting the saying's applicability to foods, but rather as underlining that it prevails even against the explicit purity rules of Leviticus itself.[10]

Jesus' statement that things from without do not "enter into the heart, but into the belly" implies a certain understanding of the human being which makes the digestive tract peripheral and emphasizes instead the organ of thinking and planning (as the heart was anciently understood to be). The force of this shift is clarified in another statement: "He went on to say, 'What comes out of the human being—*that* is what renders the person unclean. For out from within, from the human heart, come evil designs, harlotries, thefts, murders, adulteries, acts of greed, evils, deceit, license, evil eye, blasphemy, arrogance, foolishness. All these evil things come out from within and render the human being unclean'" (7:20–23).[11]

This list of what renders impure does contain some words associated with sexual acts, but they are not of a sort to suggest that one section of the old purity code is being reinstituted under a new rubric. After a general heading ("evil designs"), the next five items seem to constitute a short list drawn from the Ten Commandments.[12] "Harlotries," as first

9. So also Matt. 15:20. Neusner (*Idea of Purity,* 61–62) rightly observes that two distinct authorities are at stake—the oral tradition of the Pharisees and the written Torah. Mark and Matthew alike, however, treat the unity of the purity issue as overriding this distinction and have Jesus cancel the rules of both authorities.

10. Riches (*Jesus and the Transformation of Judaism,* 136–40) has argued that Jesus himself meant to reject the whole purity system, not merely the food laws.

11. Booth (*Jesus and the Laws of Purity,* 96–114) argues that the form of Mark 7:15 does indeed go back to the historical Jesus, but that he can have meant by it only that metaphorical purity was more important than physical purity in much the same way as Philo does (pp. 83–90). This conclusion, however, seems to have been implicit in Booth's presuppositions; see, e.g., p. 69, where he already assumes this result. Booth may have been led astray by his presupposition that Jesus could adopt only two possible attitudes toward purity—affirming or rejecting it. I am suggesting a third alternative—declaring it irrelevant. What is irrelevant becomes a matter of personal choice: one is not more righteous for practicing purity nor less righteous for ignoring it; and no one may impose its observance on another.

12. "Harlotries, thefts, murders, adulteries, acts of greed." "Acts of greed" are violations of the command against covetousness. Cf. Neyrey, "Idea of Purity," 120, although his treatment of the list neglects to take order seriously as a component of its meaning.

item in this list, thus has its metaphorical sense of "idolatrous worship" rather than literal prostitution. "Adulteries" are primarily a matter of property law, as we shall see below in part 2 of the present study. The remainder of the list seems miscellaneous. It includes "license," which may include sexual libertinism but signifies any kind of behavior lacking restraint.[13] The term describes a character trait rather than a physical impurity. Finally, "foolishness" sometimes refers specifically to sexual offenses (e.g., Deut. 22:21; 2 Sam. 13:12), but that is by no means its invariable sense. Its place as the last item in Mark's list makes it more likely that it is here serving as a general summary: all sin is "foolishness," the opposite of true wisdom.[14] Mark, then, presents Jesus as having set the whole issue of physical purity aside in favor of the metaphorical purity of the heart.[15] Since this purity is not a matter of automatic physical contagion, sexual acts are not inherently governed by it any more than foods. Only intent to harm renders a sexual act impure.

Like Luke, Mark shows Jesus as behaving in a way consistent with such a position: associating with tax collectors and sinners (2:14–17), touching a leper (1:41) or a corpse (5:41), being touched by a woman with a hemorrhage (5:25–34).[16] Jesus has no fear of contamination, but rather dominates uncleanness through his own power. Mark even calls the demons whom Jesus exorcises "unclean spirits." Jesus again and again exerts control over them, even on behalf of people who, as Gentiles, are themselves unclean and therefore, in some sense, congruent with such spirits. One of these, the man with the Legion, Jesus heals on his own initiative; and when the man asks to become a disciple, Jesus gives him the first commission to proclaim him openly (5:1–20). The other is a Syrophoenician woman whom Jesus at first scorns as a "dog"; but he heals her daughter after admitting that she has bested him in argument (7:24–30).

The uncleanness of spirits is closely linked to the uncleanness of the heart that Jesus substitutes for physical uncleanness. The spirits them-

---

13. The other New Testament usages of *aselgeia* may have a sexual connotation; but these are in Pauline writings, 1 and 2 Peter, and Jude. This is its only occurrence in Mark, and its immediate context hardly suggests a sexual reference for it here.

14. Cf. the highly general use of "foolishness" in the wisdom literature.

15. Philo, too, could say that the really *(kyriōs)* unclean person was the unjust and impious one and that this more general expression of impurity was of great importance (*Special Laws* 3.208–9); but he did not *replace* literal physical impurity with the metaphorical kind.

16. He does not reprove her for her violation of purity laws; cf. Selvidge, "Mark 5:25–34," 619–23.

selves delight in doing harm, even, as in the story of Legion, to animals (5:12–13); but beyond that, they are also a test for purity of the heart in human beings. When some of Jesus' opponents claimed that he did his exorcisms by cooperating with the demons, Jesus replied, "Amen, I say to you that all things will be forgiven the children of humanity—all the sins and the blasphemies that they commit; but whoever blasphemes against the Holy Spirit never has forgiveness but is liable for an eternal sin." He said this, Mark explains, "because they were saying, 'He has an unclean spirit'" (3:28–30). In other words, if one credits an act of loving-kindness to evil intent, this in itself is so complete a violation of the purity of the heart as to place one beyond the scope of forgiveness. The new purity thus draws as sharp a boundary as the old, but it is of a very different—one is tempted to say, "a hidden"—order. It reveals itself not in observable avoidance of the sources of impurity but in the motives which inspire action, the intentions with which action is undertaken, and the way in which one assesses the motives and intentions of others.

Mark does not reject all observance of the purity code by Christians. He shows Jesus ordering the leper he has cleansed to go show himself to the priest and make the prescribed offering (1:44), and he seems to approve of John the Baptist's denouncing Herod Antipas for marrying his brother's wife (incest according to Leviticus, Mark 6:17–18). Still, Mark is more radical than Luke in this matter, having little use for purity laws of any kind. His Jesus leaves little reason for continued observance of them. Accordingly, it is not surprising that Mark has Jesus himself authorize the mission to Gentiles, both by sending the man who had had the Legion of demons to preach (5:18–20) and by predicting that, before the end of the world, "the gospel must first be preached to all the Gentiles" (13:10). From Mark's point of view, Jesus had already cleared away the barrier of purity law.[17]

MATTHEW

The presentation of purity in Matthew's Gospel represents a complex balancing of both traditionalist and radical tendencies. On the tradi-

---

17. Neyrey ("Idea of Purity," 115–23) prefers to say that Mark's Jesus "reformed" the purity code. Neyrey can do so because he is confessedly using "purity" in two senses (p. 92). In terms of the actual purity code observed among Jews of Jesus' time, one must speak rather of his setting it aside or replacing it with something new and different. In the last analysis, I am doubtful whether "purity of the heart" can in fact function as a true purity boundary; and Neyrey's proposal of an "inclusive" kind of purity, if applied on the literal, physical level, may be a contradiction in terms. At the deepest possible level one can link literal and metaphorical purities, but even then they cannot both be practiced with equal seriousness; cf. the fine exposition by Via (*Ethics of Mark's Gospel*, 88–96).

tionalist side, Matthew's Jesus is by no means indifferent to the purity code. Except for touching a leper or a corpse in the performing of miracles (8:1–4; 9:18–26), he does not deliberately come into contact with uncleanness any more than any devout Jew of the time would have done. What is more, Matthew's Jesus reaffirms Torah in the strongest terms: ". . . till heaven and earth pass away not the least letter or fragment of a letter will pass away from the law until all things take place" (5:17–20). He even tells his followers to heed the teachings of the scribes and Pharisees, though not their example (23:1–4). He warns his hearers not to love or pray or be anxious like the tax collectors and Gentiles (5:46–48; 6:7, 32); and he confines the ministry of the Twelve to Jews, excluding even the Samaritans (10:5–6, 23). At one point, he tries to limit his own ministry in a similar way, and only the great faith of a Canaanite woman prompts him to relent (15:21–28).

One side of Matthew's Jesus, then, appears to be at least moderately traditionalist on purity issues. Another side, however, is quite different. It comes out in Jesus' preference for the company of tax collectors and sinners. Matthew makes it plain that he not only consorted with such people on a casual basis, but even included one of them in the number of the Twelve (9:9; 10:3). When challenged about his eating with such people, Jesus replies, "I have not come to call righteous people, but sinners";[18] and he justifies such action by quoting a scriptural text, "I want mercy and not sacrifice" (Hosea 6:6), thus setting the sacrificial cult, the focus of the purity system, over against another kind of ethical demand (9:10–13).[19]

This more radical Jesus even places the tax collectors and prostitutes ahead of the acknowledged religious leadership:

> [Jesus says,] "What do you think? A person had two children. He came and said to the first, 'Child, go work in the vineyard today.' He replied, 'I won't do it'; but later, he changed his mind and went. And he went to the second and said the same thing. He replied, 'I'm going, sir,' and did not go. Which of these two did what the father wanted?" They say, "The first." Jesus says to them, "Amen, I say to you that the tax collectors and the prostitutes are entering the reign of God ahead of you. For John came to you people with a way of righteousness and you didn't believe him, but the tax collectors and the prostitutes believed him. And you—even though you saw, you didn't change your minds afterward so as to believe him." (21:28–32)

18. Matthew, unlike Luke, adds no palliative "into repentance"; cf. Luke 5:32.
19. Some of Jesus' parables, such as those of the wheat and tares (Matt. 13:24–30) and the net (13:47–50), seem to be comments on the motley character of Jesus' following.

Jesus here contrasts a kind of religion that gives formal assent but not real obedience with a kind that does not give formal assent and yet does obey.

Matthew gives us little direct help in sorting out exactly what, practically, is meant in either case.[20] In part, he may simply be accusing the authorities of hypocrisy, as he has Jesus do a little further on: "They say and they do not" (23:3); they make rules which they themselves do not obey. There is also an element, however, of the contrast between purity and other ethical norms. As in Luke, Matthew's Jesus accuses the Pharisees of tithing minor herbs while neglecting the weightier aspects of the Torah, among which Matthew specifically includes "judgment and mercy and faith" (23:23). A prostitute, then, who observes "judgment and mercy and faith" may enter the reign of God ahead of one who is meticulous about purity but neglects these. The formal, observable nature of purity practices makes them a ready basis for judging the comparative religious worth of individuals; but Matthew's Jesus finds such comparisons misleading. The scribes and Pharisees, indeed, are like "whitewashed tombs, which look beautiful from the outside but on the inside are full of bones of the dead and all uncleanness." The religious leaders, too, "look righteous to people from the outside, but inside are full of hypocrisy and lawlessness" (23:27–28).[21]

The same Jesus who takes the part of unclean Israelites against the righteous also looks forward to a time when his mission will broaden out to include impure Gentiles. In Jesus' own ministry, the Gentile mission is prefigured in his praise of a centurion's faith (8:5–13), his exorcising of Gentile demoniacs (8:28–34), and his encounter with a Canaanite woman of great faith (15:21–28). He also makes certain predictions about Gentiles and how they will fare in the last judgment: many will have seats at the eschatological banquet, while "the sons of the kingdom" are shut out (8:11–12); it will be more tolerable then for Sodom and Gomorrah than for the Israelite towns that reject the minis-

20. Luke would be more helpful, since he gives us the example of Zacchaeus, whose repentance and conversion have to do not with purity, but strictly with matters of justice (19:8–9); but, of course, one cannot use Luke's Gospel in this way to explain what Matthew might have meant. I suppose that most readers of Matthew, myself included, have always assumed that the prostitutes left their trade when they followed John, but neither Matthew nor Luke specifies any such demand. It is not immediately clear how else they would have supported themselves, given the low job and family mobility of women in ancient society.

21. On the impure among Jesus' followers, see Schüssler Fiorenza, *In Memory of Her,* 126–30.

try of the Twelve (10:15); Tyre, Sidon, and Sodom would repent more readily (11:20–24); and the men of Nineveh and the Queen of the South will be found more righteous (12:41–42). The Gentiles, indeed, will be judged not by the Torah at all but simply by their acts of loving-kindness (25:31–46).

The apparent contradiction between the Jesus who upholds Torah in Matthew and the Jesus who vindicates those who fall short of its standards or live quite outside its scope is not easy to resolve. Yet, it is a part of Matthew's basic conception of the person and work of Christ. We might be tempted to suppose that Matthew has simply incorporated divergent strands of oral tradition without attempting to make them agree. Even Matthew's most distinctive contributions to his own work, however, show the same tension. His Gospel opens with a genealogy of Jesus, patterned on models in the Torah itself (1:1–17). In one sense, it is a traditionalist piece, documenting Jesus' descent from Abraham, who received the promise; from Jacob, the ancestor of all Israel; and from David, the founder of the royal line. Yet, it is also radical in its inclusion of four women who share with one another two disreputable qualities: all four were Gentiles and all four were involved in some kind of violation of the sexual codes.

The first, Tamar, was a Canaanite woman who acted the part of a prostitute in order to trick her father-in-law, Judah, into having intercourse with her (Genesis 38). To be sure, Judah was in the wrong, for he had failed in his obligations to her. He ought to have married her to his surviving son, Shelah, to beget a child in the name of Er, the deceased son who had been her original husband; when he evaded this responsibility, she simply claimed what was in some sense hers by right.[22] Judah himself admitted that "she is more righteous than I" (38:26). Yet, she had committed what appeared to be an act of prostitution and could be understood as having violated the incest rules.

The second woman in Matthew's list is Rahab, the Canaanite prostitute of Jericho who rescued Israelite spies from her fellow townsfolk (Joshua 2). She was rewarded by being spared, along with "her father's household and all who belonged to her" from the otherwise complete massacre of the city's population (6:22–25). The third, Ruth, belonged to the nation of Moab, which was forever excluded by the Torah itself

22. She had a right to Shelah, but not to Judah himself. Lev. 18:15 forbids a man to marry his son's wife, though it would not have been understood as being in force in the time of the patriarchs.

from membership in the assembly of Israel (Deut. 23:3). Moreover, she initiated sexual relations with Boaz by uncovering his "feet" (euphemistic for genitals) at the harvest celebration, well before she could be understood properly to belong to him (Ruth 3).

The fourth was "the wife of Uriah." By referring to her in this way and not as Bathsheba, Matthew underlines the act of adultery by which David first took her and the treachery by which he killed her husband and made her his own wife (2 Samuel 11). Since her husband was a Hittite, one may guess that she, too, was a Gentile. In legal terms, she would have to be reckoned as having consented to the adultery, however difficult it might have been, in practice, to refuse an absolute monarch; she was therefore as guilty in the matter as David.[23]

Thus, at the very beginning of his Gospel, Matthew presents us with a genealogy of Jesus which calls attention both to his impeccable Israelite descent and to the foreign and scandalous elements in it. Matthew underlines this motif in other ways, too. He notes that Jesus' mother was under suspicion of adultery and was saved from divorce only by the intervention of an angel (1:18–25), and he says that the first to pay homage to the infant Jesus were a group of *magoi*, Gentile priests of the god Mithras (2:1–12).

Despite his insistence on the inclusion of the impure and the foreign, Matthew does not appear to have been antagonistic toward the observance of purity law as such. It was not the observance of such rules which Matthew's Jesus condemned, but the tendency to substitute them for "the weightier matters" of judgment and mercy and faith. A comparison of Matthew's version of the controversy about hand washing with that of Mark is instructive. Mark, as we have seen, used the passage to declare all foods clean and to substitute, in a quite unambiguous way, the purity of the heart for that of the body. Matthew narrates the matter somewhat differently. His Jesus does, to be sure, reject the Pharisees' reliance on tradition (15:1–9); but rather than declaring all foods clean, he applies his argument only to the tradition of washing the hands before eating (15:20).[24] Still, the basic principle is the same as in Mark: a new purity, that of the heart, is now decisive (15:15–20).[25]

23. Cf. Deut. 22:22–27. The violated woman must cry for help if she is not to be punished as a willing partner.
24. Cf. Neusner, *Idea of Purity,* 62–63; Booth, *Jesus and the Laws of Purity,* 221–23.
25. Matthew's list of "evil intentions" that proceed from the heart includes adultery and harlotry. Since the order is different from Mark's, the sense of "harlotry" is probably different, too, but it is hard to give a confident interpretation of how Matthew understood it. He uses the term in only two other contexts, both of them suggesting that he saw *porneia* as an aspect of adultery or perhaps a synonym for it.

The same underlying principle is at work in the Sermon on the Mount, when Jesus declares that "everyone who looks at a woman to desire her has already committed adultery with her in his heart" (5:28). Such a claim excludes any understanding of adultery in terms of physical purity, for no physical "contamination" has taken place. The intention, the purity of "the heart" is the only thing that counts.

Matthew's treatment of the purity issue is thus more traditionalist than that of Luke and Mark in appearance, but it is equally radical in its implications. Matthew's Gospel pictures Jesus as a companion of tax collectors and sinners and preserves the teaching that purity of the heart, not physical purity, is central. It also portrays Gentiles and sinfully impure women as full and significant participants in God's work of salvation. It suggests that even though Matthew's church was probably predominantly Jewish, it adhered to the purity law as, at most, an expression of its membership in Israel. It could not consistently make it a point of pride in comparison to other Jews or demand its observance of Gentile converts.

Matthew saw the church as fully open to Gentiles—and not on the condition of their becoming Jews through circumcision of males. At the end of his Gospel, he has Jesus inaugurate a new era of salvation by directing his followers to begin converting Gentiles (28:19–20): "Go make disciples of all the Gentiles, baptizing them in the name of the Father and of the Son and of the Holy Spirit, teaching them to keep all the things that I have commanded you." The Gentile mission thus takes as its ethical "text" not Torah, but the commands of Jesus. In other words, it knows nothing at all about any code of physical purity.

JOHN

The Gospel of John is quite different from those we have already discussed. Indeed, on the subject of purity, it has almost no traditions in common with the three Synoptic evangelists. John notes that purification was a point of contention among Jewish groups in the time of Jesus' ministry (3:25). Yet, he has no teaching about "purity of heart" and he says not a word about associating with tax collectors. Alone of the New Testament writers, he portrays Jesus himself as administering purification rites, consisting of baptism (3:22; 4:1–2) and foot washing (13:1–17).

These differences must be seen as results of John's very individual aims in writing, which make the Fourth Gospel unique in almost all respects.[26] They do not, however, represent a radically different under-standing of the purity issue, as becomes clear in other ways. If John tells of no dinners with "tax collectors and sinners," he does narrate a long private conversation with a Samaritan woman of dubious reputation (4:4—26). Like the man with the Legion in Mark's Gospel, this foreigner becomes an effective bearer of Jesus' gospel, indeed the first truly successful missionary (4:27—30, 39—42). An independent tradition, often attached to John's Gospel, also presents him as the champion of a woman taken in the act of adultery (7:53—8:11).

The most striking element, however, in John's handling of the matter is the emphatic way he uses things impure as vehicles of the gospel. For example, in his conversation with Nicodemus (3:1—15), Jesus says that entry into the reign of God is conditional on being born *anōthen*, a term which can mean either "again" or "from above." I have argued else-where that this rebirth takes place in Christian baptism;[27] but however we interpret the saying, it is playing off the prevailing sense of impurity as defined by Torah. Giving birth, according to Leviticus, renders a woman unclean; yet John can even speak of God as giving birth to the chosen (1:13). The waters of baptism, for John, are waters of birth, comparable to the amniotic fluid; yet, they convey not impurity but intimate association with God.[28]

The other great Christian rite, the Eucharist, is even more intriguing to John in this respect. In the long eucharistic discourse of chapter 6, he presents the rite in precisely the way most offensive to purity. Jesus starts by talking about bread from heaven (6:26—33) and then makes the startling claim, "I am the bread of life" (6:35). His audience does not take this claim literally (6:41—42) until he goes on to say, "The bread that I shall give is my flesh for the life of the world" (6:51). When this, too, seems impossible to the audience, Jesus repeats it and adds to it the offensive notion of drinking his blood: "Amen, amen, I say to you, unless you eat the flesh of the son of humanity and drink his blood, you do not

---

26. Cf. Countryman, *Mystical Way,* 127—32.

27. Ibid., 29—31.

28. Early Christian baptism, it seems, was usually administered by pouring water over the head of a person standing in a pool; cf. Snyder, *Ante Pacem,* 57—58. In the Mishnah, drawn water is precisely what one must *not* use for purification, which, except for hand washing, takes place through immersion; cf. Neusner, *History,* 83—86. One must wonder whether Christians deliberately adopted for their own purification rite a form that would seem impure to rabbinic Judaism. Compare their choice of fast days different from those in use among other Jews (*Didache* 8.1).

have life in yourselves" (6:53).[29] Finally, he even switches from the ordinary word for "eat" to the more graphic "chew": "The one that chews my flesh and drinks my blood has eternal life" (6:54). The choice of motifs obnoxious to purity law and the careful and steady escalation of uncleanness throughout the discourse show that John is deliberately emphasizing the symbolic impurity of the Christian rites. It is by impure foods that one is saved.[30]

John, then, is less attached to physical purity than any of the other evangelists. Indeed, he stresses the way in which impure things have become, for Christians, the means of approach to God. There is no reason to see this as an exaltation of impurity for its own sake. The enormous tension between the Jewish-Christian communities in which John lived and wrote and the contemporary Jewish authorities has long been recognized as a major influence on the Fourth Gospel. Such a context would favor the flaunting of that in one's own tradition which was most apt to be obnoxious to one's opponents. We can find the same point, however, being made in a less polemical context in the story of the first miracle at Cana (2:1–11). There, Jesus commandeers large jars intended for Jewish purification rites, has them filled with water, and then transforms the water into wine of the finest quality to help celebrate a wedding. The miracle announces that a new means of relationship with God is here to replace the approach by way of physical purity.

CONCLUSION

The four New Testament evangelists have rather different ways of presenting the subject of purity. It would be a mistake to try to reduce their varied witness to a single synthesis; yet, there is at least one point on which they all agree: for Christians, physical purity is no longer a determinative element in their relationship with God. This does not mean that they abolished the categories of pure and impure. Even the Johannine community continued to be aware of a distinction between

29. Cf. 1 John 5:6: Jesus came "not with the water only, but with the water and the blood."

30. The same kind of point, I believe, is being made in the difficult passage at John 7:37–39. A scripture (otherwise unknown) is cited with reference to the one who believes in Jesus: "Rivers of living water will flow out of his belly." Things that flow out of the belly would include urine, menstrual blood, the amniotic fluid and other fluids associated with birth, semen, other sexual fluxes, and blood from hemorrhaging. Most of these are unclean according to the Torah; yet John, relying on an otherwise unknown text, takes them as an image of the Spirit.

clean and unclean, which gave their distinctive use of the impure its particular power. What Christians rejected was the age-old link between physical purity and access to God.[31]

Some New Testament Christians, like John, celebrated this repudiation of the purity law by speaking of even their most central and treasured rites in impure images. Others, like Mark, Luke, and Matthew, saw physical purity as giving way to an emphasis on "purity of the heart," which defined true uncleanness as consisting in the intention to do harm. One did not have to break with the old law of physical purity in order to embrace the new purity of the heart. Luke almost certainly assumed that Jewish Christians would continue to practice the whole of the Torah as an aspect of their Jewish identity; and Matthew's Gospel is by no means inconsistent with such an assumption. What every Christian, Jew or Gentile, must reject was rather the insistence on physical purity which the evangelists ascribed to the historical Pharisees.

Modern readers of the Gospels should not make the mistake of supposing that it was only or even primarily the historical Pharisees who were being attacked in this way. The evangelists were attacking any kind of religion that rates people according to externally verifiable scales—among which physical purity will always be popular. Such "pharisaism" is a generic phenomenon, as common among Christians as anywhere.[32] As Matthew saw, such religion, even if its original purpose may have been to encourage zeal in a good cause, will always wind up as a means to compliment oneself by criticizing others. That, in turn, leads to hypocrisy, for the goal of such religion eventually comes to be no more than the maintenance of a certain reputation within one's social milieu. To suppose that all the historical Pharisees turned their practice of purity into such a caricature of faith is absurd; to suppose that Christianity has been free of the same tendency is even more so. The practice of purity was not itself wrong, but lent itself to certain uses which were wrong, particularly exaltation of one's own religious excellence at the expense of others. Christianity's way of dealing with this danger was to make physical purity entirely optional, related to (and perhaps normal for)

31. Riches (*Jesus and the Transformation of Judaism*, 128–35) has argued that Jesus' own position was very close to this.

32. Thus, Forkman (*Limits of Religious Community*, 170) concludes that the Gospels have no "explicit rules which indicate which deviations lead to expulsion" and "refrain from suggesting what kinds of behavior make it impossible for a member to remain in the community."

Israelite identity, but irrelevant to salvation or to membership in the church.

The Gospels, to be sure, do not say much about sexual issues; and the ones on which they are clearest—divorce, remarriage, family, adultery—belong to part 2 of this study. If we compare our earlier discussion of purity law, however, both in its written form in the Torah and in terms of first-century Jewish practice, with the Gospel texts we have now examined, it becomes clear that the Gospels dismiss purity, not selectively, but across the board. They do not isolate some one aspect of it (food laws) for repudiation while tacitly retaining other aspects (leprosy, say, or circumcision, or sex). It is physical purity as such, in all its ramifications, that they set aside.

6

Paul and Purity

As the greatest of early Christian missionaries to the Gentiles, Paul was a key figure in the great controversy about circumcision. Acts of the Apostles and Paul's own letters, written before Acts or any of the Gospels, testify to his involvement.[1] Given this, we shall not be surprised to find that purity is an important topic in his writings or that he adopted a critical stance toward those who demanded that all Christians observe the purity code. On the present topic, his is a critically important voice in the New Testament.

It is not always easy, however, to ascertain exactly what Paul wished to say. His writings are letters, written, for the most part, to congregations he had founded and dealing with issues of immediate importance. Their content was often dictated by the occasion of writing. With the partial exception of Romans, none appears to represent a conscious, sustained effort to set forth the general outlines of his own theology or ethics. Even at Rome, which he had not yet visited at the time he wrote, he had friends, and he probably expected many in the congregation already to know much of his usual teaching. His letters, then, were occasional pieces, to be interpreted against the background of his familiar preaching and teaching—a background we no longer possess except insofar as we can reconstruct it by close examination and comparison of the letters.

1. The genuine letters of Paul are usually reckoned as Romans, 1 and 2 Corinthians, Galatians, Philippians, 1 Thessalonians, and Philemon. Colossians, though uncertain, I regard as probably his; Ephesians is probably the work of a close associate.

One thing, at least, is clear from the letters: Paul vehemently opposed those who wanted to require circumcision of male Gentile converts. This, in turn, compelled him to articulate his stance on the relationship of grace to works, of circumcision to observance of Torah, and of purity to salvation. Another aspect of his work and thought, also strongly imprinted on the letters but less commonly remarked, is a strong concern for the unity of the local congregation. The proclamation of the gospel seems at times to have unleashed an extraordinary creativity among his converts; and the new beliefs and observances thus engendered combined with the social competitiveness that was endemic to Greek society to cause strong centrifugal tendencies among the people of Paul's churches. It is important to mention this centrifugal tendency at this point, for we shall find that Paul (and, indeed, other New Testament letter writers) devotes a great deal of energy to combating it and often employs purity language metaphorically as a weapon against it.[2]

PURITY AND THE
GENTILE MISSION

In Galatians, Paul wrote about some of the events which Luke presents as connected with the Jerusalem council (Acts 15). Attempting to counteract a move by some of his churches toward the acceptance of circumcision as a requirement for membership, Paul wrote an angry defense of his mission to his congregations in Galatia. In it, he insisted that the Christian authorities at Jerusalem had acknowledged his mission to

---

2. For an interpretation of Paul's view of purity that is diametrically opposite the one I am presenting, see Newton, *Concept of Purity.* While I respond to details of Newton's arguments at appropriate places in the notes, it may be useful to sketch out my larger objections here. The first is that, as I have suggested above (chapter 3), Newton fails to make important distinctions. He does not differentiate clearly between physical purity in the strict sense and its use to reinforce other types of ethics. He fails equally to distinguish between literal physical purity and its metaphorical use to denote "purity of the heart." The second is that, having skillfully elucidated Paul's application of the temple image to the church, he then assumes that Paul will respond to the church-as-temple in a way comparable to the sectaries of Qumran. He argues in the style of "Paul as a Jew *would have* felt thus and so . . ." (see, e.g., his pp. 79, 82). This, however, is a treacherous line of argument. Paul was indeed a Jew, but one who behaved in ways quite different from those of Qumran and who was understood by some other Jews (including some Jewish Christians) as a renegade. At no point can we securely predict where he would have remained close to his Pharisee past and where he would have departed radically from it. Third, Newton lumps all sexual offenses together in English as "immorality" and assumes the same for Paul's use of *akatharsia* (uncleanness) and *porneia* without adequate analysis of that usage. Finally, Newton gives no attention to Paul's complex treatment of the question of foods sacrificed to idols and deals with Rom. 14:14 and 20, verses of central importance and unnerving clarity, in a decidedly offhand way.

Gentiles as inspired and empowered by God and had required nothing of him except to "remember the poor" (Gal. 2:1–10). There is nothing here about the council's decree—about avoiding meat sacrificed to idols, harlotry, blood, or things that have been strangled. If Luke's history of the council is accurate, this calls for explanation. Perhaps Paul's rejection of purity law was more radical than that of Luke, and he refused to convey the decree to his converts. Or again, Paul simply may have found the council's compromise irrelevant in places like Galatia, where the churches seem to have been composed almost entirely of Gentiles and there were few local occasions for conflict over table purity.

In Antioch, however, the church was mixed, and Paul told of the kind of troubles that could arise in such a situation:

> When Cephas [i.e., Peter] came to Antioch, I resisted him to his face, since he stood condemned. For before certain people came from James, he was eating with the Gentiles; but when they came, he drew back and separated himself, fearing those of the circumcision. And the other Jews joined him in his hypocrisy, with the result that even Barnabas was carried away into their hypocrisy. But when I saw that they were not keeping to the straight path as regards the truth of the gospel, I said to Cephas in the presence of them all, "If you, Jew though you are, live in the Gentile and not the Jewish way, how can you compel the Gentiles to live as Jews?" (Gal. 2:11–14)

Despite the extreme compression of this narrative, its drift is clear enough: Jewish Christians at Antioch had so far compromised their concern for purity as to eat with Gentile Christians, but pressure from strict Jews associated with Jerusalem induced them to withdraw and reerect the purity boundaries. Paul saw their behavior as proceeding not from conviction, but from political expediency. He not only objected to its inconsistency with past practice, but also insulted Peter by claiming that he was not a very faithful Jew under the best of circumstances.

To understand the Paul of this incident, we must recognize two contrary influences which were somehow united in his life. As he himself tells us, he was both the leader of the Gentile mission (Gal. 2:6–10) and a Jew of the strictest persuasion: "circumcised on the eighth day, of the nation of Israel and the tribe of Benjamin, a Hebrew of Hebrews, as to the law a Pharisee, as to jealousy [for the law] a persecutor of the church, as to righteousness by law one who had become blameless" (Phil. 3:5–6). Clearly, Paul had abandoned some aspects of this zeal in the process of becoming a missionary on Christ's behalf to Gentiles. But it was still Paul the Pharisee who could say of himself that he had "become blameless" or, of one who was not a Pharisee, that, Jew though he was, he lived like a Gentile.

Paul's conversion did not imply a wholesale rejection of his Jewish identity or of the Torah, but rather a reevaluation of the place which these had in the overall scheme of God's purpose for salvation. What had formerly been central now became peripheral: "All the things that were profit to me, these things on account of Christ I counted as loss . . . so that I might gain Christ and be found in him, having as my righteousness not the righteousness that comes from the law, but the one that comes through Christ's faith, the righteousness from God conditional upon faith" (Phil. 3:7–9).

The great issue of conversion for Paul, then, was not whether to keep the law, but whether to rely on it. Once he had become convinced that he must rely on another source of righteousness, he was no longer tied to the law, but could use it or not in accordance with the now dominant concerns associated with the "righteousness that comes through Christ's faith." Accordingly, he could subordinate his practice of the Torah to the requirements of missionary strategy: "For though I am free from all, I have made myself slave to all, in order to gain the majority. I have become to the Jews as a Jew to gain Jews, to those under law as one under law (though I am not in fact under law) to gain those under law, to those without law as one without law (though I am not without God's law, but within Christ's law) to gain those without law. I have become, to the weak, weak to gain the weak. To all people I have become all things, in order at all events to save some. But I do all things on account of the gospel, so that I might become one who shares in it" (1 Cor. 9:19–23). Only the proclamation of the gospel and one's final sharing in it were of ultimate importance; all else, including all that separated Jew from Gentile, was merely instrumental.[3]

Clearly, Paul did not consider it wrong for him to adhere to purity law, nor did he see it as an obligation—not at least where it might impede his work among non-Jews. To some degree, however, he saw his own situation as unique because of his divinely ordained mission. With those Galatians who considered accepting circumcision, he was vehement: "Look, I Paul am telling you that if you get circumcised, Christ will do you no good. And I am testifying again to every person who gets circumcised that he is obligated to keep the whole law" (Gal. 5:2–3).

---

3. Sanders, *Paul and Palestinian Judaism,* 496–99.

The assertion that "Christ will do you no good" was perhaps linked to the order of events; for a Gentile to be circumcised after conversion to the gospel implied lack of faith in Christ and a sense that something more was required. The second assertion, however—that whoever is circumcised is obligated to keep the whole law—was simply Paul's firmly held belief about the nature of Jewish identity. Israel is the chosen people; circumcision is the gateway into it for males; observance of the whole Torah is an obligation connected with that status. We need not suppose that Paul excused even himself from this obligation except insofar as his missionary responsibilities required it; he was always strongly conscious of the value of his Israelite heritage and its claim on him (2 Cor. 11:22; Rom. 2:25—3:2; 11:1–2).

TABLE FELLOWSHIP

The most significant way in which Gentiles and Jews interacted in the church was through table fellowship. The blessing of bread and wine had not yet been separated from the church's common meal to constitute the Christian Eucharist in its classic form (1 Cor. 11:17–34); instead, the common meal itself, with its anamnesis (remembrance) of Jesus, was the focus of Christian community life. Hence the particular importance of food in disputes about purity. Paul never mentions the decree which Luke attributes to the Jerusalem council, counseling against food sacrificed to idols, harlotry, blood, and things strangled (Acts 15:29). Yet, he shared at least one part of the concern—that with regard to foods sacrificed to idols.[4] He left two extensive discussions of this issue (1 Corinthians 8—10; Rom. 14:1—15:6), both of which aimed to persuade the "strong" (those whose consciences were not perturbed by eating such foods) to modify their practices so as not to cause difficulty for the "weak" who objected to them. The Strong were those whose tolerance for physical impurity was high; the Weak, those whose tolerance was low. The former group will probably have consisted mainly of Gentile Christians, the latter of Jewish Christians.

The earlier of these discussions is the one in 1 Corinthians 8—10. It is complex, for Paul employs several distinct and unrelated arguments—a practice permitted by the rhetorical teachers of the day—to achieve his

---

4. He also connects with it the issue of *porneia*, in the sense of idolatrous practices associated with foreign women (1 Cor. 10:8).

goal of changing his hearers' behavior.[5] In the first of his four arguments, Paul concedes to the Strong their basic theological claims: that idols are nothing at all and that there is no god but the One (8:4). The Strong may even think it a good thing to eat sacrificial foods to demonstrate this truth (8:8). Yet, however correct the position of the Strong may be, knowledge is less important than love (8:1–3), and they should attend to the effect their actions have on the Weak (8:9–13). Paul calls attention to his own manner of life, whereby he constantly denies himself acknowledged apostolic rights (e.g., the right to have a "sister wife" with him on his travels) "so as not to put any hindrance in the way of Christ's gospel" (9:1–18). Beyond that, Paul even "enslaves" himself to the expectations of others in order to communicate the good news (9:19–23). This is worthwhile to him if he gains even a few converts, and Paul wants the Strong to see this as analogous to the deprivations athletes voluntarily undergo in training and to join him in a kind of competition to save others (9:24–27). In summary, Paul's first argument grants the Strong their theological premise: foods sacrificed to idols mean nothing and the issue of physical purity is irrelevant. Yet, he rejects their conclusion. One does not therefore eat such foods if doing so will cause a weak Christian to stumble.

The second argument in 1 Corinthians is an admonition to the Strong not to be too sure of themselves. They should remember the exodus generation and how those people lost God's favor—precisely by indulging in foreign cults (idolatry and "harlotry") and by putting God and God's servants to the test (10:1–11). "If you think you are standing," says Paul, "watch out that you don't fall"; but then he reassures his audience that God is not about to abandon them (10:12–13). This argument serves to put the Strong on the defensive, but it adds nothing to the ethical analysis of the situation, since it does not deal with how one discerns the right course of action.

Paul follows this with a third argument, effectively reversing the premises of the first: even if an idol is nothing at all and there is no god but God, there are still demons; and idolatrous sacrifices really do involve one in their worship (10:19–20). The Christians are sharers in the Lord's table; to be sharers in the tables of demons may provoke him to jealousy (10:14–18, 21–22).

---

5. Cf. *Ad Herennium* 3.9.16–18, and Cicero *De oratore* 2.77.313–14. In a "proof," the strongest arguments were to be placed first and last, with the others, according to Cicero, in the middle as a kind of "herd," not a logical chain.

Finally, however, Paul returns to his first position. There is nothing inherently wrong in what the Strong are doing, but it is not expedient: "All things are permitted, but not all things are beneficial; all things are permitted, but not all things are constructive. Let no one seek one's own good, but that of the other person" (10:23–24). From these principles flow certain practical consequences: you may eat anything put before you unless someone specifically informs you that it has been sacrificed to an idol; in that case, you are to abstain "not for your own conscience, but for the other person's" (10:25–30). This conclusion implies that what is to be feared in relation to idolatrous cults is not any physical impurity associated with demons or with alien worship, but rather the possibility that the Weak may act contrary to their conscience. It is significant that nowhere in this whole discussion does Paul use purity language except in saying that "Some, through being accustomed to the idol in the past, eat as if the food really were sacrificed to an idol, and their conscience, being weak, is polluted" (8:7).[6]

The principle that Paul was working from in 1 Corinthians he states more clearly in his other discussion of this subject, in Romans: "All things are pure, but it is wrong for the person who eats by way of stumbling. . . . The one who is uncertain is condemned if he eats, because it is not from faith and everything that is not from faith is sin. But we who are strong have an obligation to bear the weaknesses of those who are not and not to please ourselves" (Rom. 14:20, 23—15:1). This is the heart of Paul's treatment of the subject in Romans, which is simpler and avoids the metaphysical uncertainties and conflicting arguments of 1 Corinthians. The point is simply that Christians are to accept the existence of both Strong and Weak and to avoid conflict between the two groups. The Strong are not to debate with the Weak or to despise them; the Weak are not to judge the Strong (14:1–3). Where Paul directed his discussion of the matter in 1 Corinthians mainly to the Strong, in Romans he speaks alike to the Weak, who are told at some length why they must not judge others (14:3–12), and to the Strong, who are told to make allowances for the Weak (14:13—15:3). The bottom line, however, is the same: "I know and am persuaded in the Lord Jesus that nothing is unclean in and of itself, except that for the

---

6. Newton (*Concept of Purity,* 100–101) holds that, for Paul, purity, though of no importance outside the church, is of great importance within it. Even within the church, however, Paul pleads for avoidance of sacrificial foods on the grounds of love, not purity.

person who regards anything as unclean it is" (14:14).[7] There can be no question here of impurity as a physical contagion which communicates itself automatically, as found in Leviticus. Paul's principle is that one must not do what is contrary to one's own consciousness of purity. If, by faith, that consciousness is altered, what was formerly impure would cease to be so; but if in following the example of others one transgresses one's own consciousness, that is not only impure but sinful. The only thing that is impure for you is what you yourself regard as such.

SEXUAL PURITY

Did Paul apply the same principles in dealing with sexual ethics? In one sense, it seems not. In a discussion of sexual mores in 1 Corinthians, he himself drew a sharp distinction between the two topics.

> All things are permitted me, but not all are beneficial. All things are permitted me, but I will not be dominated by any. The foods are for the belly and the belly for the foods—and God will destroy both the one and the others. The body, however, is not for *porneia*, but for the Lord, and the Lord for the body; and God both raised the Lord and will raise us through his power. (6:12–14)

Here, Paul rejected an exact correspondence between the argument about foods and that about sex. Though acknowledging that "all things are permitted," he still asserts that there are reasons to avoid certain sexual acts. Does this mean that he retained purity as an ethical principle in the sexual sphere? That must depend on what he meant by *porneia*. We have already seen that this term is difficult to pin down in the New Testament writings; and we shall discuss below some of its range of metaphorical meaning for Paul. In the context of the quotation above, however, we can be quite specific about it; it means the use of prostitutes by male Christians, which is the subject of the whole section (6:12–20). Since prostitution was as much an issue of property ethics as of purity, Paul was saying that repudiation of the purity code did not

---

7. Neusner (*Idea of Purity*, 59) describes this as "a highly rabbinic conception." If I have understood him correctly, however, it is also different from the rabbinic concept in an important way. For the rabbis, intention enters into the purity system in the way it makes items, by associating them with human use, susceptible of impurity (*Idea of Purity*, 16; *History*, 92–93). If one were to touch a corpse without understanding it as unclean or intending to become unclean oneself, this would not alter the outcome. Paul, however, implies that the purity system is entirely in the conscience (or consciousness), so that if one ceases to regard a corpse as unclean, it ceases to be so.

leave sex, like food, entirely outside the range of ethical concern, for another ethical principle still applied.[8]

As far as purity itself is concerned, Paul does treat sex in terms comparable to food. That is, he demands only the purity of the heart. For example, in 1 Thessalonians, he writes:

> This is God's will, your sanctification—for you to keep away from harlotry *(porneia),* for each of you to know how to possess his own vessel in holiness and honor, not in a passion of desire like the Gentiles who do not know God, for each of you not to overreach his brother in the business and take what belongs to him, for the Lord is avenger in all these matters, just as we have also told you before and borne witness. For God has not called us for uncleanness, but in sanctification. So, then, the person who treats [another] as of no account is despising not a human being but the God who has put his Holy Spirit into you. (1 Thess. 4:3–8)

If one reads only as far as "the Gentiles who do not know God," the passage seems to encourage a purity ethic, reinforced by a Hellenistic suspicion of passion. It is only in the following phrase, however, that Paul specifies the offense that concerns him here—adultery, overreaching a male fellow Christian by taking what is rightfully his. What Paul calls "uncleanness" is the intent to harm another (in this case, the woman's husband). For Paul, the great evil in the act of adultery is that one man is treating another as of no human value. Worse yet, this offense, if directed against a fellow Christian, is really directed at "the God who has put his Holy Spirit into you."[9]

Paul did speak of "impurity" fairly often in making lists of vices, and some have assumed that he used this term as a generalized expression for all sexual wrongdoing, perhaps even retaining the Levitical purity code in this regard.[10] The occurrence of terms in lists is not, of course, very informative in and of itself, since they carry with them little context to tell us how they were being used. Among Paul's contemporaries, their meaning will have depended on what they understood to be his usual

---

8. Forkman (*Limits of Religious Community,* 150–51) speaks as if Paul regarded impurity as grounds for expulsion from the church, but this is simply a momentary carelessness in use of terms. Elsewhere, he speaks more precisely of "fornication" (141–47) and its link with "dissension" (172).

9. The association of *pleonexia* with sexual offenses was noted, but regarded as inexplicable, by Gerhard Delling (*TDNT,* s.v. *pleonexia*). I am gratified to find that Yarbrough offers a detailed exegesis of the text from 1 Thessalonians comparable to the one offered here in his *Not Like the Gentiles,* 65–76.

10. See Newton, *Concept of Purity,* 103.

teaching in the matter. Did he normally use this vocabulary in its literal, physical sense or in a metaphorical sense (purity of the heart)? Unfortunately, we no longer have independent access to Paul's teaching: the most we can say is that his use of "impurity" in 1 Corinthians, Romans, and 1 Thessalonians does not encourage us to think that he would ever use it as a simple and unambiguous reference to physical impurity of a sexual kind. Still, it will be useful to look at the lists themselves and note how they are organized, for the grouping of words within lists is frequently our best clue to the meaning of individual items.[11]

Perhaps the most complete list is the one found in Galatians, enumerating "the works of the flesh" (5:19–21). ("Flesh," in the specialized sense which Paul gives the term, means not the body or even specifically what is material, but rather the whole human being in opposition to God.)[12] The list includes "harlotry, impurity, license, idolatry, sorcery, enmities, strife, jealousy, rages, selfish ambitions, dissensions, sects, envies, drunkennesses, carousings and things like these." For the most part, the list is easily divided into its component subgroups. The last two categories ("drunkennesses" and "carousings") are examples of excess in drinking and eating, perhaps with some public exhibition of the loss of control. The long central section of the list (from "enmities" through "envies") is composed of offenses against the internal peace of a community. "Idolatry" and "sorcery" go together here just as they do in Leviticus. The question, then, is how "harlotry," "impurity," and "license" fit into the list. Do they go with "idolatry" and "sorcery" to form a single group of terms referring to the cults of foreign gods? That is not at all impossible. We are already familiar with both "harlotry" and "impurity" in that context, and Paul noted elsewhere that the idolatry of the people in the wilderness included licentious behavior (1 Cor. 10:7). Or do they form a separate group by themselves? And if so, do they refer to sexual practices? And if so, how were those sexual practices defined?

The same three terms appear together in another passage, where Paul is reproving the Corinthian church and threatening them with an unpleasant visit from him:

11. Zaas has argued convincingly that lists of vices and virtues are not mere set traditions flung haphazardly into the epistles, but are integrated with the epistles' subject matter; see his "As I Teach Everywhere," 1–59, and "Catalogue and Context." I am inclined to think that context and grouping of words within the lists are, in most cases, our only serious clues to the meaning of the otherwise rather vague individual terms. As Zaas observes, such catalogues were reminders of catechesis, where the vices had previously been defined in ways now lost to us.

12. Robinson, *Body,* 17–26.

> I am afraid that somehow when I come I will not find you what I want and that you will find me not what you want; that somehow there will be strife, jealousy, rages, selfish ambitions, denunciations, gossipings, conceits, disorders; that when I come again my God will humiliate me in your presence and I will grieve over many of those who sinned before and have not repented for the uncleanness and harlotry and license that they committed. (2 Cor. 12:20–21)

Commentators have compared Paul's reference in 1 Cor. 5:1 to a man who "had his father's wife." Since Paul did refer to that act as a case of "harlotry" might he not be speaking of similar problems here? On the other hand, Paul has already made it clear that the specific dangers which he feared to encounter had nothing to do with sexual impurity and everything to do with the internal peace of the community.

The sudden and unprepared shift of subjects, if that is what it is, from social turmoil to sexual impurity has been a difficulty for interpreters.[13] It would be at least equally reasonable, and perhaps more so, to suppose that what Paul meant by "uncleanness and harlotry and license" was in fact the same thing as "strife, jealousy, rages, selfish ambitions," and so forth. The desire of individual church members to take charge of the local community and subject it to their own control, a problem abundantly documented throughout Paul's Corinthian correspondence, would certainly qualify as an "impurity of the heart." We know that Paul did see license of all kinds as one of the typical causes of discord in the community. In Romans, he contrasted the love which is the "fullness of the law" with "carousings and drinking bouts, acts of sexual intercourse and license, strife and jealousy" (13:8–14). We have no evidence, however, that he ever singled out sexual impurity in the physical sense as the supreme example of sinfulness. What he feared would humble him was rather the "unclean" disunity and jockeying for advantage to be found at Corinth.

If we return to the list in Galatians, then, we have three possible ways of analyzing it. One would be to read the list as composed of three basic categories: idolatry (including "uncleanness and harlotry and license"), internal divisions, and acts of excess. The other two would make four categories by separating off the first three items in the list; but they would differ as to whether this first category should be understood as

13. Cf. Barrett, *Second Epistle*, 329–32. He observes that the two lists of offenses in vv. 20 and 21 are difficult to tie together unless the latter is "violently allegorized." He proposes instead an accidental link of history, arising from the fact that some of those who were causing internal strife in the Corinthian community were also teaching sexual libertinism.

sexual impurity or as the desire to place oneself first in the community. Of these three options, the one that emphasizes sexual purity, though not impossible, is the least likely. There is little, if anything, elsewhere in Paul's writings to suggest that he regarded sexual purity as the leading Christian virtue, while there is a good deal to suggest that he so regarded humility and peaceableness within the community.

If this interpretation seems odd to the modern reader, that is largely because we read Paul's letters now as part of a larger body of literature which includes Leviticus. "Uncleanness," to our mind, does not readily equate with "social greed."[14] Paul's original audience, however, would have heard his letters not just in the context of Scripture but also in that of Paul's oral teachings. If Paul habitually used "uncleanness" as an equivalent for "greed," his audience will have had no difficulty following him. Since his teachings, however, were oral and are accessible to us now only through his incidental written references to them, we must proceed cautiously. We have already noted Paul's identification of greed with uncleanness in 1 Thessalonians. Further evidence that this was his predominant teaching comes from two letters which are of uncertain authorship but which are closely associated with Paul. If Paul was not their actual author, they were possibly written by his subordinates in his own lifetime and authorized by him. I refer to Colossians and Ephesians.

In each of these letters, references to uncleanness always link up with references to greed. This greed (pleonexia) is not merely the private vice of lust, the desire to have something for oneself, but rather the social one of covetousness, the desire to have more than another or even to have what rightfully belongs to another. In Ephesians, the author warns the audience not to behave like the Gentiles, who, "having grown callous, surrendered themselves to license for working all uncleanness in greed" (4:19). License, uncleanness, and greed all work together here; for the abandonment of restraint and of concern for the rights of others is what produces the impurity of heart which the Gospels treat as the only significant form of uncleanness. The same point is echoed elsewhere in Ephesians: "Let harlotry and all uncleanness or greed (pleonexia) not even be named among you. . . . for know this: that a person given to harlotry or an unclean or a greedy person (pleonektēs), that is, an idolator, has no inheritance in the reign of Christ and God" (5:3,5). For the

14. Cf., however, such English expressions as "He did me dirt" and "dirty tricks."

author of Ephesians, uncleanness, harlotry, and even idolatry seem to be synonyms of *pleonexia*.

The author of Colossians takes a similar but more complex approach. Having admonished his audience to respect their baptism, in which they have died to this world and been raised with Christ, he continues: "Put to death, then, the members that are on the earth, harlotry, uncleanness, passion, evil desire, and the greed *(pleonexia)* which is idolatry, on account of which things the wrath of God is coming upon the children of disobedience" (3:5–6). Here, one can easily detect an association of harlotry and uncleanness with sexual acts, because of the association with passion and evil desire (about as close as New Testament Greek comes to an unambiguous designation of "lust"). This need not mean, however, that the author is resurrecting the idea of physical unclean- ness. More probably, here, as in 1 Thessalonians, the preeminent exam- ple of *pleonexia* is the desire to possess some other person's sexual property through adultery. This understanding of the passage is borne out by the following list of specific vices which the author wants Chris- tian folk to reject: anger, rage, badness, blasphemy, shameless conversa- tion, and lying (3:8–9). This list barely even alludes to sexual activities, and the corresponding list of virtues which caps the passage (3:12–15) is concerned entirely with the peace of the community.

Paul and the Pauline tradition, then, appear from the evidence dis- cussed thus far to have little, if any, concern with sexual purity in the physical sense. Impurity, for them, consists rather in trying to get the better of someone else; in other words, impurity is competitive greed— mainly for influence in the community or for sexual property. Thus far in our analysis of Paul, we have found him to be in broad agreement with the Gospels. He is familiar with the purity code of the Torah and with that of Pharisaism, and he does not object to their continued observance. The purity that counts, however, is that of the heart, which Paul identifies as the opposite of *pleonexia*. In comparison with the Gospels, Paul is unique, it seems, in one respect only—he also expands the understanding of purity of the heart so that physical purity becomes an aspect of it for those who believe it to be so (Rom. 14:14).

PURITY, HOMOSEXUAL ACTS, AND SIN

We must still examine one passage of great importance—the only pas- sage in which Paul freely and repeatedly used the language of impurity in its physical sense. I refer to the discussion of homosexual acts in Romans 1:18–32. The usual modern interpretation of this passage understands Paul to be saying that God, as a punishment for the sin of idolatry, has abandoned the Gentiles to another sin—that of homosexual acts (vv. 18–25). In addition, as punishment for this "error" (the homosexual acts), God has also inflicted on Gentile males some further, unspecified "recompense" (vv. 26–27). The homosexual acts are part of a larger group of characteristically Gentile sins, all of which deserve death (vv. 28–32). This understanding of the passage has a long history; but, so far as I am aware, no one has identified its true age or origins. If it is correct, it means that Paul, in Romans 1, assumed a very different understanding of purity from that which he took for granted elsewhere in his writings, a doubtful proposition at best.

A closer examination of the passage, however, will show that this common interpretation is not only inadequate to the text itself, but also improbable. To begin with, it assumes that Paul was treating homosexual acts here as sinful. In fact he did not apply the vocabulary of sin to them here at all. Paul had a rich store of words to refer to sin: sin *(hamartia, hamartēma),* lawlessness or transgression *(anomia),* unrighteousness *(adikia),* impiety *(asebeia).* This kind of language appears in our passage twice: at the beginning, it refers to idolatry (1:18–23); and, at the end, it forms the heading for a whole list of wrongs—a list which includes *pleonexia* and many other offenses against social peace, but nothing sexual (vv. 29–31). The idea that Paul was labeling homosexual acts as sinful can be upheld only if one can show that he used other terms here with an equivalent meaning.

Paul's basic argument here runs thus: Idolatry was the root sin of Gentile culture. In the creation, God left ample evidence of his goodness, power, and divinity, so that any people should have known enough to worship and give thanks to him alone. The Gentiles, in the stupidity of their hearts, chose instead to worship "a likeness of an image of a perishable human being and of birds and beasts and vermin" (1:23). This was a voluntary act, effected in full knowledge of its meaning; and it is the reason why "God surrendered them in the desires of their hearts to uncleanness" (v. 24). Paul did not, of course, mean that every Gentile invented idolatry individually or that each began to experience homosexual desire as a direct result of individual sin. He was thinking in terms of Gentile culture as a whole, not of individuals: the original forebears of the Gentiles committed the sin of idolatry, in which their descendants, in the normal course of events, have followed them; and this is why God has also decreed that certain unclean practices are to be characteristic of their culture. Compare Paul's similar treatment of God's dealings with Israel as a nation in Rom. 11:11–36.

Did Paul understand these unclean practices as also being sinful? That is not inconceivable, for the religious tradition of Israel and of Christianity was willing to entertain the idea that God might punish one sin by causing the sinner to commit another.[15] In order to determine whether that is Paul's meaning here, however, we must look carefully at the vocabulary he used in discussing homosexual acts. Unfortunately, the existing English translations, having been made with the presupposition that Paul regarded these acts as sinful, tend to predetermine the conclusions of anyone using them. For those readers who cannot consult the Greek text directly, there is a need for a more neutral translation, which I shall supply as we proceed.

To begin with, Paul wrote:

> For this reason [idolatry], God surrendered them in the desires *(epithymiai)* of their hearts to uncleanness so that they would dishonor *(atimazō)* their bodies among themselves—these people who exchanged the truth of God for the lie and revered and worshiped the creation instead of the Creator, who is blessed forever, amen. (1:24–25)

The classic English translations of this passage have usually taken *epithymiai* as equivalent to "lusts," but that is not necessarily appropriate here. Paul did use the term for the most part in a negative sense—sometimes, in continuity with its use in the Greek version of the Tenth Commandment, as meaning "covetousness" (Rom. 7:7; cf. Exod. 20:17 LXX). What is more important, however, is that the word's basic meaning, "desire," could always carry a variety of tones and be judged in various ways. Stoicism, the prevailing ethical philosophy among Greeks in the New Testament period, was, like Paul, typically critical of desire; yet, this had not deprived the word of all positive meaning. Paul himself could use it positively, as when he wrote to the Thessalonian church, "We, brethren, having been bereft of you for some time in face, though not in heart, have been all the more eager to see your face with much *epithymia*" (1 Thess. 2:17). Here, the term requires some quite positive translation, such as "eagerness." I do not suggest a positive translation,

---

15. Sanday and Headlam, *Romans*, 45. Cf. the teaching of 2 Macc. 6:12–17 that God waits to punish the Gentiles until they "have reached the full measure of their sins" (RSV).

to be sure, in Romans—only a neutral one, so that we do not decide the question of Paul's evaluation of homosexual acts before we have examined it thoroughly. Paul says, then, that God dealt with the *desires* of Gentiles in such a way as to hand them over to uncleanness. In other words, Paul took the frequency and acceptability of homosexual acts in Gentile culture as evidence that "the desires of their hearts" were different from those of Jews and then went on to conclude that this was the result of an act of God, who had "surrendered" them to this state.[16]

Along with the uncleanness of these acts goes also an element of social disgrace, which Paul describes as the "dishonoring" of bodies. Paul was by no means the first to link uncleanness and dishonor, a combination of motifs that one finds already in the Scriptures of Israel. The household of Jacob, for example, regards it as dishonorable for their women to be given to uncircumcised men (Gen. 34:14). Ezekiel uses the phrase "death of the uncircumcised" as equivalent to "disgraceful death" (28:10) and says that the man who has intercourse with a menstruating woman has shamed her (22:10; cf. 18:6). Job refers to the cult prostitutes as the lowest of the low in society (36:14). The incidental way in which biblical writers thus combine uncleanness and dishonor shows that this was a familiar fact of life in their world: those at the bottom of the social scale were assumed to be habitually unclean, and those who were chronically unclean (e.g., lepers) were shifted to the margins and, often, the bottom of society. We shall find that Paul moves easily, in the rest of our present passage, between the language of purity and that of social status.

Paul continues the discussion by reiterating his original point and making it more explicit:

> On account of this [i.e., the sin of idolatry], God surrendered them to passions *(pathos)* of dishonor *(atimia)*, for their females exchanged the natural use for that over against nature *(para physin)* and in the same way the males, too, having left the natural use of the female, burned with their desire *(orexis)* for one another, males accomplishing shamelessness *(aschēmosynē)* with males and receiving the due recompense *(antimisthia)* of their error *(planē)* among themselves. (Rom. 1:26–27)

16. Boswell (*Christianity, Social Tolerance, and Homosexuality,* 109–10) correctly observed that Paul was talking about a *change* which he understood to have taken place as a consequence of the sin of idolatry. People who formerly experienced desire for the opposite sex now committed homosexual acts. Boswell was mistaken, I think, only in treating this as a matter of individual experience, whereas Paul was writing about Gentile culture as a whole.

As in the preceding verses, we find terms for desire *(pathos, orexis)* which can be understood either positively or negatively. Insofar as Paul, like his Gentile counterparts the Stoic teachers, regarded desire as something for the mature person to subdue, he will be looking askance at it here. This is the same Paul, however, who wrote to the Corinthians that, even though he preferred for single persons not to marry, "it is better to marry than to burn" (1 Cor. 7:9). In other words, Paul was willing, if need be, to accept the legitimacy of sexual desire and its appropriate satisfaction.

We also find again, in vv. 26–27, the language of social dishonor, including the term "shamelessness" *(aschēmosynē)* which Paul applies to homosexual acts among males. In the ancient world generally, the most important social imperative was to maintain or improve the standing of one's family, whether positively by increasing its public honor or negatively by avoiding anything that might shame the family. "Shamelessness" meant being deficient in concern for the latter. It was thus a synonym for dishonor, not a term denoting sinful behavior. King James's translators found a suitable equivalent in the English of their day: "that which is unseemly." Paul's choice of this particular term in Greek also ties his argument back to the purity code itself, for the Old Greek version of the Old Testament uses the term to denote (among other things) sexual violations of the purity code, genitalia, and human excrement.[17] Paul does not question that what the Gentiles do is contrary to the Israelite code of purity and therefore certainly dirty from a Jewish perspective. This still does not settle, however, the question of whether it is sinful for them to commit unclean acts.

A new element that Paul introduces in vv. 26–27 is the statement that homosexual intercourse is an abandonment of "natural use" for what is "over against nature." This terminology is not easy to interpret, since the terms "nature" and "natural" can mean a great many different things, particularly in the context of ethical discourse.[18] Paul's own use of the

17. For violations of the sexual code, see the LXX of Leviticus 18 and 20 *passim;* on the genitalia, Exod. 20:26, 22:26 (27MT); on excrement, Deut. 23:13 (14MT).

18. Paul's usage was dependent on that of contemporary Stoicism, as its association with *kathēkonta* in v. 28 shows. In the absence of any evidence of a direct acquaintance on Paul's part with Stoicism, however, one must assume that he drew these terms from popular contemporary usage, especially within the Hellenistic Diaspora; cf. Schnackenburg, *Moral Teaching,* 290–92. In strict Stoic usage, acts "over against nature" and "improper acts" *(ta mē kathēkonta)* were synonymous with "sins." More popular usage, however, was far from precise or rigorous. Cicero, despite his intellectual and educational advantages, got the whole system of distinctions badly garbled according to Rist (*Stoic Philosophy,* 97–111). Paul's contemporary Philo could even speak of "acts *according* to nature" as being

term "nature" elsewhere offers us some important help—not so much in clarifying his usage as in warning us against certain misapplications of it. In most instances, he uses the term to refer to the continuity of an organism with its past; thus, he distinguishes branches that are still attached to their original tree (*kata physin*, according to nature) from those that have been grafted into a tree of another species (*para physin*, over against nature) (Rom. 11:24); or he speaks of those who "by nature" are without law (Rom. 2:14) or uncircumcised (2:27) or Jewish (Gal. 2:15).[19] If this is the sense Paul has in mind in Rom. 1:26–27, he is simply reiterating the idea he has already hinted at—that Gentiles experienced only heterosexual desire before God visited uncleanness on them and have therefore changed their "nature," that is, lost a certain continuity with their remotest past.

In another passage, Paul gives a different sense to "nature." In an effort to convince the Corinthian church that women must cover their heads when they prophesy in the Christian assembly, he adduces a number of independent arguments, among them the following: "Judge among yourselves: is it proper for a woman to pray to God uncovered? Does not nature *(physis)* itself teach you that if a man wears his hair long it is a dishonor *(atimia)* to him but if a woman wears her hair long it is her glory? Because the hair has been given her in place of a covering" (1 Cor. 11:13–15). Here, "nature" seems to mean something like "widespread social usage." Paul draws an argument by analogy from such usage: just as women in his world were expected to wear their hair long and men to wear theirs short, so, too, women ought to wear something on their heads when leading worship while men should not. This usage of "nature," however, is less likely to be relevant to the passage in Romans 1. Since "widespread social usage" in the Greek world in fact accepted homosexual intercourse, the argument would fall flat.[20]

---

blameworthy if indulged to excess (*Special Laws* 3.9)—something no true Stoic could have said. If Paul's usage here is equivalent to that of Philo or of pseudo-Phocylides, "natural" would mean "procreative," as applied to sexual acts, and "over against nature" would mean "nonprocreative." Paul's own normal usage, however, as I have analyzed it in the text, offers a more satisfactory interpretation, for Paul elsewhere shows no concern for begetting children in "these last days."

19. Hays ("Relations Natural and Unnatural," 198–99) has skillfully brought out the outrageous character of the usage in Romans 11, where God, in effect, is said to perform "unnatural acts." He has not observed, however, that this passage makes any equation of "unnatural" and "sinful" in Paul's usage extremely difficult.

20. Hays, in his useful though intemperate article "Relations Natural and Unnatural," 191, suggests yet another possible definition of "natural," namely, as a reference to the creation narrative of Genesis 1—3. There is no strong evidence for such a conclusion,

It remains to ask, with regard to the verses above, what Paul meant by saying that Gentile males were "receiving the due recompense of their error among themselves." The common interpretation of this statement understands the "error" to be homosexual behavior and the "recompense" as some evil which punishes it. The RSV goes so far as to speak of a "penalty" that they suffered "in their own persons," though the latter must be reckoned an unlikely translation of *en heautois* ("among themselves"). Two difficulties attend this interpretation. First, no one has yet given a satisfactory explanation of what this "penalty" might have been. Although hemorrhoids and sexually transmitted disease have been suggested, neither is suitable, since they are in no way confined either to homosexuals or to Gentiles.[21] The common interpretation thus makes nonsense of the text itself at this point. The second problem lies in supposing that Paul used the term *planē* (error) with reference to sexual acts. This term and its near relatives appear a good many times in Paul's undoubted writings, but always with reference to wrong belief rather than desire or action. Even in 1 Thessalonians, where "error" appears alongside "uncleanness" and "deceit" (2:3), a perusal of the whole passage will show that Paul refers to a kind of false teaching framed with a view to deceiving the audience and enriching the teacher (2:5–6). To take *planē* in Rom. 1:27, then, as referring to homosexual behavior is to suggest that Paul altered his normal usage without apparent reason.

The common interpretation, then, whether of the "recompense" or of the "error," is impossible to maintain. How can the phrase be interpreted with greater fidelity to the text and to Paul's normal usage? The simplest solution—and one fully in accord with the context here—would be to take the "error" as idolatry and the "recompense" as the uncleanness of Gentile culture. In this way, *planē* retains its otherwise invariable sense of "wrong belief." In other words, Paul is reiterating

---

however, either in Romans 1 or in contemporary usage. In Romans 1, Paul alludes in a variety of ways to Genesis 1, but never explicitly to the creation of male and female or to the institution of marriage. Moreover, as noted above (chapter 3), *para physin* in Hellenistic Jewish authors refers not to a theology of creation but to the issue of whether sexual acts are procreative. Paul himself seems to have had little interest in procreation.

21. E.g., Enslin, *Ethics of Paul*, 147 n. 45. Scroggs (*New Testament and Homosexuality*, 115–16) suggests that "the distortion of homosexuality" was its own punishment. This seems quite unsatisfactory, however, in rhetorical terms: a critic of Gentile culture would be dissatisfied with so intangible a penalty, and the Gentiles themselves may not have thought it a punishment at all. Philo wrote of the "female disease" (effeminacy) that afflicted the younger partner and of the emotional and financial ruin of the elder in pursuit of a beloved (*Special Laws* 3.37–40; *Abraham* 136; *The Contemplative Life* 59–62); but these were, of course, far from inevitable accompaniments of homosexual relationships.

once again, at the end of v. 27, the point he had made previously in vv. 24 and 26: because the progenitors of the Gentiles forsook the true God to worship idols, God visited on them and on their progeny a characteristic kind of uncleanness, namely the desire for and practice of homosexual relations. This is not a matter of individual idolators receiving a recompense for their errors; it is a cultural phenomenon, as Paul says: "receiving *among* themselves the due recompense [uncleanness] of their error [idolatry]."

Finally, Paul concludes his discussion of the subject by saying that God's visiting of this uncleanness upon the Gentiles was justified not only by their idolatry, but by other sins which they also accepted and practiced:

> And just as they did not agree to keep God in recognition, God surrendered them to a disagreeable mind, to do things that are not proper *(kathēkonta),* since they were already filled *(peplērōmenous)* with all unrighteousness, evil, greed *(pleonexia),* badness; full of envy, murder, strife, deceit, craftiness; gossips, slanderers, God-haters, proud, arrogant, boasters, contrivers of evils, disobeyers of parents, unintelligent, unfaithful, unloving, unmerciful—people who, though knowing God's judgment that those who do such things deserve death, not only do them but also offer approval to those who do. (Rom. 1:28–32)

These verses offer us a list of sins that Paul treats as characteristic of Gentiles. Interestingly, the list does not include anything of a sexual nature, but concentrates on the sins of social disruption that concern Paul so often elsewhere. The Gentiles "were already filled" with these vices[22] and gave them cultural validation.[23] Only thereafter did God "surrender" them to homosexual behavior, described in these verses not as sin, but as "things that are not proper." The deeds that make people "deserve death" are not, of course, the "improper" acts of homosexual intercourse, but the vices in the list itself, beginning with "unrighteousness."[24]

We thus find that a close reading of Paul's discussion of homosexual

22. The perfect passive participle *(peplērōmenous)* indicates that this was already the case before God surrendered the Gentiles to a "disagreeable mind." This, I think, makes impossible Scroggs's proposal *(New Testament and Homosexuality,* 113–14) that homosexual acts and the vice catalogue of vv. 27–31 were, for Paul, interchangeable illustrations of human sinfulness.

23. Cf. Philo's similar condemnation of both wrongdoers and those who take their part, in *Special Laws* 3.19.

24. The rules of syntax require this conclusion, for the demonstrative *toiauta* ("such things") must ordinarily refer to the nearest possible antecedent, which would be the list of vices, not the references to homosexual acts.

acts in Romans 1 does not support the common modern interpretation of the passage. While Paul wrote of such acts as being unclean, dishonorable, improper, and "over against nature," he did not apply the language of sin to them at all. Instead, he treated homosexual behavior as an integral if unpleasingly dirty aspect of Gentile culture. It was not in itself sinful, but had been visited upon the Gentiles as recompense for sins, chiefly the sin of idolatry but also those of social disruption. This reading of the passage also brings it into reasonable accord with what we have seen of Paul's attitude to purity elsewhere.[25] Paul did not deny the existence of a distinction between clean and unclean and even assumed that Jewish Christians would continue to observe the purity code. He refrained, however, from identifying physical impurity with sin or demanding that Gentiles adhere to that code.

Some have asserted that another passage in Paul's writings does, however, contain an unambiguous condemnation of homosexual persons as sinners. The passage in question is a list: "Neither those given to harlotry nor idolators nor adulterers nor *malakoi* nor *arsenokoitai* nor thieves nor the greedy *(pleonektai)*—not the drunken or the abusive or the rapacious will inherit God's reign" (1 Cor. 6:9–10). The interpretation of the two terms I have left untranslated here is the crux of the matter and has long proven troublesome. *Malakoi* means, basically, "soft," and the King James Version translated it "effeminate."[26] *Arsenokoitai* is of uncertain meaning. It contains within it basic elements referring to the male and to sexual intercourse, and the King James translators, presumably relying on the guidance of etymology, used the peculiar phrase "abusers of themselves with mankind." The original edition of the Revised Standard Version combined the two terms and translated them "homosexuals." The second edition substituted "sexual perverts."

The difficulty is that *arsenokoitai* never appears in a passage that would give us a clear sense of how the term was used or exactly what it meant either to Paul or to Paul's audience. There is no certain instance of it

25. Sanders *(Paul, the Law, and the Jewish People,* 123–32) has argued that in fact Rom. 1:18—2:29 is a synagogue sermon that Paul simply incorporated for convenience' sake. In that case, one could not expect consistency with his own thinking in Romans 14. But would Paul have begun an important letter with materials in conflict with a conviction expressed as strongly as Rom. 14:14?

26. *Malakos,* however, cannot simply be equated with "effeminate," for it was applicable to any male who was seen as less than upstanding or respectable. E.g., Philo applied the term to the man who remarries his former wife, *Special Laws* 3.30–31.

prior to the New Testament writings, and it occurs only one other time in the New Testament itself—again in a list and this time without *malakoi* (1 Tim. 1:10). While its etymology could very well suggest some such meaning as "a man who has intercourse with another man," etymology is a notoriously bad guide to the actual, live meanings of words. In English, for example, "outbuilding" and "outhouse" are synonymous in terms of etymology but quite different in usage. Usage is the real determinant of meaning.

The next thing to be said in this regard is that the term "homosexual" and the concept behind it are modern coinages. Ancient Greeks and Romans seem to have assumed that human beings are attracted sexually both to their own and the opposite sex. They could even debate the relative merits of the two types of love.[27] The idea of the homosexual person as one who is exclusively or predominantly attracted to members of the same sex appears to have been unknown to them. They lacked even a behavior-based category for people who showed a fixed preference for partners of the same sex. Accordingly, we cannot expect a text written in ancient Greek to address the modern concept of homosexuality in so many words.[28]

The terms and concepts available were all more limited in scope. The classic form of same-sex partnership was pederastic, the love of an adult male (*erastēs*, lover) for a youth (*erōmenos*, beloved). This was similar to the pattern of marriage, where the bride was usually much younger than the groom. In the classical age of Greece, the youth was typically freeborn and the relationship could be quite open, approved, and honorable. In the Roman era, the beloved was more commonly a slave and entirely at his master's bidding; and freemen did not like to surrender control of their sons in this particular way. There were also male prostitutes who serviced both sexes. It was degrading for an adult male to be penetrated in intercourse, though this does not, of course, mean that it did not happen.[29]

There have been two major scholarly efforts to shed light on Paul's terms in recent years. One, put forward by Robin Scroggs, proposes that *malakoi* and *arsenokoitai* functioned together as Greek equivalents to

---

27. E.g., Achilles Tatius *Leucippe and Clitophon* 2.35–38.
28. See Petersen, "ΑΡΣΕΝΟΚΟΙΤΑΙ," 187–91.
29. Veyne, "Homosexuality," 26–35. Cf. the discussion of homosexual acts among adult males under similar circumstances in modern Greece by Horner (*Eros in Greece*, 54–65).

technical terminology in rabbinic Hebrew which designated, respectively, the "passive" and "active" partners in male homosexual intercourse. The terms, on this interpretation, would have been closely tied to the purity law of Leviticus and its interpretation in the scribal tradition.[30] The other position, proposed by John Boswell, holds that there was no intrinsic connection between *malakoi* and *arsenokoitai,* that the former word, if it had anything at all to do with sexual activity, meant "masturbators," and that the latter was probably a vulgar expression meaning "male prostitutes." If this is correct, it would make it unclear whether Paul's use of the term was meant to condemn them for homosexual acts or for acts of prostitution or for both.[31]

It would be unwise to imagine that we can know clearly or definitively what the terms meant to Paul. The evidence is too meager to allow for much more than an educated guess. Of the two proposals outlined above, however, that of Boswell seems to me the better grounded, for three reasons. First, if Scroggs's argument were correct, we should expect the two terms *malakoi* and *arsenokoitai* to form an invariable pair; since neither would mean the same thing without the other, they would be unlikely to appear independently. Yet, in its one other occurrence in the New Testament, *arsenokoitai* appears without *malakoi* and is associated rather with "those given to harlotry" and "kidnappers" (1 Tim. 1:10). Second, if Paul was indeed reproducing technical terminology used in the synagogue and reaffirming it in the context of the church, we should expect knowledge of this to continue; but the later record is at best mixed, with little evidence for *arsenokoitēs* as meaning anything like "homosexual."[32] Third, Scroggs's hypothesis is more complex, requiring

---

30. Scroggs, *New Testament and Homosexuality,* 62–65, 83, 101–9.

31. Boswell, *Christianity, Social Tolerance, and Homosexuality,* 338–53. Wright ("Homosexuals or Prostitutes?" 125–53) has attempted to refute Boswell's position, but has succeeded only in removing much of Boswell's evidence without in fact proving his hypothesis untenable or demonstrating another hypothesis in its place. What Wright has demonstrated is that antagonism on the part of some Christians toward those who engage in homosexual intercourse goes back to at least the second century and almost certainly shows direct continuity with the same sentiment in Hellenistic Judaism. In relating these data to the New Testament, one must not forget that Paul was almost certainly more radical with regard to all such questions than his second-century successors; for he lived at a moment when institutional boundaries were being broken down, they at a time when they were being rebuilt. For a helpful corrective to Wright's work, see Petersen, "ΑΡΣΕΝΟΚΟΙΤΑΙ," 187–91.

32. Boswell (*Christianity, Social Tolerance, and Homosexuality,* 346–48) argued that the term never meant simply "homosexual" as distinct from "male prostitute." Wright ("Homosexuals or Prostitutes?" 125–53) argued the reverse. In both cases, the contexts on which the arguments depend are meager and make any certainty difficult.

us to understand the vocabulary in terms of a double linguistic and cultural tradition, whereas Boswell's hypothesis stays entirely within the bounds of the Greek-speaking world. This does not, of course, mean that Scroggs is necessarily mistaken; but, other considerations being at least equal, the simpler hypothesis is always preferable.[33]

The result, it seems to me, is that the reference to *arsenokoitai* in 1 Corinthians is, regrettably, not helpful to us in the present connection. Whatever we are going to learn of Paul's attitude toward homosexual behavior we must glean from the first chapter of Romans; and that, as we have seen, indicates that Paul regarded it as unclean but not therefore sinful. Indeed, it is difficult to see how he could have done otherwise, for his whole mission was predicated on the principle that Gentiles did not have to become Jews in order to be Christians. This was not merely a question of whether their males must be circumcised, but also included differences with regard to Sabbath observance (Rom. 14:5–6) and purity. Even in the matter of eating food sacrificed to idols, with the implied danger of participation in alien cults, Paul found it impossible to prohibit the behavior of the Strong on grounds of impurity; instead, as we have seen, he merely discouraged it on grounds of consideration for the Weak.

If Paul, however, did not regard homosexual acts among Gentiles as necessarily sinful, why did he open a letter in which he proposed to make a major statement of his understanding of the gospel with an extended passage emphasizing the unclean nature of this aspect of Gentile culture? The answer lies in the demands the Roman situation made on Paul and the rhetorical means he chose to respond to them.[34] The Roman church was not of Paul's founding, nor had he ever visited it hitherto. Since he was himself a controversial figure, he was perhaps in some doubt as to what kind of reception he would meet with when he did go there. The letter, therefore, had not only to lay out the main

---

33. I shall suggest below (in chapter 7) that an analysis of the list in 1 Timothy supports Boswell's hypothesis with a slight modification.

34. In the following discussion of the literary structure of Romans, I am heavily indebted to the work of Sinclair ("Christologies," 25–55). He outlines Romans in the following large units:

I. 1:1–16 Introduction: The Gospel is for Jew first and also Greek.

II. 1:17–15:13 Body of letter:
   A. 1:18–8:39 Jew must not boast over Greek.
   B. 9:1–15:13 Greek must not despise Jew.

III. 15:14–16:24 Personal Appendix: Both Strong and Weak should support Paul's ministry.

outlines of this theological stance but to do so in such a way as to gain the approval of all parts of the congregation. At Rome, as elsewhere, the outstanding question was how unclean Gentiles and Jews concerned for purity were to coexist in a single community. Since Paul's own work was so intimately bound up with the Gentile side of that problem, he had to begin by conciliating the Jewish part of the congregation, so as to persuade them that they could and should tolerate the presence of the Gentiles. Then he could lay out the ways in which he expected the Gentiles to cooperate in the matter.

The main body of Romans begins with a strong statement that the gospel is for "Jew first and also Greek" (1:16), and the remainder of the book addresses the two groups in this same order. In 1:18–32, Gentiles are spoken of as "they" and described in negative terms. Then, in 2:1, Paul begins reproving an anonymous critic of the Gentiles in the second person singular: "So you are without excuse, you fellow, whoever you are, sitting in judgment; for when you judge the other, you condemn yourself, for you that judge do the same things." Only in 2:17, does Paul reveal that the critic he is addressing is in fact the Jewish Christian. He has thus taken care to bring the Jewish part of his audience along with him gradually. Rather than confronting Jewish Christians directly, he begins with a critique of the dirtiness of Gentile culture in which he expects that they will silently join him.[35] He then questions whether this condemnatory attitude toward Gentiles is justified by unimpeachable virtue in the critic. Only then does he spring the rhetorical trap with his "Thou art the man"—or, as he puts it, "But if you bear the name Jew . . ." (2:17). (Paul does not explicitly address the Gentile members of the Roman church until 11:13, though he begins to speak of Jews in the third person in chap. 9.) The vivid account of the origins of Gentile uncleanness which Paul gives in Romans 1, then, is serving the rhetorical function of *captatio benevolentiae*, that is, of capturing the sympathies of the audience—or, in this case, of one part of the audience.

Still, one asks, why the specific choice of homosexual acts as the illustration of that uncleanness? One reason must have been that it was a very obvious and oft-belabored difference between Jewish and Gentile cultures. A second must have been that it was not a point of contention

---

35. Scroggs (*New Testament and Homosexuality,* 85–98, 109–110) showed that Paul's words about homosexual acts were entirely conventional in the context of Hellenistic Judaism.

between the two groups in the Roman church.[36] Food purity, as we have seen in our study of Romans 14—15, very much was; and to have begun with it would have exacerbated the tensions within the audience—something no competent rhetorician would do when one of his goals was to heal divisions. Paul had to begin from a noncontroversial point in order to lay the groundwork for an irenic treatment of that question by discussing the relationship of the Torah to salvation. A third reason was that homosexual acts were clearly a purity issue; no other reason was assigned for their prohibition in Leviticus. This meant that the original audience would be able easily to distinguish what Paul had to say about Gentile sin from what he had to say about Gentile uncleanness. The "debate" with the anonymous Jewish critic in chapter 2 was thus freed to be a debate about sin, not about impurity. Having granted in chapter 1 that Gentiles are unclean, Paul could insist in chapter 2 that they are not therefore necessarily more or less unrighteous than Jews. Thus, the Jewish interlocutor's sense of superiority is distinguished from a true right to judge.

Finally, an important reason for choosing homosexual acts as the prime illustration of Gentile uncleanness must have lain in the Gentile part of the audience itself. The most difficult part of Paul's rhetorical task was to gain the good will of the Jewish part of the audience without losing that of the Gentiles. Although Paul largely ignores the Gentiles until chapter 11, they were present and responding to the whole letter as they heard it read. When he was being critical of them, therefore, he had to speak in such a way as not to alienate their support of him. He might criticize their culture freely with respect to sin, since all Christians were expected to acknowledge their past sinfulness (cf. Rom. 3:9); but he must not suggest at any point that it was uniquely sinful, so that they had to cease being Gentiles and become Jews in order to be Christians— in other words, that being an unclean Gentile was somehow in itself a sin. The Gentiles would have been familiar with the repulsion Jews felt toward homosexual acts; and, given their own relative lack of interest in purity, they would have regarded this reaction as a Jewish peculiarity. Since Paul already had a large number of connections with the Roman church (Romans 16), they also would have known that Paul defended

---

36. Hays ("Relations Natural and Unnatural," 194–95) assumes that both Gentile and Jewish Christians would have been united in their condemnation of homosexuality as a vice of pagan Gentiles. But that is to assume his conclusions as the basis of his argument. Moreover, it makes nonsense of the singling out of the *Jewish* critic in Rom. 2:17.

the right of Gentile Christians to remain unclean in the physical sense. As he would put it, later in this same letter, "I know and am persuaded in the Lord Jesus that nothing is unclean in and of itself, except that for the person who regards anything as unclean it is" (14:14). Thus, by singling out the uncleanness of homosexual acts as an example of Gentile behavior, Paul can conciliate the Jewish part of his audience by inviting them to share with him a sense of their superiority, and yet not alienate the Gentiles who already know where he stands on the whole issue of purity.

Surprising as it may seem, then, the text (Rom. 1:18–32), which has perhaps been most used in recent Christian debates to justify the continuation of some kind of purity ethic, probably bears witness to a situation exactly opposite that envisioned by most modern interpreters. Instead of demonstrating Paul's retention of Levitical purity law as regards homosexual acts, it makes rhetorical sense only on the presupposition that he kept, in the realm of sex as well as that of food, a consistent distinction between impurity and sin. Indeed, Romans 1 becomes intelligible rhetorically only on the hypothesis that no one in the Roman church ever thought that Paul would wish to apply the purity laws of Leviticus to Gentiles. The argument is simply this: "We all know Gentiles have sinned. Only look at the dirtiness into which God plunged them as a consequence. But what of the Jew who criticizes them? Are you claiming to be sinless?"

CONCLUSIONS

Paul's assessment of purity in relation to the gospel is distinguished from those of Matthew, Mark, Luke, and John by a greater subtlety and more complete articulation. Where the evangelists simply know a distinction between physical purity and that of the heart, Paul also recognizes that purity of the heart may require physical purity in the case of the Weak, that is, those who cannot successfully distinguish between the two. And where the evangelists give a somewhat miscellaneous account of what constitutes impurity in the heart, Paul moves toward a particular stress on socially defined greed *(pleonexia)* and other wrongs that create social discord. Also, Paul clarifies the status of the purity code in the specific area of sex, both by the clarity of his general principles ("nothing is unclean in and of itself") and by the careful distinction he observed in Romans 1 between the impurity manifest in homosexual acts and the sins of idolatry and social disruption for which God imposed such impurity as "recompense."

7

The New Testament and Sexual Purity

We have seen that the evangelists and Paul rejected physical purity as a prerequisite of salvation or of membership in the Christian community. They did not deny its reality: dirt, as they understood it, was still dirt. They asserted, however, that the gospel transcended or even transformed it. Insofar as purity continued to be an important category for them, it now took the form of the metaphorical "purity of the heart." For them, real dirt consisted not of specific foods or sexual acts or of leprosy or corpses, but of arrogance, greed, and other sins of social oppression or disruption. If certain sexual acts, such as adultery, were still "unclean" in this new sense, it was for reasons quite different from the purity ethics in Leviticus. Greed, not physical contamination, rendered them so.

One could argue that the agreement of the evangelists and Paul in this matter constitutes a kind of presumption that this is the authentic New Testament teaching on the issue of purity. It is worthwhile, however, to examine the remaining books of the New Testament to see how congruent their teaching is with that of Paul and the Gospels. Some of them, indeed, have little to add. The three letters of John, for instance, scarcely use purity language; and only their close relationship with the Gospel of John enables us to interpret what little they do say. They provide us, then, with no independent evidence on our present topic. On the other hand, some of the late New Testament documents give us the opportunity to see the repudiation of the purity ethic being adapted to new circumstances, while a couple of them give us glimpses of an abortive search for new purity codes distinctive to the various churches. After examining these texts, we shall be in a position to sum up the ethics of purity as they are dealt with in the New Testament writings.

THE PASTORAL EPISTLES
AND 1 PETER

Among the latest New Testament books are the three letters addressed, in Paul's name, to Timothy and Titus (usually called, as a group, the "Pastoral Epistles"). They were probably written a good many decades after Paul's death, perhaps as late as the early second century. Their author wished to claim Paul's authority for his own development of the Pauline teaching and adaptation of it to the needs of his own time. The letters show a substantial shift of perspective from Paul's own writings. Their characteristic concern is for stability in the church's inner organization, for exclusion of false teaching, and for behavior that will accredit the church as respectable in the eyes of outsiders. The author wants the church, for example, to accept the leadership of established male householders whose sobriety and administrative talent are proven and who enjoy a good reputation with the larger public (1 Tim. 3:1–13; Titus 1:5–9). He also wants to exclude certain Christian teachers with whom he disagrees and to ensure that Christians look and behave by the standards of the general culture. In pursuing the goal of respectability, he is prepared to sacrifice some of the freedom characteristic of Paul's own time, particularly the prominent role which women played in Paul's original foundations.

It would not be surprising if such an author returned to the use of purity rules, since respectability in itself typically constitutes a kind of purity code or is at least hedged about with purity restrictions. Yet, our author stands by the Pauline tradition in this respect and even gives us one of its most emphatic formulations: "All things are pure for the pure; for the polluted and faithless, however, nothing is pure, but both their minds and their consciences are polluted" (Titus 1:15). The "faithless" in question are insubordinate teachers "from the circumcision," who disrupt the congregations with teachings that involve "Jewish myths" and "human commandments"—and perhaps also "genealogies and conflicts and battles about the law" (1:10–14; 3:9). Thus, with an authentically Pauline twist, our author condemns the very advocates of physical purity as impure by reason of their lack of faith.

The great virtues for the faithful pastor, who is the opposite of these disruptive teachers, are "a pure heart and a good conscience and a faith without pretense," all of which combine to produce love (1 Tim. 1:5). Such a pastor, strengthened by purity of the heart, will reject the impositions of the heretical teachers, who even go beyond the purity code of Israel, "forbidding people to marry" as well as "telling them to abstain from foods" (4:3a). "These things," says our author, "God created for those who are faithful and know the truth to receive with thanksgiving, because everything God has created is good and nothing is to be rejected when received with thanksgiving, for it is hallowed through God's word and through prayer" (4:3b–5). The author even requires, perhaps in opposition to such asceticism, that bishops and deacons be married, albeit only once (1 Tim. 3:2, 12; Titus 1:6).

Two elements in the Pastorals may at first seem to suggest a tendency to reaffirm some kind of purity law unique to these post-Pauline communities. One is the author's use of *hagnos* and related terms, which English translations tend to render with such words as "pure" and "chaste" (e.g., in the RSV, "set the believers an example . . . in purity," 1 Tim. 4:12; "train the young women . . . to be . . . chaste," Titus 2:4–5). There may be no better choice of vocabulary, in many cases, in English; in biblical Greek, however, there is a significant distinction between *hagnos* and *katharos,* the more common term for "pure." *Katharos,* which is used, for example, in the declaration "All things are pure for the pure" (Titus 1:15), emphasizes separation from what is impure. It defines boundaries. *Hagnos* characterizes dedication to some serious, often religious purpose. It might better be translated "dedicated," "devoted," or "consecrated."[1]

The author wants the Christian leadership to be dedicated to the peace of the community. Thus, he directs Timothy to treat each element within the community appropriately, without displaying partiality (1 Tim. 5:1–21); and then he sums up his directions with reference to ordination by saying, "Do not lay hands on anyone rashly and do not share in another's sins. Keep yourself *hagnos*" (5:22). The concern is not for physical purity. If Timothy were to ordain people who then introduce factions into the church, he would become a participant in their sins. He will avoid this mistake if he remains dedicated *(hagnos)* to his own ministry, which is to preserve the unity of the church and its teaching. The same matter is at stake elsewhere, when the author warns him to

---

1. The same terminology is found in 1 John 3:3, which speaks of forming oneself on the pattern of a future hope, as yet dimly understood, not on a static definition of pure and impure.

"flee the passions of youth" (2 Tim. 2:22). While the modern reader may at first take these passions as sexual in nature, the following verses, which encourage peace, gentleness, and the avoidance of fights, make it clear that the author is concerned rather about the tendency of the young to be proud, hasty, and quarrelsome.

The second element in the Pastorals which may suggest an interest in purity is the inclusion of the term *arsenokoitai* (which the RSV here translated "sodomites") in a list of transgressors (1 Tim. 1:8–11). We have already seen how difficult it is to define this term with precision (see above, pp. 117–20); but we may at least be able to recover some sense of what it meant for the author of the Pastorals by an analysis of the list in question. The passage begins with a received truth: "We know that the law is good if anyone uses it lawfully, knowing this—that law does not apply to a righteous person but to lawless and insubordinate people . . ." (vv. 8–9a). None of this would be new in the context of the Pauline tradition. Paul himself invoked the law as a guide for Christian behavior, provided it was not understood in ways that counteracted the teaching of grace.[2]

The righteous, to whom the law does not apply, are those "made righteous [or justified] by his grace" (Titus 3:7); the insubordinate, for the author of the Pastorals, would at least include the teachers of purity (1:10–16). In the immediate context, the "lawless and insubordinate" are best understood as a general heading for the list that follows. This list gives an accounting of people who are without internal law and do not subject themselves to God's will and who therefore must be told by some external authority that they are in the wrong. The specific items of the list begin with two pairs, "irreverent and sinners, unholy and profane." This language describes people who commit offenses against the worship of God. The next pair is "patricides and matricides." A pattern thus begins to emerge, following that of the Ten Commandments: first, offenses against the worship of God, and then those against parents. If this is the controlling model of the list, we should now expect references to murder, adultery, and theft. What we find is "killers of men, people given to harlotry, *arsenokoitai*, stealers of men." The list then concludes with "liars, perjurers, and whatever else is opposed to sound teaching." The reference to liars and perjurers corresponds to the commandment

2. On the complexity of Paul's treatment of the subject, see Sanders, *Paul, the Law, and the Jewish People,* 93–114.

against false witness, and the author leaves the list unfinished both to involve the audience silently in its completion and to avoid giving the impression that it is an exhaustive catalogue of wrongdoers.

Where, in terms of the pattern drawn from the Ten Commandments, do the *arsenokoitai* belong? There are two possibilities, falling as the word does between "those given to harlotry" *(pornoi)* and the "stealers of men." In other lists, we have seen references to *porneia* as a synonym for idolatry; here it is almost certainly standing in for adultery. *Pornoi* may have a generalized sense of "sexual wrongdoers"; or, if it refers, as it may, specifically to *men* who visit prostitutes, it could represent a redefinition of adultery to include all sexual acts of husbands outside marriage. The "stealers of men" (probably kidnappers for the slave trade), on the other hand, appear here in relation to the prohibition against theft. If we take the *arsenokoitai* more closely with the *pornoi,* we shall need to understand them specifically in relation to adultery, that is, violation of the marriage bond. Since use of the word *pornoi* implies at least the metaphor of prostitution, Boswell's hypothesis that they were male prostitutes becomes particularly apropos (see above, p. 119). Even more to the point, such men were accused in antiquity of cultivating the elderly for the purpose of obtaining legacies.[3] From the family's point of view, such a legacy represented a theft of its goods; and this links the *arsenokoitai* to the category of theft as well as that of adultery, exactly the intermediate position they hold in the list itself. While we shall probably never have any real assurance as to the meaning of the term, this use of it, in one of its earlier occurrences, suggests strongly that it refers to legacy hunters who used sexual attraction as bait. There is no reason to suppose that our author used it, contrary to his overall ethical stance, as a reference to the Levitical purity rule against homosexual acts.

The author of the Pastorals certainly had a sexual ethic, but it was a property, not a purity, ethic. He was anxious that the church become more orderly and respectable, and he knew of Christian teachers who urged the adoption of purity codes, whether Levitical or of later origin. Yet, his letters still represent a firm commitment to the principles enunciated by Paul. Physical purity is irrelevant to salvation or to church membership; "all things are pure to the pure." Yet, purity of the heart, which restrains a Christian teacher from becoming involved in divisive quarrels and struggles for power, is a fundamental necessity.

3. Cf. Juvenal *Satires* 1.37–42, taunting a rich woman for such lovers. I am indebted for this interpretation of the *arsenokoitai* to Linda Clader of Carleton College.

Of the other New Testament letters, 1 Peter stands close to the Pastorals in this matter. It is a difficult work to date, but it shares the Pastorals' concern that Christians appear respectable in their neighbors' eyes. There is no clear reference to any code of physical purity. A "pure heart," however, is held up as the source of love within the community (1:22). Christians are to avoid "fleshly passions" as part of a campaign to maintain a good reputation among their Gentile neighbors (2:11–12).[4] The time for wild and idolatrous banqueting is long past (4:1–6); they are to replace it with moderation, sobriety, love, and hospitality (4:7–11). As in the Pastorals, purity is thought of not as a physical state, but as a dedication to humble and loving behavior.

HEBREWS

On purity, as on almost every topic, Hebrews occupies a distinctive position. The date and authorship of this work have been much debated; but since its theological stance is nearly unique in the New Testament, perhaps it does not much matter for us who wrote it or when. Purity is very important to the author, but in a way otherwise almost unexampled in the New Testament. Like the Qumran community, he believes that all sin is in some sense impurity and therefore demands rites of purification. This is the significance of Christ's work: he has "accomplished purification of the sins" (1:3).[5] In this, the author means to explain what Christ has done by comparing it to the sacrificial cultus which the Torah required. This cultus he sees as no more than a shadowy representation of the real sacrifice that Jesus alone could perform; in comparison, the work of Jesus must always be seen as superior to that performed at the earthly altar.

One way this author has of describing Jesus' superiority is to say that the Tabernacle cultus had to do only with external, physical purity. He refers to "the present time, in which both gifts and sacrifices are being offered that cannot perfect the worshiper with respect to conscience, but only with reference to foods and beverages and various washings. [These sacrifices are] ordinances of flesh, in force until a time of correction" (9:9–10). Christ's sacrifice is correspondingly superior: "For if the

---

4. Cf. 1 John 2:16, where the "desire of flesh . . . eyes . . . world" is connected with the "boasting of status in life" (*bios*, not *zoē*). The easy modern assumption that "flesh" equals "sexual desire" does not sufficiently explain New Testament usage. Weil, I believe, caught the sense of the latter correctly in saying that "the flesh impels us to say *me*" (*Waiting for God*, 54). Flesh is whatever shuts out the neighbor.

5. One finds comparable language in 1 John 1:7, 9. On Qumran, see above, chapter 3.

blood of goats and bulls and a heifer's ashes, sprinkling the defiled, sanctify for the purification of the flesh, how much more will the blood of Christ, who through eternal Spirit offered himself up without blemish to God, purify our consciences from dead works to worship a living God?" (9:13–14).

The uniqueness of Christ's sacrifice is a sign of its finality. The sacrifices of the Tabernacle were repeated again and again—a sign, for our author, that they were ineffectual (10:1–4). Christ's sacrifice was once for all, with the consequent danger that anyone who sinned after once receiving its benefits would be beyond help: "For if we sin voluntarily after receiving the knowledge of truth, no further sacrifice for sins is left, but a certain fearsome expectation of judgment and a jealous flame that is going to devour the opposition" (10:26–27). There is no hope for the person "who has trodden the son of God underfoot and deemed the blood of the covenant, by which he was sanctified, profane and insulted the Spirit of grace" (10:29). In sum, all sins, not just violations of the purity code, require purification; and only the sacrifice of Jesus can achieve this. The sacrifices prescribed by the Torah purified one only from violations of the purity code, but left the conscience untouched.

In practical terms, Hebrews agrees with the other New Testament writings we have studied in holding that purity of foods is of no ultimate importance among Christians: "It is a good thing for the heart to be strengthened by grace, not by foods; those who frame their conduct by them have not benefited" (13:9). In terms of sex, "marriage is to be honored among all and the bed undefiled"; and these instructions are grounded on the belief that "God will judge those given to harlotry *(pornoi)* and adulterers" (13:4). The defilement of the bed, then, consists in violations of the property ethic through prostitution and adultery. This is confirmed by the ease with which the author moves directly on to say, "Let your manner of life not be money-grubbing; be content with what you have" (13:5). It is also confirmed by the picture of the archetypical *"pornos* and profane person," provided elsewhere in the book, who turns out to be not a noted libertine, but Esau in the act of selling his birthright (12:16).

The treatment of Esau is also significant for what it tells us about both *porneia* and its opposite, about both pollution and cleanness. The relevant passage begins with an exhortation to "Pursue peace with all people and sanctification, without which no one will see the Lord, watching out lest anyone falling short of God's grace, lest any root of bitterness springing up cause trouble and through it many be polluted" (12:14–15). For Hebrews as for the Pauline school, pollution is whatever gives rise to discord in the community; Christian purity means pursuing peace with all. In Hebrews, then, even given its unusual emphasis on the "purification" of sins, we find a basic attitude toward purity, physical and metaphorical, that is coherent with that of the evangelists and Paul. Purity of the heart is determinative; physical purity does not "benefit" anyone.

JAMES

The Epistle of James is heavily influenced by the traditions of moral exhortation developed in Greek-speaking Judaism—so much so that some later Christian thinkers, such as Luther, have felt that it had little to do with Christianity. It offers an interesting test case, then, of the picture we have gained thus far of New Testament attitudes toward purity. Here, if anywhere, we might expect to find expressed the attitude of those early Jewish Christians who insisted on the retention of the full purity code (Acts 15:1).[6] Indeed, the document is attributed to the very James whom Paul blamed for the troubles at Antioch (Gal. 2:12), though it is difficult to say who actually wrote it or when. James gives clear evidence, however, of sharing the broader New Testament perspective we have already become familiar with. The work's famous definition of religion is a good place to begin: "Religion pure *(katharos)* and undefiled in the presence of the God and Father is this—to take responsibility for orphans and widows in their tribulation, to keep oneself unblemished from the world" (1:27).[7] The first element of this definition, the care of the needy, is an expression of love, of the purity of the heart. What about the second part—keeping oneself "unblemished"?

The author does not give a direct answer, but there are clues as to his meaning. A little earlier, for example, he told his reader to discard all "dirt" (or "shabbiness," *rhyparia*); and there he did explain what the image entailed: "Let every person be quick to listen, slow to speak, slow

6. James becomes still more interesting as test case if we read it as midrash on Lev. 19:12–18 with Johnson ("Use of Leviticus 19," 391–401). James ignores surrounding purity materials in Leviticus in abstracting these verses. If Johnson's comparison of James with pseudo-Phocylides be accepted, then the omission is still more remarkable, since the latter author did incorporate portions of the purity code touching on sex.

7. Note that there is asyndeton (lack of connective) between the injunction to care for the defenseless and that to keep oneself unblemished. This apposition suggests that the latter is simply another way of saying the same thing as the former and not at all a statement about physical purity.

to anger, for a man's anger does not work God's righteousness. Therefore, putting aside all dirt and excess of wickedness by means of gentleness, receive the implanted word that is able to save your souls" (1:19–21). Here, "dirt" characterizes the efforts of angry people to assume leadership in the community while ignoring the thoughts and contributions of others; purity, by implication, is what delivers from this dirt, namely, gentleness.

In another passage, our author writes of the tongue as a source of pollution. "The tongue is fire. The tongue takes its place among the members as the order (or universe) of unrighteousness; it blemishes the whole body and kindles the cycle of becoming and is kindled by Gehenna" (3:6).[8] The tongue is thus the shaping factor in human sin, but in what specific sense? The following verses suggest that discord in the community is still the key issue: with the tongue one blesses God and curses "human beings made in God's likeness" (3:9–10). The truly wise person will demonstrate that he acts "with the gentleness of wisdom"; but those who "have jealousy and selfish ambition" at heart, will boast and lie "against the truth." Such are the sources of social disruption (3:13–18). Here, then, as in chapter 1, James identifies pollution with whatever induces people to create discord in the community, especially by claiming unique knowledge or understanding.

The author does say that one is obligated to keep the whole law (2:10), a formula that leaves room for him to insist on the purity code. Yet, the examples he gives are not purity issues, but rather the commandments against adultery and murder (2:11). He tells sinners to cleanse their hands, but also to consecrate their hearts (4:8); and, after telling them to mourn and repent, his practical direction about behavior is that they not slander one another (4:11). If the author had any particular concern about physical purity, it does not come to the fore in this work. Indeed, like Matthew (1:5) and the author of Hebrews (11:31), he takes Rahab the harlot as one of his positive examples, saying that she was justified by her works when she received the spies

8. This is a difficult passage, not least because of the strange expression "the cycle (or wheel) of becoming" *(ton trochon tēs geneseōs)*. In Matthew and Luke, *genesis* occurs in the sense of "birth"; but in James (the only other New Testament author who uses the term), it appears only here and in the equally curious reference to a man who "sees the face of his *genesis* in a mirror" (1:23). The easiest way to explain both instances of the word in James is to take *genesis* in a Platonic sense as referring to the turbulent and temporary world of becoming in contrast to the stable world of being. The whole phrase, then, would be equivalent to the "wheel of life" in *Sibylline Oracles* 2.87, which speaks of the constant but unpredictable reality of change in this life.

and sent them safely on their way (2:25). For James, as for our other authors, the essential purity is the purity of the heart, which sends people out to care for the needy and keeps them unblemished by worldly desires for power and domination. Such desires, wreaking havoc within the community of faith, are the only real pollution.

JUDE AND 2 PETER

The Epistle of Jude, short and undatable as it is and totally absorbed in fierce denunciation of sectarian teachers, might seem unlikely to contribute anything to the present discussion. It does, however, confirm some of what we have already seen. It identifies the rival teachers as people who, following their desires *(epithymia)*, are willing to divide the church for the sake of personal gain (16–19). "Desire," here, clearly has more to do with greed than with "lust" as it is now commonly understood. Also, by a clever pun, the letter indicates that its author regards fomenters of discord as the true blemishes on the church. In a long and sometimes chaotic metaphor drawn from a storm at sea, he calls them "the *spilades* in your love feasts," *spilades* meaning both "submerged rocks" and "spots" (12).

Jude gives evidence of a new purity rule which seems to be unique to this letter. It takes the form of an otherwise unexampled explanation of the sin of Sodom. In asserting the reality of God's judgment, he reminds his readers of three instances of divine punishment from ancient times: the members of the exodus generation who did not believe, the angels who came down to earth and had children by human females (Gen. 6:1–4),[9] and the Cities of the Plain (Genesis 19). The latter two cases he links closely together: "The angels who did not keep their own place in the hierarchy, but left their proper dwelling he has kept under darkness in eternal chains for the judgment of the great day, just as Sodom and Gomorrah and the surrounding cities, having committed the same kind of harlotry as these did and having gone off after other flesh, provide an example by undergoing a judgment of agelong fire" (6–7).

The passage is difficult for the modern reader because our presuppositions about angels are different from those of many biblical writers. Two phrases are the key to Jude's interpretation of the matter: first, he says that Sodom and Gomorrah committed the *same kind* of harlotry as the Watchers (as the angelic beings of Genesis 6 are commonly called);

---

9. Jude seems to be drawing more on *1 Enoch* here than on Genesis.

second, he describes this harlotry, in an unusual phrase, as "going off after other flesh." The "men" that Lot received into his house in Sodom were, according to Genesis, really angels. Thus, Jude's understanding of the sin of Sodom is that the men there wished to have sexual intercourse with angels.[10] The widespread notion that the sin of Sodom was homosexuality will not fit Jude's language at all, for there would be no parallel with the deeds of the Watchers, and homosexual acts would surely have to be described in terms of "going off after the same flesh" rather than "other flesh."[11] The long-standing Christian presupposition that angels are immaterial beings, whatever its origins may have been, has obscured for us the meaning of the phrase, but Jude clearly shares the conviction of Genesis and *1 Enoch* (which offers a longer and more circumstantial account of the incident) that angels are capable of entering into physical sexual relations with human beings.[12]

Jude may have introduced this subject in response to his opponents. In the following verse, he says that these people, too, "in the same way both pollute the flesh in their dreams and negate dominion and blaspheme glories" (8). "Dominion" and "glories" here are probably names for grades of angelic beings, and Jude's language suggests that certain sectarian teachers were claiming to have sexual intercourse with them.[13] All this is quite beyond the scope of the purity code of Leviticus. Even Genesis, if it disapproves at all of what the Watchers did, does so only on the grounds that humanity must not be immortal (6:3). For Jude, however, it appears to be a transgression of a purity rule analogous to that which prohibits bestiality; in other words, it is a mixing of kinds.

The author of 2 Peter, whose letter is probably the latest of all New Testament writings, seems to agree with Jude that some early Christian teachers practiced sexual rites. Since this author reused virtually the whole of Jude in his letter, it is difficult to be clear how far the material reflects his own concerns and how much of it merely carries over from Jude. Still, 2 Peter generally edits Jude in a way that brings it closer to the New Testament mainstream, and this suggests that what the author

10. *Testament of Naphtali* 3.4 may have the same interpretation in mind when it makes a similar comparison between Sodom and the Watchers, but it is less clear than Jude.

11. The King James translators must at least have perceived the problem, for they translated "strange flesh." The RSV committee substituted the arbitrary phrase "unnatural lust"—not a translation at all and quite misleading in this case.

12. On the physical character of angels, see *Jubilees* 15.27, which holds that those of the highest rank were created without foreskins.

13. Very likely, Jude was disturbed by something like the rites and ideas intimated in the *Gospel of Philip;* cf. Buckley, "Cult-Mystery," 570–75, 579–81.

kept he kept deliberately. For example, there is no hint here (2:6–8) of Jude's unusual explanation of the sin of Sodom; 2 Peter substitutes quite general language about "unlawful acts" and "license." One cannot be certain what the author means by these vague terms. He still threatens judgment, however, against unrighteous people "who go after flesh with a desire for pollution and despise dominion" (2:10; cf. Jude 8).

According to 2 Peter, the behavior of sectarian teachers blended license, adultery, and greed (*pleonexia*; 2:1–3, 12–14). The letter's omission of any clear reference to intercourse with angels may mean that it was unknown to the author or only that it was irrelevant to his purposes. What remains is a description of the dangers of early Christian prophecy that can easily be paralleled from the *Didache*, or *Teaching of the Twelve Apostles*, a work which probably antedates 2 Peter by some decades, though it was not finally included in the New Testament canon. The *Didache* warns against prophets who, while seeming to speak in the Spirit, order up fine meals for themselves or command that money be given them or perform a "mystery of the church," presumably a sexual act of some sort.[14] Those who would profit from meals or gifts the *Didache* brands at once as false prophets; those who perform a mystery, however, it tolerates as long as they do not teach others to do the same.

REVELATION

The Revelation of John was written in a time of great stress for Christians, perhaps in the last decade of the first century. The circumstances were exactly the sort in which one would expect to find a threatened community raising barriers of purity between itself and the surrounding, hostile world. The book does, in fact, use the language of purity with some frequency; but, given its highly imagistic nature, it is often difficult to know how the author might have applied the language in practical situations. Thus, he speaks often of the "abominations," "uncleanness," and "harlotry" of Babylon (emblematic, it seems, of Rome; 14:8; 16:19; and quite often in chaps. 17—18). The New Jerusalem, by contrast, is clothed in clean, shining linen, which is the righteous deeds of the saints (19:8); and this city will be forbidden to anyone who commits abomination or lie (21:27). It would seem easy to understand these passages in terms of physical purity, particularly in the light of similar motifs in Hellenistic Jewish apologetic.

14. *Didache* 11.

There are materials at the beginning and end of the book, however, that help us to connect these apocalyptic images with the particularities of the author's immediate milieu and so give them more precise content. First, at the beginning of the book, we encounter two groups of people whom he accused of committing harlotry. One is a group of people in the church at Pergamum who followed "the teaching of Balaam, which he taught Balak to put a stumbling block in front of the children of Israel—to eat things sacrificed to idols and commit harlotry" (2:14). The other is the congregation at Thyatira which tolerated "the woman Jezebel, who calls herself a prophetess and teaches and misleads my slaves to commit harlotry and eat things sacrificed to idols" (2:20). He also described certain people as "committing adultery with her" (2:22).

In view of what we have read in Jude and 2 Peter, one would not wish to be hasty in ruling out an actual sexual component in these charges. Indeed, the reference to Balak may confirm it, as the narrative in Numbers suggests that the Moabite women used sexual enticements in luring Israel from its proper worship (Num. 25:1–2). The connection of "harlotry" with sacrificial food, however, is explicable without such a hypothesis (see above, pp. 72–74); and Jezebel's historical prototype was known for her devotion to Baal, not for licentiousness (1 Kings 18:4, 19; 19:1–3). In the end, we cannot know whether the author knew and objected to specific sexual practices at Pergamum and Thyatira. What we can be sure of is his antagonism toward Christian participation in idolatrous rites, for this is a dominant theme in his work.

At the end of Revelation, we find two closely related lists of sinners who will be, in the one case, consigned to the second death (21:8) or, in the other, excluded from the New Jerusalem (22:15). The first list is the longer one and includes: cowards, unfaithful people, those who have become abominable, murderers, those given to harlotry, sorcerers, idolators, and "all lying people." The common association of harlotry, sorcery, and idolatry points to the importance of the alien cult in this list; and what we know of the persecution of Christians under the early Roman Empire explains why this was of great concern for the author of this work. The courts sought to persuade those accused as Christians to commit apostasy by performing an act of worship before the images of the gods.[15] Since those who did so were typically released without

15. Pliny the Younger *Letters* 10.96.5.

further ado, the offering of a pinch of incense or tasting of a single morsel of the sacrifice would have seemed a small price for one's life. Many gave way at once. The practice of the courts in this matter—and its evident success—explains why the list begins with the cowardly, unfaithful, and polluted, in other words, those Christians who have apostatized through offering sacrifice to the idols. Murderers belong to this same context; they are the informers who gave the names of other Christians to the authorities. All these people can be summed up as "liars" who, having claimed to be servants of Christ, finally betrayed that commitment.

The shorter list, in chapter 22, is not significantly different except for its opening insult: "Outside are the dogs and the sorcerers and those given to harlotry and the murderers and the idolators and everyone that loves and practices a lie" (22:15). This list covers the same group of people: apostates and informers. The stress on the "lie" makes it clear that these have committed impurity of the heart and not just incurred simple physical contamination through idolatry. The author of Revelation, then, links impurity with idolatrous worship because of its connection with the persecution of Christians and with apostasy. This, in turn, explains why he also connected it to sectarian teaching in local churches. The "teaching of Balaam" and that of Jezebel must have justified Christians who saved their lives by offering the sacrifices. Accordingly, our author sees these teachers as themselves polluted in the same way as the apostates.

Apart from this, one other reference to purity appears in a single passage of Revelation. It is difficult to interpret because of its isolation not only within this one book but in the whole New Testament. In chapter 14, the seer beholds the Lamb, standing on Mt. Zion and, with him, one hundred and forty-four thousand men who have the Lamb's name and that of his Father engraved on their foreheads and who sing a new song that only they may learn. They are not angels, but human beings "purchased from the earth." The seer tells us, "These are they who have not polluted themselves with women, for they are virgins; these are they who follow the Lamb wherever it goes; these have been purchased from among human beings as firstfruits for God and the Lamb and in their mouth has been found no lie. They are blameless (or, unblemished)" (14:4–5).

Nowhere else in the New Testament is there a comparable evaluation of virginity, much less of specifically male virginity.[16] One can find related materials outside the New Testament canon in books, such as the second-century *Acts of Paul,* which preached the doctrine of "encratism," namely, that only the sexually continent can be saved. Even the encratites, however, seem to have been equally interested in both male and female virginity. Given his powerful image of the woman clothed with the sun who brings forth a male child (12:1–6), it is unlikely that our author wished to exclude women altogether from the company of the elect. It is somewhat easier to imagine that he accepted encratite principles and regarded all sexual acts as contrary to Christian teaching. Yet, there is no straightforward statement to that effect in the book. One is left without a final answer; for the rest of Revelation, as I have shown, knows no purity concern other than that connected with apostates and informers.[17]

CONCLUSION

Close study of the passages dealing with sexual and other forms of purity reveals a high level of agreement on this subject among the New Testament authors. With the possible exception of Jude and Revelation, all the documents that dealt with physical purity at all agreed in rejecting it as an authoritative ethic for Christians as such. Gentile Christians, in particular, were understood to be entirely free of it, and this was what made possible the inclusion of Gentiles in the church without circumcision being required of their males. Jewish Christians, it seems, were still expected in a general way to keep the purity law as an expression of their Jewish identity; even in their case, however, it cannot have been a requirement for church membership since that would have meant making salvation conditional on something in addition to "the grace of Christ" (Acts 15:11). Even Jude and Revelation do not return to the purity code of Leviticus. Though they reveal that Christianity had the capacity to begin generating its own purity rules, the particular rules they give evidence for have not commanded lasting assent in the mainstream of orthodox Christianity since the first century.

Many modern Christians suppose that early Christians made a sharp

16. Cf., however, 1 Cor. 7:1 and 1 Tim. 4:3, both of which suggest that there were teachers on the fringes of the Pauline communities who demanded complete sexual abstinence.

17. Schüssler Fiorenza (*Book of Revelation,* 181–92) argues that the male virgins are not to be understood literally at all. If she is correct (and her argument is a strong one), then even this exception to the New Testament rejection of physical purity falls.

distinction between purity rules touching on foods and those touching on sex, rejecting the former and retaining the latter. There is no justification for this position in the New Testament itself, which reveals that physical purity was—and had to be—rejected as a defining note of Christian identity. The dirty Gentile was as welcome to the church in all respects as the pure Jew. There was a difference, for the New Testament writers, between the ethics of food and those of sex; but it did not lie in a distinction between one kind of purity and another, for Levitical purity was of a piece. The distinction lay rather in the availability of other kinds of ethical principles with reference to sex and the lack of same with reference to food.

Once the purity ethic was abolished, there was no ethic left to distinguish permissible from impermissible foods. To enable Christians to eat together, the Jerusalem council sought a practical accommodation, by which Gentiles would avoid foods tainted by idolatry and blood, while Jews waived all other purity demands. Paul counseled the Strong to respect the Weak without surrendering their convictions and the Weak to respect their own consciences without being critical of the Strong. In neither case was the Levitical purity code imposed on anyone. The gradual disappearance of a strong Jewish constituency from the church meant that both the council's and Paul's recommendations became, in due course, irrelevant. The author of Revelation expressed an absolute opposition to foods sacrificed to idols; but even this was not simply a rule of physical purity, but rather the result of an absolute insistence on avoiding apostasy. With sex, on the other hand, the abolition of purity rules still left in place a whole realm of ethics based on property considerations. Accordingly, the New Testament writers still considered sex to be an area subject to ethical demands, whereas food had practically ceased to be so.

The early Christians did not cease to be conscious of a distinction between clean and unclean. What they had abolished was the link between physical cleanness and divine favor. The distinction as such continued, particularly for Jewish Christians, as a socially defined reality. Clean and unclean still carried with them at least the degree of attraction and repulsion that clean and dirty do for the modern Gentile reader. The power of clean and unclean thus remained as a powerful social reality, and New Testament writers applied that power freely to other purposes: some by calling upon all Christians to keep the metaphorical purity of the heart, others (mainly the Johannine school) by rejoicing in the power of unclean rites to convey salvation.

From the New Testament onward, all genuinely Christian ethics had to explain themselves in terms of purity of the heart, which is itself defined primarily as willingness to respect and unwillingness to harm the neighbor. The war waged in the epistolary literature on the sins of social competition and disruption is perhaps the New Testament's most significant contribution to the explication of this purity. In part, this was a reaction to the centrifugal qualities of church life in its earliest decades.[18] The preaching of the gospel and the formation of new communities around it unleashed a flood of theological creativity and a sometimes fierce struggle as to who would determine the shape of the new society and on what principles. Still, the rejection of social competition by Paul and others was also a basic Christian ethical insight dependent upon the cross itself. The cross represents God's willingness to be least and weakest and creates thereby a model for all Christian behavior characterized by love and humility. It is to this insight that the language of purity, when used positively by New Testament authors, most often refers.

Some early Christians heard the repeal of the purity code as signifying an abolition of all sexual morality and its replacement by unrestricted libertinism. To them, Paul and his successors reaffirmed the existence of another kind of sexual ethic, which was still authoritative. At the other extreme, some Christians supposed that their new faith demanded complete rejection of all sexual activity. Unguarded use of the language of purity in its metaphorical sense may well have encouraged such a mistake; the Christian demand for purity of heart may have been heard, by the ill-instructed, as an appeal for the avoidance of all physical dirtiness. The principal impulse behind this ascetical movement, however, must surely have lain in the widespread and still poorly understood revulsion which many sorts of people in late antiquity were beginning to feel toward sexuality. In other words, the more extreme suspicions of sex which Paul combated at Corinth (1 Cor. 7:1–2) and the author of Revelation perhaps accepted in his vision of the hundred and forty-four thousand male virgins—these originated more in the spirit of the age

18. The character of Greek culture and other tensions specific to the churches played a significant role, as I have suggested elsewhere with respect to wealth (*Rich Christian,* 149–73).

than in that of the gospel.[19] On the whole, the New Testament writers were neither negative nor naively approving toward sex. Their rejection of the code of physical purity originated not in a program to revise sexual ethics as such, but in their determination to break down the barriers that purity rules erected between human communities and against the marginal people in a given society. Jesus' own example, confirmed by the later decision to admit uncircumcised Gentiles to the church, demanded this; and the church quickly came to understand that this was a fundamental expression of the triumph of God's grace in the cross.

The results which I have just set forward will, of course, be very difficult for many modern readers to accept. One problem, the less difficult one, lies in the New Testament writings themselves. Their authors shift freely and without warning between two quite different uses of purity language: the literal, in which it denotes what I have called "physical purity," and the metaphorical, in which it points to various applications of the Christian "purity of the heart." When the New Testament writers insist on purity as a standard of Christian conduct, they intend this latter, metaphorical sense. Most of their original hearers will have been familiar, through the life of the community itself, with the general outlines of Christian ethical teaching. On the whole, they were not so much learning new things from the writings that now form our New Testament as hearing known truths confirmed or disputed issues reexamined. Our own, latter-day position is, of course, much more difficult. In our effort to understand the New Testament writings on their own terms, we must seek to recover from them not only what they say but what their original audiences already knew. At most, we can hope for a close approximation of such knowledge—and not even that unless we are prepared to place our modern presuppositions at risk in the process.

This brings me to the other and greater barrier which modern readers must overcome in accepting the New Testament witness on the subject of purity—our own traditional preconceptions. Sex is not a primary concern in the New Testament writings nor is physical purity an accepted principle there. To those who read the New Testament in the light

19. Cf. the account of the further development of sexual asceticism among Christians by Brown ("Late Antiquity," 263–67).

of modern Western Christianity this will always be difficult to comprehend or accept, for a long history of pietism, both Protestant and Catholic, has made physical purity a major principle and sex a primary concern among us. A private kind of morality that stresses sexual purity (sometimes hedging that purity about with prohibitions on dancing, dating, kissing, and so forth) has been widespread in Western Christianity. Many American Protestants have added a form of food purity (total abstinence from alcohol) as well. An authentically New Testament ethic, which emphasizes gentleness, unity, love, and justice, is likely to seem an innovation in such a context. One result is that modern Christians find it hard to believe that the New Testament writers were, in fact, ethically indifferent to what we would call "dirty" behavior and that they adopted this stance of indifference in response to the demands of the gospel itself. If the gospel is indeed "God's power for salvation to every one who believes" (Rom. 1:16), then it must welcome the leper, the menstruant, the uncircumcised Gentile, indeed all the unclean without exception.

How did Christianity become so different in this respect? The full story is far from clear and too complex to be included in this study. The widespread revulsion toward the body in late antiquity affected Christians as well as others. From at least the second century onward, there were Christian sects who held that salvation was contingent on sexual continence (the encratites) or that the material world was wholly evil and sex was to be rejected on that account (Marcionites and some Gnostics). By the fourth century, there were also orthodox writers, such as Jerome, who were obsessed with physical purity. The legalization and subsequent establishment of Christianity as the imperial religion in that same century may have contributed to the development of a new purity code, for the church would have felt the need of new boundaries to replace the unarguable ones martyrdom had previously drawn around it. (A comparable response to a similar situation is found in the experience of the nineteenth-century Mormons.)[20] Closer to the present time, pietism and revivalism made major contributions to the development and propagation of this purity code. The subject calls for full and careful investigation in its own right. I mention it here only as an aspect of the intellectual and spiritual presuppositions of the modern reader. The serious student of Scripture must be prepared to set aside such precon-

20. Shipps, *Mormonism*, 109–11, 124–25.

ceptions, however treasured, at least for the time required to give the New Testament a careful reading on its own terms. The historical, cultural, and ecclesiastical distance between the world of the New Testament and that of today is vast, and one must resist the temptation to read the ancient texts only in terms drawn from one's own immediate experience and the tradition which has shaped it.

At no point is the distance more evident or more critical than in the subject which has been under discussion in the preceding chapters. The Jesus who regularly preferred the company of the impure to that of the religious authorities of his day or who predicted that tax collectors and prostitutes would more readily gain entrance into the reign of God than the devout would not have been a popular figure in the church itself in most of the succeeding Christian centuries. He would have been seen as undermining public morality; and, insofar as the church itself adopted a purity ethic from the fourth century onward, that accusation would have been apt. In its accommodation with Constantine's empire, the church in the Roman world effectively inherited, in its own social realm, the role the Pharisees and the early rabbis had held in the realm where the New Testament books were being written. Faithful reading of the New Testament, then, demands of the modern Christian at least a temporary distancing of oneself from that role so that one does not forbid Scripture to speak things unheard of in our narrow experience. One thing it so speaks is the end of the ethic of physical purity.

2

Dirt
GREED
Sex

8

Women and Children as Property in the Ancient Mediterranean World

In the ethic of purity, "dirtiness" is defined as wrong and therefore to be avoided, corrected, and/or punished. Since the purity ethic, with its concern for bodily boundaries, has a certain natural affinity for sexual acts, people often, in a casual way, reduce all issues of sexual ethics to that of purity; and, once we learn that "all things are pure for the pure" (Titus 1:15), we may assume that, for the New Testament writers, sexual ethics have ceased to exist. This is far, however, from being their position. They turn, instead, to another ethical principle deeply rooted in their world—one, moreover, on which Jews and Gentiles were broadly agreed—the principle of respect for sexual property.

"Property" denotes something which is understood as an extension of the self, so that a violation of my property is a violation of my personhood. It is a difficult concept, as both ancient and modern thinkers have recognized; for, pushed to extremes, it can license self-aggrandizement at the expense of or in indifference to the welfare of the larger human community. Early Christians were at least attracted to the idea of a fully communal existence and even claimed to have practiced it on occasion (e.g., Acts 2:43–45).[1] Yet, Christian thinkers of the more orthodox sort, at least, did not include in this claim the idea of sexual communism. Tertullian, in the late second or early third century, wrote, "All things are without distinction [of ownership] among us except wives."[2]

There were ancient thinkers who suggested sexual communism, in-

1. Countryman, *Rich Christian*, 76–81.
2. Tertullian *Apology* 39.11.

147

cluding one youthful gnostic Christian teacher, Epiphanes, the son of the better-known Carpocrates. On the whole, however, Christians held firmly to the notion of private sexual property and made this the foundation for constructing their sexual ethic. If impurity or dirtiness no longer served to define sexual sin, *greed*, the desire to have more than one's own fair share of goods, did.[3]

Greed is, of course, a social offense which enhances one's own property at the expense of another or which revels in possessing more than another. Since we have already seen that Paul and other New Testament writers set great store by unity and peace in the community and even characterized the virtues contributing thereto as "purity of heart," we shall not be surprised to find them opposing acts of greed, which are by definition disruptive of the community. The way in which sex figures here, however, will be difficult to follow unless we first gain some insight into what sexual property meant in the ancient world. The following discussion will focus, once again, on Israel; but the results are broadly applicable, with appropriate exceptions, to the Greco-Roman world of the first century as well.[4]

THE PATRIARCH AND HIS FAMILY

If the purity concerns of ancient Israel are strange to the average modern reader, the other side of its sexual ethics is likely to be no less so—at least to those readers who are part of the predominantly individualized culture of the West. The distance between us and the biblical writers becomes evident in passages that are, quite simply, unintelligible when read in the context of modern family life. Take, for example, the attitude toward wife and children manifest in the Book of Job. At one point in the book (chap. 31), Job invokes on himself a series of conditional curses: if I have committed such-and-such sin, may some appropriate punishment befall me. It is a way of asserting his innocence in the strongest possible way; and the passage forms, in fact, the peroration of his self-defense. Among the sins listed are deceit in business, inhumanity toward servants, indifference to the poor, trust in riches, idolatry, taking pleasure in the ruin of an enemy, concealment of crime, misap-

3. Since ancient cultures generally assumed a world of "limited good," not the expanding universe of modern capitalism, they tended to define the fundamental offense against property as greed rather than, say, theft. Acquisition of new wealth could fall under this condemnation even when fully legal, if it were seen as gained at the expense of another.

4. See the useful survey of Greco-Roman sources by Yarbrough (*Not Like the Gentiles*, 31–63).

propriation of land, and adultery. Here is how he speaks about adultery. "If my heart has become simple over a woman *(ishshah)* and I have lain in wait at my neighbor's gate, let my wife *(ishshah)* grind[5] for another man and other men bow down on her" (31:9–10).

In the modern West, if one asks, "What is the *wrong* of adultery?" one is likely to be told that it is a betrayal of trust. On the basis of such an understanding, Job ought to invoke some punishment on *himself* if he had committed the offense. In a similar vein, he says that if he has ignored the needs of the poor or been cruel to them, he should suffer the loss of the arm that committed the sin (31:16–23). Yet, in the case of adultery, he suggests that an appropriate punishment would be for his *wife* to become another man's household servant and be used sexually, like a prostitute, by a number of men. This curse becomes intelligible only when we note that it is parallel to others in the chapter which deal with property offenses: if Job has practiced deceit, let his own crops be rooted out (31:5–8); if he has taken another's land, let his own grow weeds instead of good crops (31:38–40). If he has taken another man's wife, let another take his. The wife was a form of property; adultery was violation of the property of another and should therefore be punished with violation of one's own.

What was true of the wife was true also of the children. At the beginning of the story, Job has seven sons and three daughters (1:2), all of whom are killed by Satan, acting under God's authorization (1:6–19). At the end of the story, after God has, in some sense, vindicated him (42:7–9), Job acquires greater riches than he had to begin with (42:10–12). In addition, he sires a new family, identical to the old in numbers and distribution between the sexes, and he lives on to see his great-grandchildren (42:13–17). From the perspective of the modern reader, this is not likely to seem very satisfactory. It is one thing to have fourteen thousand sheep in place of seven thousand, one sheep being much like another; but surely ten new children, however loved in themselves, do not really replace the ten destroyed. We are inclined to think of each child as a unique and irreplaceable individual. Yet, the conclusion of Job makes sense only if we understand that, in its author's

---

5. It has been suggested that one should read this verb, with different vowels, to mean "be ground," in a sexual sense. That would make the two halves of v. 10 completely synonymous, but seems unnecessary. Part of a woman's value as property lay in her contribution to the work of the household.

day, children, like wives, were first and foremost possessions.[6] The new ten would serve as well as the old to perform the basic function of these possessions, which was to reproduce and carry on the family. There is no further reason for Job to complain in the matter.[7]

The offense which the modern reader finds in this resolution of the story arises not from individual callousness on the part of the author of Job, but from the great cultural distance between antiquity and our own day. Mediterranean antiquity, whether Jewish or Gentile, did not take the average individual as its basic building block. The value of every individual, which is so fundamental to modern democracies, was inconceivable in that context. In its place stood the value of the family, which was the basic social unit. The eunuch and the bastard, who were inevitably individuals, since they were by definition incapable of being related to a family, were permanently excluded from the assembly of Israel (Deut. 23:1–2); they had no place in a society where the family was the basic social unit.[8]

Job himself is no individual—no independent adult male on the modern pattern. He has meaning and significance in his world as the embodiment of his family, as its patriarch, its male head who ruled it within and represented it in its dealings with outsiders. In the latter role, he was the family's vital link to the larger world. Widows and orphans, lacking any connection with a patriarch, were marginal people whose interest could easily be trampled on. The patriarch's task was to maintain the family's wealth and public standing in the community, even, if possible, to enhance it. He was not a free agent, but the servant of that larger and ongoing unit which he embodied only for his own lifetime. Other members of the family were agents and tools for the patriarch, sharply subordinated to him in the pursuit of his lifelong task. One of them, the eldest surviving son, would also be his successor (Deut. 21:15–17).

6. Compare the easy way in which the Torah links human with animal offspring and even with agricultural produce; e.g., Exod. 13:2, 11–16; Deut. 30:9.

7. Israel was unlike its Greek and Roman neighbors in its rejection of abortion and infanticide. While the Scriptures of Israel do not make a point of this, later Hellenistic Jewish apologetic did, e.g., *Sibylline Oracles* 2.252–82, 3.762–66, and pseudo-Phocylides 184–85. It is still true, however, that children were a form of property in Israel as much as among the Gentiles.

8. The occasional exception, such as Nehemiah who was a eunuch, "proves" the rule in both the original and modern senses of that verb. That is, he puts the rule to the test and demonstrates its accuracy. In his own right, he had no standing whatever among his own people; it was purely and solely his connection with the Persian ruler that gave him the power he wielded in Jerusalem.

If the patriarch was not an individual, those below him in the hierarchy of the family were even less so. Children existed for the sake of the family—practically speaking, for the sake of their parents, as the Torah shows by its stress on reverence for parents (Exod. 20:12). The striking of a parent (Exod. 21:15) or even habitual rebelliousness against them (Deut. 21:18–21) was grounds for the death sentence. The wife was brought in from another family in order to preserve and sustain that of her husband through the bearing of children and the wise administration of the household. The portrait of the ideal wife in Proverbs 31, though attributed to the mother of a Gentile king, is in harmony with expectations that were equally fundamental in Israel: she is her husband's confidante, a hard worker, an intelligent businesswoman, a charitable almsgiver, a good household administrator, and a fine seamstress; and her children rise up to call her blessed. She is perhaps not beautiful (31:30), for the point of the poem is to call attention to other qualities, ministering not so much to the husband's personal gratification as to the building up of his and his forebears' family.

THE PLACE OF WOMEN

Biblical Hebrew and ancient Greek felt no need, it seems, to make the distinction that English makes between "woman" and "wife." (In Hebrew, the word *ishshah* does duty for both; in Greek, *gynē*.) There was little occasion to make such a distinction, for it was the ideal destiny of an adult female to be some man's wife. In childhood, a woman was a member of her father's household and she might become so again in the event of divorce or widowhood—particularly if she were childless. Normally, she was transferred to the household of a husband at about the time of puberty, and from this time onward, she lived in a kind of familial limbo, being a full member of neither household. Marriage was not equivalent to a blood relationship, though it did alienate a woman to some degree from her own blood kin. The Torah gives a good illustration of the ambiguity involved, in the form of restrictions imposed upon priests in the matter of mourning. A priest was allowed to mourn only for members of his immediate family, and this included neither his wife nor his married sister (Lev. 21:1–4).

A woman never became truly a member of her husband's family, since she could be separated from it through divorce. The Torah gave the right of divorce only to the husband, preserving a unique power to him in the relationship (Deut. 24:1–4). To be deprived of the right of divorce was a serious punishment. If a man forcibly violated an unbetrothed virgin, he had to pay the bridal price to her father and marry her without possibility of divorce (Deut. 22:28–29). Or, if a man accused his lawful wife of not having been a virgin bride and the accusation proved false, he lost the right ever to divorce her (Deut. 22:13–19). There were some protests in the Scriptures of Israel against the power given the husband in the right of divorce. Malachi objected to the prevalence of divorce (2:13–16); and the second creation narrative in Genesis spoke of marriage as a reunion of Adam's separated parts to form "one flesh"—a phrase which makes of marriage a familial, not simply a contractual relationship (2:24).[9] Among the Pharisees of the first century, the School of Shammai allowed divorce only on grounds of sexual wrongdoing by the wife. There is no reason to doubt, however, that the law of divorce in Deuteronomy expressed the normal understanding of marriage.

The power of the father and then of the husband meant that a woman could enjoy, at most, only a secondary role in whatever household she belonged to—a status pointedly underlined by the right which the Torah gave to her father (before her marriage) or her husband to annul even her vows to God (Num. 30:3–15).[10] In fact, her position could be worse than just secondary. The ideal for a woman was to be a wife, but many found themselves in various grades of slavery, while even those who had achieved the status of wife might lose it through divorce or widowhood. The slave-woman was subject not only to the patriarch, but to a whole internal family hierarchy, including the patriarch's wife. The consequences could be devastating, as one sees in the case of Hagar, Abraham's Egyptian slave-woman. In this case, the patriarch was not ill-disposed toward her; but the jealousy of his wife Sarah and her influence with her husband resulted in Hagar's being degraded and expelled into the desert (Gen. 16:1–16; 21:9–21). Yet, even Sarah's power over Hagar was less her own than a result of her place as wife within the hierarchy of the family.[11]

In a culture where wives, children, and slaves were all property of

9. Malina (*New Testament World,* 108–9) is right in this interpretation of Gen. 2:24, but wrong, I think, in assuming that it represented the dominant understanding of marriage in ancient Israel.

10. In the Roman world, too, the wife could aptly be described as "like a grown child" from the point of view of the male head of household. See Veyne, *History of Private Life,* 39–40.

11. Trible, *Texts of Terror,* 10–13. Trible's analysis of the Hagar narratives, though primarily literary, is very helpful in clarifying the social dynamics of such a household.

male heads of household, hierarchy within the family group was the principal expression of these property relations. Not all property was governed by the same rules; human property could not be disposed of in exactly the same ways as animals or land. The Torah prescribed that slaves, for example, were not to be treated in the same way as cattle: one might deal with one's cattle as one wished, but one must not deliberately kill one's slave (Exod. 21:20–21). On the other hand, the punishment of a master who kills a slave is left unspecified, whereas the Torah is quite clear in demanding the death penalty for one who kills a freeman (21:12–14). The household was highly stratified and complex in its hierarchy, particularly since it was usual for those men who could afford it to have more than one wife.

One can glean from the pages of Torah some indications of the various grades of sexual property.[12] The lowest grade was the slave-woman taken captive in war. Deuteronomy specifically prohibits Israelites from taking male enemies alive—or even female captives from Canaan, though such might be brought from further away (20:10–18). (In one specific case, this is limited to women who have never had sexual relations; Num. 31:17.) Restrictions of this sort were related to the question of which foreign women could be accepted as wives for Israelite men: they should be virgins, to ensure that they are not bearing foreign children, and they must be from a distance so that they will not involve their husbands in Canaanite cults. Israelite men might indeed marry such women, but the woman's status, even as a wife, remained poor. A law on the subject (Deut. 21:10–14) provides that the captive must be given time to mourn her parents before the consummation of the marriage and that her master cannot afterward sell her for money, though he may send her out on her own if he comes to be displeased with her. Since she had no family to return to, this sort of expulsion would be disastrous for her. Such a woman, with no native country left and without any natal family to protect her interests, was in fact only one step removed from any other sort of slave. The gesture of constituting her as a "wife" can only have been in the interest of procuring legitimate heirs, as when Sarah gave Hagar to Abraham for the same purpose (Gen. 16:1–3).

12. These differed somewhat among Gentiles; but they too recognized distinctions between slave-women whom their masters used sexually, concubines of various sorts, and legitimate wives. For the Hellenistic world, see Pomeroy, *Goddesses*, 127–30, 139–41. For the Romans, see Veyne, *History of Private Life*, 33–35, 75–79.

The Gentile slave was a true chattel according to the Torah (Lev. 25:44–46). Hebrew slaves, however, enjoyed certain advantages. For example, males were to be released in the jubilee, celebrated every forty-nine years (Lev. 25:40) or even in the seventh year of their slavery (Exod. 21:2; Deut. 15:12). The male Hebrew slave might have entered slavery with his family or might have been given a wife by his master. In either case, a certain difficulty arose, since the relation of husband to wife was analogous to that of master and slave-woman. Who, then, owned the wife of the slave? Exodus settled the issue by discerning which ownership has precedence in time. If marriage preceded the man's entry into slavery, the wife was primarily his and went with him when he returned to freedom; if slavery came first and the wife was a gift of the master, then both she and her children belonged to the master (Exod. 21:3–6).[13]

The state of the female Hebrew slave was less clear. Deuteronomy assured her of freedom after six years (15:17). Exodus, however, makes the assumption that she was originally purchased to serve as wife for either her master or his son. Accordingly it did not provide for them to release her, but it did place certain restrictions on their control of her. Her master could not sell her to foreigners. If she was to be his daughter-in-law, he must also behave toward her in the place of her own father. After all, she would have no family to defend her interests. If she was to be his own wife, he might not discard her or slight her in favor of a better match later on. If he violated any of these rules, she automatically gained the right to her freedom—though in her case, as in that of the captive woman, this may have been a dubious advantage (Exod. 21:7–11).

A man might also take a free woman as concubine. The Torah does not define the status of concubine, but it must have been something less than that of full wife—even where the wife was of slave origin. One may guess that concubinage was a way for a younger man to acquire a first sexual partner without committing himself to treating her children as his heirs. Under some circumstances, it might be more profitable for him

---

13. Lev. 25:41 treats the children as the slave's property, but says nothing about the wife. This stems from the logic of the jubilee year, in which every father's house in Israel was to be restored to its original allotment of land. Since the purpose of the jubilee was to ensure the continuation of each individual family on its land, the freedman must be able to take his children, but he does not require his wife, since there are already children and since he will have the means to support himself again and, in due course, either ransom his slave-wife or marry another.

to postpone marriage until he was better established and could attract the attention of richer and more powerful future in-laws. The benefit to the concubine's family would come from not having to provide a dowry. That such arrangements could be mutually satisfactory to the men involved is evident from the story of the Levite's concubine (Judges 19:3–9). The social insignificance of the concubine is equally evident in that narrative: the woman is never named nor consulted as to her wishes, and finally her master brutally sacrifices her to the mob to save himself (19:22–30)[14]

The status of full wife was, generally speaking, the best position to which a woman could aspire in ancient Israel. The marriage would be arranged by the woman's father in a process that intimately concerned his own prestige. The ability to attract a favorable match depended not only on the young woman's personal qualities, but on her family's wealth, power, and civic repute. Her well-being in the marriage might also depend on these, since she would always remain, to some extent, a stranger in her husband's family. If he chose to take another wife or otherwise came to lose interest in her, she had little protection except his unwillingness to offend her family.

Although the wife did not, properly speaking, become a member of her husband's family, she did become his property; Deuteronomy routinely equates the acquisition of house, vineyard, and wife (20:5–7; 28:30).[15] Like these other major possessions, the wife became the property not merely of her husband, but of his family. Hence the law of levirate marriage (marriage with the husband's brother). A family took a wife for a son in order to ensure an heir. If the son died without producing one and he had surviving brothers, it was the duty of the next brother to take the widow himself. The first child of this union, however, was considered the child of the deceased brother, not of the brother who had joined in its conception. It was a disgrace for a man to refuse this duty, since he would be setting his private interests ahead of those of the family (Deut. 25:5–10). The woman does not appear to have had a choice; on the whole, however, the arrangement would have been in the widow's interest as preserving her existing social position.

It thus appears that, in general, women had little authority of their own in the society envisioned by the Torah. A partial exception lay with

14. Trible, *Texts of Terror,* 76–82.
15. Cf. the excuses of those invited to the great supper in Jesus' parable: one has bought a field, one has bought five yoke of oxen, one has married a wife (Luke 14:18–20).

the woman who was an heir in her own right. Job is presented as making his daughters heirs alongside his sons (Job 42:15); but Job was not an Israelite. The Torah recognized female heirs only when there were no sons, as in the case of the daughters of Zelophehad (Num. 27:1–11). Perhaps we meet such a person in the Shunammite who hosted Elisha (2 Kings 4:8–37). She is described as an "important woman" (4:8); she dwells among her own people (4:13), not those of her husband; and she, not her husband, is the principal initiator of action in the story (4:9–10, 22–27).[16] Such women created anomalies, however, in the system of inheritance, for in the usual course of events, their property would pass to their sons who would be members not of the women's but of their husbands' families. Accordingly, Torah required them to marry among their father's kin (Num. 36:1–12).

The picture which the Torah offers of the place of women in the family seems to have been generally stable over a very long period of time, into and past the New Testament era.[17] There were changes, of course, in detail. Jews in Jesus' lifetime, for example, had little occasion to concern themselves with the law about a woman captured in war. Polygamy, moreover, had largely faded away, perhaps in adaptation to Greco-Roman culture, which was monogamous. The *Temple Scroll* from Qumran actually forbade polygamy altogether for the king (56.18–19). It appears that marriage contracts sometimes gave the bride the right to divorce her husband.[18] In the centuries before and after Jesus, women were occasionally accepted as something like religious equals: the prophet Joel predicted the revival of prophecy among both men and women (2:28–29); the contemplatives called "Therapeutae" accepted women into membership;[19] and some women held responsible positions in Greek-speaking synagogues.[20] Wives, however, continued to be a particular class of property, whose function was to produce heirs and help administer the husband's household.

16. Cf. the anxiety of some Greco-Roman writers about the rich wife's domination of her husband; see Yarbrough, *Not Like the Gentiles*, 44–50.

17. E.g., Philo regarded public life as the male sphere and "household management" as the female one. He wrote abusively of women who violated this division and even used it to justify the barbarous law (Deut. 25:11–12) which required that a woman who, when intervening in a fight on her husband's behalf, touched another man's genitals should have her hand amputated (*Special Laws* 3.169–75).

18. Brooten, *"Konnten Frauen,"* 65–73.

19. Philo *The Contemplative Life* 32–33, 68.

20. Brooten, *Women Leaders*, 5–99.

OFFENSES AGAINST SEXUAL
PROPERTY

Adultery

The preceding discussion makes it sufficiently clear why adultery was a crime against sexual property. The continuity of the family was entirely dependent on its acquiring of legitimate heirs. While other ancient cultures, notably the Romans, were willing to achieve this end through adoption as well as through conception, this seems never to have been a usual alternative in ancient Israel.[21] Hence, there was a very strong concern for the legitimacy of heirs and the purity of the family line. For the same reason that an Israelite man was reluctant to marry a woman who was not a virgin, he was also anxious that his wife not have sexual intercourse with any other man.[22] If an outsider did have intercourse with a married woman, this constituted a theft of her husband's right to legitimate offspring. Like any loss of property to another, this also shamed the husband and reduced the family's status in the community.[23]

It is no surprise, then, to find that the commandment against adultery is in proximity to that against theft (Exod. 20:14–15) or that one is forbidden, in the same breath, to covet the neighbor's house or wife or servant or ox or ass or other property (20:17). Even the intervening commandment against bearing false witness is not unrelated, since the object of bearing false witness was to improve the status of one's own family at the expense of the neighbor's (20:16). It is also no surprise that adultery, in this context, referred purely and simply to a man's having intercourse with a married woman. The man's own marital status was irrelevant, for it was not a matter of violating his own vows or implicit commitments of sexual fidelity, as in a modern marriage, but rather of usurping some other man's property rights in his wife.

---

21. Even among the Romans, bastards could not inherit or, in theory at least, be adopted by their father as legitimate children; Veyne, *History of Private Life*, 76–79. Hence, marriage remained important for family continuity.

22. E.g., Philo (*Special Laws* 3.11) treats adultery as a threat to society at large because it defeats "hopes for children."

23. The Greeks, on the whole, seem to have held an equally dim view of adultery, though there were variations at different times and places; Pomeroy, *Goddesses*, 36–37, 86–87, 128–29; Licht, *Sexual Life*, 24, 61–62. The Romans were perhaps a little more indifferent to it, for their understanding of family continuity centered on name more than on blood kinship; Veyne, *History of Private Life*, 17–18, 38–40.

Adultery was different, to be sure, from other property violations in one significant way, for it involved the consent of the property. Accordingly, the Torah required that both parties to adultery, if caught in the act, should be punished (Deut. 22:22). The fact that the prescribed punishment was death is reminiscent of the concern of the Holiness Code to purge certain types of uncleanness from the people; and, in fact, that Code did treat adultery as a violation of purity (Lev. 20:10). On the whole, however, the Torah saw in adultery a property violation. The death penalty for the woman was a kind of limited (and backhanded) recognition of her humanity, that is, of her ability to make decisions for herself—and perhaps also a recognition that, having once received another man's semen, she was no longer of any use to her husband in the matter of legitimate offspring.

A woman became her husband's property even before entering his household, at the time of betrothal. From then on, as far as the Torah was concerned, any violation of her was a form of adultery. If the woman had entered voluntarily into the liaison, both parties were to be put to death; but not if the man had forced her. Accordingly, the Torah distinguished between an incident occurring in the city, where the woman, had she resisted, would have been heard and rescued, and one that took place in the country, where the man might have used force but no one would have heard the woman's cry for help. In true cases of adultery, both man and woman were to be executed; in cases of forcible violation, only the man (Deut. 22:23–27).[24]

Since a woman, before she became the property of her husband, was the property of her father, adultery could also become an issue, by analogy, even before she was married. Daughters were less valuable to a family than sons; Job's seven sons and three daughters were no doubt considered the perfect sort of blessing where posterity was concerned. Daughters, after all, did not continue their father's family but those of their husbands. Still, daughters were advantageous as providing the wherewithal to form marital alliances, thus affording their natal families influence and political security. The virginity of a daughter was essential to this purpose, for if she were not a virgin, she would not be suitable for marriage.[25]

24. Strictly speaking, the passage refers to a betrothed rather than a married woman; but, as Philo observed in commenting on it, there was no practical difference (*Special Laws* 3.72).

25. See Deut. 22:13–21, the case of the man who falsely claims that his bride was not a virgin. The damage done is not only to the woman but also to her parents' reputation; cf. Philo *Special Laws* 3.79–82.

The man who took an unbetrothed daughter's virginity without having acquired it properly through marriage negotiations and the consent of her father was, like the adulterer, a thief. There was no death penalty in such a case, but the Torah provided that the seducer must pay her father the bride price and, if the father consented, marry her—without any right to divorce her later (Deut. 22:28). She was unlikely, after all, to find another husband. Even if the father refused to accept the marriage, the man still had to pay him the equivalent of the bride price, since the daughter was of no further value in the marriage "market" (Exod. 22:16–17). Similarly, as we saw above (pp. 36–37), in a case of adultery with a woman who belonged to two men at once (as slave to one and betrothed to the other), no one was executed, but a penalty had to be paid (Lev. 19:20–21).

The understanding of adultery, both in the Torah and in the New Testament era, thus proves to have been quite different from that current in the contemporary Western world. Among us, sexual activity outside the marriage on the part of either partner is understood as adultery; in antiquity, only such activity on the part of the wife (or the betrothed woman) qualified. The husband could commit adultery only by having intercourse with the wife (or betrothed) of another man; if he had sexual relations with a slave, a prostitute, a concubine, or a divorced or widowed woman, this did not constitute adultery against his own marriage. Again, our own explanations of what is wrong in adultery usually focus on the betrayal of trust and of formal commitments between spouses, whereas the ancient understanding of adultery assumes rather that it is a violation of another's property. What for us is analogous to betrayal was for them a species of theft. The treatment of adultery in the New Testament documents is almost certain to be unintelligible if we do not keep these distinctions in mind.

Incest

We have already seen that the concept of incest in ancient Israel was quite different from ours. Where we define it primarily in terms of shared genetic endowment, Torah defined it as violation of the intra-family hierarchy (above, pp. 34–35). This hierarchy was an expression of property relations, a way of exercising ownership over human property, whether slaves or concubines or children or wives, which could not merely be manipulated like real estate or domestic animals. Where both owner and owned were human beings, their relationship had to find some expression other than the simple right of the master to dispose of the property when and as he pleased. The solution was found in the interactions of dominance and deference which characterizes hierarchical relationships. In the matter of incest, the outstanding concern of the Torah was that younger male members of a household should not usurp the rights of their seniors or of their age-mates.

The details of Israel's laws of incest are often difficult to follow, and it will be necessary to look closely at them in order to comprehend how different they are from our own and what concerns animated them. The reader may be helped if I set out my conclusions in simple form at the start. The incest code can be summarized comprehensively in three general principles, all dependent on matters of hierarchy. First, a man must not infringe on the sexual property of other males who rank above him or on the same level as he in the family hierarchy. Second, a man must not interfere with the sexual property of his sons and daughters (i.e., their wives and daughters), since any affront to the honor of other members of his household would reflect on his own honor. Third, a man must not put two women in a position which would force them to violate the hierarchy prevailing among female relatives.

In order for a modern Western reader to make sense of the laws about incest, one must recall that, for ancient Israel, husband and wife were not kin to one another, even though the wife was a kind of extension of her husband. The husband remained a member of the "father's house" in which he was born. The wife remained, in some sense, a part of her family, too, and would return to them if she were divorced or left widowed and childless (e.g., Lev. 22:13).[26] Generally speaking, men were kin to their mothers and to both the men and the women of their father's house while women were kin only to their sons and to their immediate female relatives—at least, for purposes of the law of incest.[27] These realities were reflected in the precise language of the laws against incest, to which we must give close attention.

The most serious form of incest was a son's violation of his father's wife, whether it was his own mother or another wife;[28] this was "un-

26. So, too, among the Greeks (Pomeroy, *Goddesses*, 87) and Romans (Veyne, *History of Private Life*, 73–75).

27. The Essenes at Qumran reinterpreted the law so that degrees of affinity counted the same for both males and females (*DR* V,7–11; *Temple Scroll* 66.12–17). The *Mishnah*, however, maintains the old point of view; Vermes, *Dead Sea Scrolls*, 166.

28. The Greeks and Romans were monogamous, but since divorce was common and children remained with their father, it would not be unusual among them for an adolescent son to be living in the same household with a stepmother (Veyne, *History of Private Life*, 34).

covering the father's nakedness," which was a violation of the son's subordination to his father (Lev. 18:7–8; cf. Deut. 23:1, ET 22:30).[29] Thus, Absalom had intercourse with his father David's concubines to make the break between him and his father irreparable (2 Sam. 16:20–22). In the same way, incest with the wife of one's father's brother was "uncovering the nakedness" of the uncle (Lev. 18:14); with the wife of a brother, it was "uncovering the brother's nakedness" (Lev. 18:16). In each case, the language makes clear that the incest was an offense not so much against the woman violated as against her husband.

The respect owed the father also extended to his immediate female kin. The Torah specifies that the father's sisters and daughters were placed off-limits by reason of their relationship to him rather than to the son (18:9, 11–12). There is at least a suggestion, however, that the father's link with his female relatives was weaker than with the males. In the case of a half-sister who shared only the same father, the son had to be reminded that "she is your sister," as if it might not be obvious (18:11). Indeed, in great houses with several wives, it may not have been, for the children of each wife would have tended to form a distinct subhousehold. The callousness of Amnon after forcing his half-sister Tamar may have arisen from a common social perception that she was not truly a close relative as well as from his own exceptional lack of moral feeling (2 Sam. 13:1–19). No equivalent reminder was given in regard to those who were half-sisters sharing only the same mother; but the opportunity for this type of incest scarcely existed. If children remained with the father's family after divorce or the father's death, such half-siblings rarely would have been found in the same household.

A man was not obliged to pay any particular respect to the younger members of his household. Nephews and nieces, on the whole, did not enter into the reckoning of incest. The one exception is that the nephew must avoid his father's brother's wife. There was no comparable law, however, prohibiting the uncle from having his niece or his nephew's wife. A man was, to some extent, forbidden to have his children and grandchildren; but the justification for this hinged on his own paternal honor, for he could not be warned off on grounds of owing deference to his son. This reasoning was made explicit in the prohibition of incest with grandchildren: "You shall not uncover the nakedness of your son's daughter or of your daughter's daughter, for their nakedness is your own

---

29. *Jubilees* 33.8 makes it clear that when Reuben violated Bilhah, his father Jacob's concubine, it was an offense against Jacob himself.

nakedness" (18:10 RSV). In other words, incest with his granddaughter (who would then no longer be a marriageable virgin) would shame his whole family, for which he was ultimately responsible. Similarly, a man was not to have sexual relations with his daughter-in-law because it would dishonor his son (18:15), and implicit in any dishonoring of his son was a dishonoring of his own house. Intercourse by a man with his daughter, however, was not explicitly prohibited as such, perhaps because a patriarch had to be recognized as owning the female members of his household, so that in some sense this would be an exercise of his rights.[30]

The male was also obligated to respect his mother, though her honor could never be distinguished from that of his father. Hence, the Israelite was told: "You shall not uncover your father's nakedness and your mother's nakedness; she is your mother; you shall not uncover her nakedness" (18:7). Incest with the mother was a violation of both parents at once. The son's kinship with his mother also extended a prohibition to her sister and daughter, that is, her closest female relatives (18:9, 13). This did not, however, extend to her male relatives, for, though the mother's brother might seem to be as closely related to a man as the father's brother, his wife was not in fact forbidden under the incest code.

There was a similar phenomenon in the case of siblings. A man's sisters were all prohibited, whether full sisters or half-sisters—the latter whether he shared a common mother with them or a common father. The Holiness Code further specified that this was true whether they were born in the same household or not (18:9). Since the unmarried woman was reckoned to her father's household, it would be conceivable to think of a marriage being contracted between two half-siblings who shared the same mother but belonged to different households, and the code guarded against this. No similar stipulation was made, however, in the case of half-*brothers* who belonged to different households; and, given the solidarity of the father's house, it is possible that the protection of a brother's wife extended only to those brothers who shared the same father.

Finally, within the purely female sphere, certain relationships were

---

30. Lev. 18:17 forbids intercourse with a woman and her daughter or granddaughter. This would, in effect, prohibit the patriarch from having intercourse with his own daughters—but only as part of a larger group including his stepdaughters as well.

inconsistent with women's acting as co-wives. A woman could not be co-wife with her mother or grandmother (18:17).[31] This provision would effectively prevent a man from marrying his own daughter, but that does not appear to have been its main import. The point rather was to prohibit marriage with his mother-in-law, as the phrasing of the law elsewhere shows (Lev. 20:14; Deut. 27:23). Such a marriage would create grave problems of hierarchy, for the daughter, as first wife, would have precedence over her mother, but would still owe her, as daughter, a respect inconsistent with that position. For similar reasons, two sisters could not be co-wives (Lev. 18:18).[32]

We can form some impression of how gravely the Torah regarded the various kinds of incest from the punishments it prescribed. Leviticus imposed the death penalty for three kinds of incest: with the father's wife, with the son's wife, with a woman and her mother (Lev. 20:11, 12, 14). Of these, it required death by fire for the last, suggesting that the most aggravated form of incest was for a man to marry his mother-in-law. A less grave level of incest consisted of intercourse with one's sister or half-sister and was to be punished by "cutting off" (20:17). A third level, which God would punish with childlessness, consisted of intercourse with a brother's wife or father's brother's wife (20:20–21). Intercourse with the father's or mother's sister was condemned, but no penalty was named (20:19). The remaining offenses from the list in Leviticus 18 (wife's sister; grandchildren) receive no notice in chapter 20. A slightly different listing of worst offenses is found in Deuteronomy, which curses just three kinds of incest: with a man's father's wife, his sister or half-sister, and his mother-in-law (27:20–23).

While the Holiness Code in Leviticus and the curses of Deuteronomy 27 both treated incest as a violation of purity, purity considerations alone are not sufficient to explain the exact nature of the rules themselves. They were purity rules in that they forbade the combining of distinct social roles, but the social roles in question were themselves

31. MT must be correct here as against LXX and RSV. The point is not that these women are the *man's* kinswomen, but one another's.

32. Philo offers essentially this same explanation of the commandment against marriage with two sisters: it would occasion jealousy or allow one sister to profit at the other's expense, both being violations of their sisterly relationship (*Special Laws* 3.27–28). In the case of Lot's daughters (Gen. 19:30–38), it is hard to say whether the reader is expected to blame the women for incest or praise their heroic devotion to the duty of preserving their father's line.

expressions of a sense of property and hierarchy—one vastly different from the familial presuppositions of the modern West.[33]

Prostitution

The Torah had little to say on the subject of secular prostitution. We have seen that it prohibited parents from dedicating their children as sacred prostitutes, but there is nothing to tell us whether its authors would have objected equally to the idea of a master's making his slave-woman a secular prostitute or even a father's doing so with his daughter. There are only two references to secular prostitution which offer any details as to how it was regarded. In both cases an unmarried woman is understood to have chosen this course of action on her own and thereby brought disgrace on her father. In one passage, a priest's daughter who "plays the harlot" is condemned to be burned for having "profaned" her father (Lev. 21:9). One may guess that she is part of her father's household, either as not yet married or as divorced or widowed. Her activity threatens the state of purity vital to the household, since its food comes largely from the altar of the temple.

In the other passage, a man charges that his wife was not found to be a virgin on her wedding night. If this is true, she is to be stoned for having "played the harlot in her father's house" (Deut. 22:13–21). In other words, she has engaged in sexual intercourse when she ought to have been guarding her virginity carefully in order to be a suitable bride. In the process, she has exposed her father to the shame of having misrepresented her state in negotiating her marriage. It is not clear from the passage that she has actually received payment for her services; the point seems to be, rather, that she has deprived her father and prospective husband of their rights in her. What was wrong with prostitution, from the perspective of ancient Israel, was not so much the giving or receiving of payment for sexual intercourse as it was the removal of sexual intercourse from the framework of property and hierarchy which normally contained it and ensured that it was placed at the service of the family.

Such an interpretation is made explicit in a more extensive critique of prostitution found in Proverbs. After warning the reader against the

33. Ancient Greek definitions of incest appear to have been simpler. Marriage between ascendants and descendants was forbidden; there was some variation in attitudes toward brother-sister marriage, which was, however, widely tolerated. A man could at least be criticized for marrying his mother-in-law, but this also violated the norm of monogamy. See Licht, *Sexual Life*, 516–18.

wiles of the loose woman, the author contrasts the positive ideal of possessing a wife with the negative prospect of wasting one's resources on a courtesan:

> Drink water from your own cistern.
>   flowing water from your own well.
> Should your springs be scattered abroad,
>   streams of water in the streets?
> Let them be for yourself alone,
>   and not for strangers with you.
> Let your fountain be blessed,
>   and rejoice in the wife of your youth,
>   a lovely hind, a graceful doe.
> Let her affection fill you at all times with delight,
>   be infatuated always with her love.
> Why should you be infatuated, my son, with a loose woman
>   and embrace the bosom of an adventuress?
> For a man's ways are before the eyes of the LORD,
>   and he watches all his paths.
> The iniquities of the wicked ensnare him,
>   and he is caught in the toils of his sin.
> He dies for lack of discipline,
>   and because of his great folly he is lost.
>
> (Prov. 5:15–23 RSV)

One might sum up the sage's message by saying that, in matters sexual, one should buy, not rent.

One cannot, of course, treat wisdom literature as if it were the same genre as legislation; and it is clear that Proverbs agrees with the Torah in understanding prostitution as a violation of God's will, not merely as something to be avoided for prudential reasons. Still, the justification offered for the prohibition is instructive as to the ethical framework in which the prohibition itself belonged. Prostitution was wrong because it stood outside the normal patriarchal system in which the male head of household owned one or more women as sexual partners. As such it threatened the interests of the family. The man might feel that he had gotten full value for his expense, but the family gained nothing at all from his patronizing of the prostitute. His action, therefore, was a betrayal of his responsibilities, since he existed not to gratify his own desires but to maintain and enhance the fortunes of his "father's house."

What the Torah and Proverbs agree upon, then, is the condemnation of those who place personal gratification ahead of family duty. The Torah condemns the unmarried woman who prefers sexual pleasure above her obligations as a good daughter of the household who must preserve her marriageability—which is, indeed, the family's investment in her. Proverbs condemns the man who spends family resources on private pleasure which benefits the family not at all. He must marry and content himself with his wife, who not only gives him sexual pleasure but also provides legitimate heirs and additional labor for the household.

What is absent here is condemnation for the woman who, whether as an obedient slave or as a free woman separated from any family group, has become a professional courtesan. Proverbs was concerned to make the prostitute sound as unscrupulous and unattractive as possible; but its reproof was not for her, but for the man who would visit her. The Torah was speaking to the woman who was trying to behave as an unattached individual in the pursuit of pleasure while still remaining under the protection of her father. Either, way, the heart of the problem lay in the tension between private inclination and family responsibilities.[34] The modern moralism which attacks the independent female prostitute and says little against those who patronize her is a world removed from the Scriptures of Israel.[35]

SUMMARY

The ethics of sexual property in ancient Israel included both an ideal picture of what was to be desired and a set of prohibitions indicating what was to be avoided. The ideal defined the household, the fundamental building block of society, as consisting of a male head who possessed one or more women as wives or concubines, and children who would either carry on the family (sons) or be used to make alliances with other families (daughters).[36] There were no "individuals" in the modern sense, unless eunuchs and bastards might fit that cate-

34. Gentile society was more tolerant of prostitution. Prostitutes were frequently slaves and were generally allotted a low social rank, even when they were educated, witty, and influential courtesans. There was little ethical antagonism toward them, however, apart from the anxiety that young men would waste their patrimonies on youthful pleasures. See Pomeroy, *Goddesses,* 88–91, 139–41; Licht, *Sexual Life,* 329–42, 354–56; Veyne, *History of Private Life,* 23, 25–27. In the late first and second centuries c.e., medical notions, backed by Stoic philosophy, began to discourage all intercourse on the part of young males (Veyne, *History of Private Life,* 24–25).

35. *Sibylline Oracles* 3.43–44 condemns the widow who becomes a prostitute. This is unusual, however, and the passage is not one of the older parts of the work.

36. In the Roman era, pseudo-Phocylides advised his readers to marry with an eye to preserving their family wealth (205–6) and to guard their beautiful children closely in order to keep them away from seducers (213–17).

gory. Those persons, such as widows and orphans, who had no connection with a patriarch were necessarily marginal to the society.

This property ethic gave rise to certain prohibitions deemed necessary to protect it. Adultery was wrong because it was theft of a neighbor's property. Incest was wrong because, being defined primarily as a revolt of the young against the old, it upset the internal hierarchy of the family. Prostitution, though a less serious concern, was wrong insofar as it represented the triumph of individual gratification over against the principle of subordination to the family.

There is little evidence of significant development in this ethic between the writing of the Torah and the time of Jesus. Apart from the waning of polygamy and an occasional protest against the abuse of divorce, the Torah's definition of sexual property and the ethic relative to it was the one which Jesus and Paul found current in their own time.[37] In contrast to their treatment of the purity ethic, the early Christians accepted this property ethic in principle. Yet, as we shall see, they also modified it drastically by redefining the ownership of sexuality, by undermining the autonomy of the family, and by subordinating all human goods to the reign of God.

37. On the Greco-Roman side, one should observe that the theory of marriage was undergoing a major shift at this very time, with the husband-wife relationship increasingly spoken of in terms of "friendship." It is less clear how far the realities had shifted. Cf. Veyne, *History of Private Life,* 36–49.

9   Family and Sexual Property
in the Gospels

If we wish to understand the ethic of sexual property in the Gospels, the first step is to see what they have to say about family. One of the most striking features of Jesus' teaching, as it is preserved in these works, is the way in which he distanced himself from contemporary culture in his estimate of the importance and value of the family. For the religion, as for the social structure, of Israel, family was a given and a central necessity. Since membership in the chosen people was primarily through descent, family was crucial for the continuation and definition of Israel. Descent also defined the priesthood and the expected Davidic messiah. Moreover, the whole contemporary world knew virtually no social imperative more compelling than the one which required a man to devote himself to the maintenance and the improvement of his family's well-being. The peace of the local community was of recognized importance; and national loyalty could become an issue in times of oppression or open war. Yet, one's basic loyalty was to the "father's house"; and only extraordinary circumstances, such as would threaten the welfare of all households, caused other loyalties to take precedence.

The Gospels tend to dismiss family or at least to downgrade it in significant ways. They express this not only in direct references to family as such, but also in their treatment of women and of divorce and adultery. Each of the evangelists presents a distinctive portrait of Jesus and his teachings on this subject. The broad picture, however, indicates a far-reaching revision of contemporary attitudes on all these subjects.

MATTHEW

Family

The inherent centrality of the family must have been as close to a self-evident truth as any in ancient Israel. Given this, Jesus' negative judgment on it must have seemed startling and even outrageous. Matthew, in fact, presents him as expressing himself in deliberately outrageous ways. For example, when a would-be disciple asked leave to go and perform the final filial duty of burying his father, Jesus rejected his request by saying: "Follow me and leave the dead to bury their own dead" (Matt. 8:22; cf. Luke 9:60). The words have never ceased to trouble interpreters, who have sometimes invented fanciful explanations of them to avoid acknowledging their negative import. Their meaning, however, is not far to seek. Commitment to one's family, even the respect for parents mandated in the Ten Commandments, was of no significance in comparison with the claim of discipleship. Or, as Jesus said elsewhere, "The person who loves father or mother more than me is not worthy of me, and the person who loves son or daughter more than me is not worthy of me" (Matt. 10:37; cf. Luke 14:26).

In practice, this seems to have meant that Jesus' disciples had to sever their family ties in order to follow him. He took James and John away from their father, depriving him of their labor in his fishing business (Matt. 4:21–22). He promised that "everyone who has left houses or brothers or sisters or father or mother or children or fields for the sake of my name will receive a hundredfold and inherit eternal life" (19:29). Jesus told at least one would-be disciple not to turn his abandoned property over to other members of his family, as the prevailing culture expected and as the Jewish contemplatives called "Therapeutae" are known to have done.[1] Instead, he was to give it to the poor (19:21), a practice sure to arouse enormous antagonism on the part of other family members. It was not surprising, then, when Jesus predicted that the Twelve, during their ministry, would meet with the utmost opposition from their family members, including even betrayal and murder (10:21). What was surprising was his claim that this was in fact one of the goals of his work: "Do not suppose that I have come to cast peace on the

---

1. Philo (*The Contemplative Life* 13–17) asserts that the conduct of the Therapeutae was superior to that of Anaxagoras or Democritus, who simply abandoned their property rather than giving it to their kinsfolk.

earth. I have not come to cast peace, but a sword. For I have come to set a person in opposition against his father and a daughter against her mother and a bride against her mother-in-law; and one's enemies will be the members of one's own household" (10:34–36).

Jesus' own behavior reflected this same distancing of family. He left home and spent his ministry as a wanderer with "no place to lay his head" (8:19–20). He publicly replaced his mother, brothers, and sisters with his followers, making them his true family (12:46–50). He said that the people of his own town and household were uniquely incapable of recognizing and honoring him as prophet (13:53–58). And though the crowds at Jerusalem greeted him as "Son of David" (21:9), he told his opponents there a riddle suggesting that, even if he were so, it was not the key to understanding his real significance. If he was David's son, he was also, and more importantly, his own ancestor's lord (22:41–46)—a concept which turned normal family hierarchy on its head.

This may well have been the significance, for Matthew, of the virgin birth. Matthew carefully placed Jesus in the Davidic royal line by means of the genealogy with which his Gospel begins, tracing this ancestry through Joseph (1:16). Yet Joseph, according to Matthew, was not in fact Jesus' father (1:18). Accordingly, Jesus' identity as "Son of David" had to be understood as something other than a true familial relationship of physical descent. If this interpretation is correct, the virginity of Mary was important to Matthew not because of a relationship between virginity and purity (a connection important to later Christians, but one which Matthew never actually drew), but rather because it broke the physical connection of Jesus with his own "father's house." Jesus' own birth was thus a paradigm of the separation from family which he would subsequently require of his followers.

The reign of the heavens,[2] which was central to the gospel Jesus proclaimed (4:17), demanded not only separation from one's own family, but also a drastic reorientation in one's view of the world. Already in the present age, the hierarchical organization which characterized the family ceased to be acceptable in Jesus' ministry; and in the age to come, the family as a focus of human life was expected to disappear altogether. Jesus' treatment of children is the clearest example of his overturning of

2. This, rather than "reign of God," is Matthew's usual phrase. "The heavens" was a standard Jewish circumlocution of the time for the name of God (or even the word "God"), which the pious avoided uttering to ensure that they did not violate the commandment against taking God's name in vain.

the family hierarchy. When people brought children to him for his blessing, his disciples tried to keep them away, probably because they thought them too insignificant to deserve his attention. Jesus stopped them with the words, "Of such is the reign of the heavens" (19:13–15).

The meaning of this statement is elucidated by another episode. The disciples asked Jesus who would be greatest in the reign of the heavens, and he placed a child before them and said, "Unless you turn and become like the children, you will never enter the reign of the heavens. So, whoever will lower himself [to be] like this child, that person is the greatest in the reign of the heavens" (18:1–4). Interpreters have differed as to what characteristic of children was being praised here, but the language of the passage, in fact, leaves little doubt. It was the low station of children in the hierarchy of the family—and of society in general. One enters the reign of the heavens by "lowering oneself," giving up all claim to social status, security, and respect. When the mother of the sons of Zebedee asked Jesus to grant them the two foremost places in his reign, he answered that, among his disciples, leaders must not seek to lord it over the others, the way Gentile rulers did, but must accept the position of slave (20:20–28). The same principle stands behind Jesus' admonition to his followers not to accept such titles as "rabbi" or "teacher." "You are all brothers," he said; "and do not call anyone 'father' on earth, for you have one father—the one in the heavens" (23:8–12). In the new "family" of Jesus' followers, there are only children, no patriarchs. The family of this age is completely overturned.[3]

This was not merely a transitional arrangement during the interim of expectation, while the disciples waited for the full unveiling of the reign of the heavens. It was to be understood as a feature of the heavenly life itself, which, according to Jesus, knows nothing of marriage. This was the point of his controversy with the Sadducees and, indeed, explains why the account of it was preserved in the oral tradition of Jesus' teachings even after 70 C.E., when the Sadducees themselves disappeared as a religious-political force (22:23–33). The Sadducees, who rejected belief in the resurrection, raised a very difficult question about it based on the institution of levirate marriage. Suppose that, in a family of seven brothers, the first married a woman and died childless; the second, as was his duty, married the widow, but also died childless; and so on through all seven. In the resurrection, all eight persons would be

---

3. Cf. Schüssler Fiorenza, *In Memory of Her,* 147–51.

alive at one time, and what the law of levirate marriage commanded in the present world would create an inevitable violation of other laws in the world to come. Since ancient Israel did not accept the marriage of one woman to several men at the same time, she must be either the wife of the first brother or of a later one. If one of the later husbands kept the woman, he would be violating the law which defines intercourse with the living brother's wife as incest (Lev. 18:16). On the other hand, if the first husband took her back, this would violate the law forbidding the remarriage of a couple after the woman had been married to another man (Deut. 24:1–4). The Sadducees had thus produced an astute argument to show that the idea of a general resurrection was actually inconsistent with the Torah. Jesus answered them by denying that the institution of marriage had any place at all in the life of the resurrection. The family and its internal hierarchy would, of course, fall along with the institution of marriage, leaving no more reason for the levirate law than for the problems it threatened to create.

The teaching about the family in Matthew is not entirely negative. Jesus upheld the honor ascribed to parents in the written Torah against exceptions made to it in "the tradition of the elders," that is, the oral Torah of the Pharisees. Their tradition allowed dedications to the Temple *(qorban)* to take precedence over duty to parents, and Jesus rejected this (15:3–9). Again, when the rich young man asked him about the way into life, Jesus included the honor due to parents among the commandments of which he reminded him. Respect for parents is the only point of contemporary family hierarchy Matthew treated in this positive way, and the few examples of it form a rather minor countertheme in his Gospel as a whole. Still, it is important to ask what it is doing there, in the context of so much antifamily teaching. One possibility is that it was introduced into the tradition of Jesus' teaching as the result of increasing social conservatism in the early churches. Such a development can be documented elsewhere (see below, pp. 224–29). This conclusion is not necessary, however, for another explanation lies ready to hand, which can accommodate the apparent conflict within the limits of Jesus' own ministry.

Jesus had followers at more than one level of commitment. Those nearest to him, the male disciples and the women who accompanied him on his travels, had surrendered the safety of their households in order to take up that peripatetic existence. (Not everyone who was invited to join their circle was willing to make the sacrifice; e.g., the rich young man, 19:16–22.) On the other hand, the great majority of those who took Jesus' message seriously, who welcomed his disciples and came to hear him preach when he was nearby, must have continued to live much as before, in families that seemed but little changed.[4] In that context, it was right to honor parents and to preserve the stability of the household. Accordingly, the oral tradition of Jesus' teaching contained at least a moderate endorsement of respect for parents. Yet, even for these followers in the wider circle, the teaching of Jesus and the ongoing example of the inner circle which had abandoned family to be with him would have served as a constant witness that, for his followers, family was no longer a central and unquestioned value. One must at least be prepared to sacrifice it to enter the reign of the heavens.

Divorce

Even for this wider circle of followers, Jesus altered marriage and family life in a highly significant way through his prohibition of divorce. This issue is important in our contemporary conflicts about the encouragement of family life. It is also entangled in controversy about the maintenance of the Western Christian tradition which, unlike that of the East, enforced the prohibition of divorce rigidly in the past and, in some denominations, still does. These debates, of course, have little if anything to do with the reasons for Jesus' original prohibition or what it may have meant to his original audience. We must try to separate ourselves from them for the moment in order to appreciate what Jesus was saying. Fortunately, Matthew provides, alongside the prohibition itself, some material which indicates what its contemporary significance may have been.

The account opens with the Pharisees asking Jesus for an interpretation of the law: "Is a man permitted to divorce his wife for any reason at all?" (19:3). This was, in fact, a difficult legal point and the subject of some controversy between the two principal divisions of the Pharisees in Jesus' time, the Schools of Shammai and Hillel. The Torah did not legislate directly on the matter of divorce, but simply alluded to it in passing as something which a man might do if he found in his wife "anything improper" (Deut. 24:1). The phrase could refer to sexual impropriety, for one of the Hebrew terms in it refers primarily to the female genitals. This is how the Pharisees of the School of Shammai

---

4. Theissen, *Early Palestinian Christianity,* 17–23.

took it, thus limiting divorce to cases of sexual wrongdoing. On the other hand, it could be understood more broadly, as the Septuagint translators apparently did in rendering it as *aschēmon pragma* "an unseemly thing." This was the position of the School of Hillel, thus allowing divorce for a wider variety of causes. Jesus was being asked to involve himself in this debate between the schools.

Jesus' response, however, was to dismiss the whole question by reference to another passage of Torah, the creation narratives at the beginning of Genesis. The gist of his argument, which thus took the form of an interpretation of Scripture, was that the will of God as originally revealed in the act of creation could not subsequently be annulled by any rule communicated through (or even created by) Moses during the exodus from Egypt. (Paul used the same type of argument to show the superiority of the promise to Abraham over the Torah in Gal. 3:17.) Jesus, relying on the first creation account in Genesis (1:27), argued that the female was as human as the male: "from the beginning He made them male and female." Male and female, therefore, participate equally in the image of God. Again, relying on the second creation narrative (Gen. 2:24), he held that the man and woman (or husband and wife) become "one flesh" in marriage.

As we have seen, the family structure of ancient Israel did not, in fact, acknowledge either an equality between male and female or a complete unity of flesh between married persons. The wife, though she was in some ways an extension of her husband and was an important part of his household, did not become truly and fully a member of his family and was certainly not his equal. His right to divorce her was the ultimate expression of both these realities; he could dismiss her in a way analogous to his dismissal of a slave, though, as befitted her higher status, he must allege a reason; that is, he must find in her "something improper." This right of the husband to divorce the wife nullified, to all practical purposes, both the "one flesh" God created in marriage and the equality of "male and female" as God originally created them in the divine image. Divorce, then, could not be seen as part of God's original creation, but only as Moses' concession to male hardheartedness (19:8). In this way, Jesus abolished one part of Scripture, the divorce law, on authority of another, the creation accounts.[5]

This abolition of divorce was of immediate and far-reaching conse-

5. Cf. the astute analysis in Schüssler Fiorenza's *In Memory of Her,* 143.

quence, particularly since Jesus combined with it a redefinition of adultery: "I tell you that anyone who divorces his wife except for *porneia* and marries another is committing adultery" (19:9). The exemption for *porneia* (harlotry) must refer to the provision in Torah which allowed a man to reject a wife who had not shown proof of virginity on her wedding night (Deut. 22:13–21). Such a bride was said to have "played the harlot" (*ekporneuō* in the Septuagint) in her father's house.[6] Since the consummation of such a marriage showed that the bride was not a virgin, it was no marriage at all from the ancient family's point of view and Jesus allowed the man to terminate it. Divorce for any other reason, however, if followed by remarriage, was now to be understood as adultery. Jesus' pronouncement implies a complete redefinition of adultery. Under the provisions of the Torah, it was strictly a matter of one man having intercourse with a woman married to another man. The marital status of the man committing the offense was irrelevant, for it was impossible for a man to commit adultery against his own married state. In a single phrase, Jesus created such a possibility and thus made the wife equal in this regard, too. He not only forbade the man to divorce his wife, but also gave her a permanent and indissoluble claim on him as her sexual property. Henceforth, his sexual freedom was to be no greater than hers.

The same notion of marriage as constituting a unity of flesh, a permanent and indissoluble claim, lay behind the other Matthean pronouncement on divorce, found in the Sermon on the Mount. This earlier statement, however, was less far-reaching, since it implied only that the husband retains a permanent claim on the wife. In contrast to the law of divorce in the Torah, Jesus said, "*I* say to you that everyone who divorces his wife except for reason of *porneia* makes her commit adultery and whoever marries a divorced woman is committing adultery" (5:32). Here again, *porneia* rendered the original marriage invalid. Divorce for any other reason, however, rendered adultery in this new sense more or less inevitable since the rejected woman would normally marry again if she could. This passage is thus related to the one in chapter 19 but is less

6. Alternatively, one may, with a long interpretive tradition, understand the exception as sanctioning divorce in cases where the wife commits adultery; but one would expect the more explicit word *moicheia* in that case. Jesus' original pronouncement on the subject seems *not* to have given permission for divorce of an adulterous wife—in shocking contrast to the culture's insistence on it. See Riches, *Jesus and the Transformation of Judaism*, 138.

comprehensive and less threatening to the social order since it does not explicitly render the husband property of the wife.

Just how threatening the pronouncement of chapter 19 was and in what way becomes evident from the discussion between the disciples and Jesus which follows it. The disciples objected, "If this is the man's legal situation with his wife, it is not advantageous to get married" (19:10). The man, after all, has lost both his sexual freedom and his ultimate authority within the household. Jesus replied, "Not all receive the saying, but those to whom it has been granted. For there are eunuchs who were born so from the mother's womb, and there are eunuchs who have been made eunuchs by human beings, and there are eunuchs who have made themselves eunuchs on account of the reign of the heavens. Let whoever can receive it receive it" (19:11–12). The eunuch, as we have seen, was one of the few "individuals" in the ancient world—a man with no intrinsic relation to a family. Jesus was acknowledging, then, that his prohibition of divorce effectively dissolved the family and made eunuchs of all men, for it deprived them of the authority requisite to maintain their patriarchal position and keep their households in subjection to themselves as the unique representatives of their families. What may appear to be a pronouncement about details of sexual ethics (divorce and remarriage) actually spelled the end of the entire hierarchical institution called family. The prohibition of divorce and redefinition of adultery, while they may appear, from a modern perspective, to protect the family, were actually undermining it in its ancient form.

Adultery

Jesus, as we have seen, redefined adultery as part of his prohibition of divorce. Henceforward, since marriage was, really for the first time, to constitute an indissoluble unity of flesh and to recognize the equality of the sexes in the image of God, even the most legal of divorces and remarriages must constitute a case of adultery. This might appear to be a form of physical purity code reasserting itself, as if to say that a spouse automatically became henceforward sexually impure to all others during the lifetime of the partner. In fact, however, Jesus recognized, here as elsewhere, the necessity of conscious and intentional participation in any act that was to be defined as sin. In saying that his pronouncement could be "received" only by those to whom it was granted, he indicated that one could not regard the general public as guilty according to these new definitions. To accept these new principles at all was in itself a gift from God. This was not, in other words, an automatic form of pollution which operated of itself wherever the new set of rules was violated. It was a new conception of marriage to be received voluntarily and as an act of renunciation by Jesus' followers. The key here, as with all of Jesus' ethics, was intention.[7]

This emerges, too, in Jesus' other major statement on adultery: "You have heard that it was said, 'You shall not commit adultery.' But *I* tell you that every man who looks at a woman to desire (or covet) her has already committed adultery with her in his heart" (5:27–28). The statement is ambiguous as to exactly what the man has done. Has he simply desired[8] the woman, in a way that is more or less automatic and prior to conscious control? In that case, Jesus was saying that all sexual desire is implicitly adulterous, since it takes no account of the marital status of either the desirer or the object of desire. This, in turn, would imply that adultery is an inescapable sin. While such a statement is outrageous, it is not therefore impossible. The Jesus who could say, "You shall be perfect as your heavenly father is perfect" (5:48), was capable of making other outrageous demands, too. Immediately following the statement about desire, we find, "If your right eye makes you stumble, pluck it out and throw it away; it is better for you to lose one of your members and not have your whole body thrown into Gehenna" (5:29). The tradition of interpretation seems to be united in understanding this last verse as an instance of outrageous hyperbole designed to bring one to a recognition of the gravity of one's situation. The identification of all sexual desire as implicitly adulterous could serve the similar function of revealing how deep is the human indifference to the rights of others.

Another possible interpretation would take note of the fact that the Greek verb in question is the one used in the Septuagint's translation of the Tenth Commandment ("Thou shalt not covet . . ."). In this case, Matthew has Jesus saying that covetousness, the desire to deprive another of his property, is the essence of adultery. Jesus was then reaffirm-

---

7. This passage also makes it clear that Matthew understood Jesus' prohibition of divorce as a spiritual and ethical goal, attainable only by those to whom it is granted; it is not a new law for Christians. Cf. Grant, "Impracticability of the Gospel Ethics," 90–91. Mark saw a similar tension in Jesus' ethical demands, which are both realizable and unrealizable in that they are dependent on the reign of God, which is both present in the gospel and yet to come in the fullness of the new age; see Via, *Ethics of Mark's Gospel,* 121–24.

8. The English phrase "lusted after" is an overtranslation here. The Greek verb in question is not invariably pejorative.

ing a quite traditional understanding of what is wrong in adultery. In this case, however, Jesus was asserting that adultery does not consist primarily in the sexual union of two people at least one of whom is "one flesh" with another person; it consists rather in the intention, accomplished or not, to take what belongs to another. Matthew gave us no clue as to which meaning of the Greek verb should predominate here. Perhaps there is no need, in fact, to decide between them. Both interpretations are consistent with the teaching of Jesus as presented in this Gospel. No human being is free of sin, but the nature of sin lies in impurity of the heart rather than in the physical act by itself.

Incest and Prostitution

The other basic offenses against sexual property receive little notice in Matthew's Gospel. The only reference to incest has to do with the arrest of John the Baptist, who had admonished Herod Antipas, tetrarch of Galilee, for taking his brother's wife, Herodias (14:3–4). The other Synoptic evangelists also report the same information (Mark 6:17; Luke 3:19–20). One may guess that Matthew and the others agreed with John's position, but it is difficult to be sure of their exact reasons. Under the Torah, Herod had committed incest in compelling his brother to divorce his wife in order to marry her himself. By Jesus' definition, however, this was also adultery. On what basis did the evangelists disapprove? It seems impossible to say.

The matter of prostitution receives only slightly more attention, but it appears in a significant pronouncement of Jesus. The tax collectors and the prostitutes, he said, were entering the reign of the heavens ahead of respectable religious leaders (the chief priests and elders) because they believed the preaching of John the Baptist (21:23–32). Since John preached repentance (3:2), one may suspect the prostitutes ceased to be such when they came to believe his message. It proves difficult, however, to be certain. The tax collectors presumably did not cease to be tax collectors. (In Luke 19:1–10, the tax collector Zacchaeus, upon his conversion, gave half of his property to the poor and made amends to those he had defrauded.) A prostitute would have found it singularly difficult to emerge from her low place in the community. We know little about them in the Jewish world of the time. In the contemporary Gentile world, however, most of them were slaves, who could not legally abandon their status. Even free prostitutes, if poor, would have had only the most limited of options, since they would not have been acceptable as wives. Our own presuppositions, then, may perhaps dictate whether we think of these women as giving up prostitution or not; there is nothing in Matthew's Gospel to settle the question.[9] The most significant thing is that Jesus held them up to the religious leadership as a model of repentance for them to follow, thus implying that the respectable are not unlike prostitutes in respect to sin.

MARK

Mark's Gospel, though closely related to that of Matthew, is much shorter and contains less of Jesus' teaching. In light of this, it is remarkable how much Mark and Matthew share on the subject of the family. Most of the relevant material found in Matthew is also in Mark, where it forms a larger proportion of the whole work than in Matthew. What is more, Mark often underlines the material more strongly than Matthew. Matthew, for example, shows us James and John in the boat with their father Zebedee and then has Jesus call them away as his disciples, so that they "leave the boat and their father" (Matt. 4:21–22); this makes it clear enough that they are abandoning their parent. Mark, however, includes a detail to suggest that they were Zebedee's only sons and that their departure left him without anyone to carry on his family: "At once [Jesus] called them; and, leaving their father Zebedee in the boat *with the hired hands*, they went off after him" (Mark 1:20; emphasis added). Again, both Matthew and Mark recount the story of how Jesus replaced his mother and siblings with his followers as his true family. Mark alone precedes the story with the statement that Jesus' relatives had come looking for him out of a conviction that he was out of his mind (3:21). When they arrived, they could not reach him for the crowd. The people told him they were asking for him, but he said, "Who are my mother and brothers?" And looking round at the crowd, he announced, "Look! My mother and my brothers. Whoever does God's will, this person is my brother and sister and mother" (3:31–35).[10]

Mark reports Jesus' prohibition of divorce in a form almost identical

9. Cf. Luke 7:36–50, where Jesus is anointed by a woman who is a public sinner. While she is not called a prostitute, that is one possible conclusion about her. Jesus accepts her attentions, contrasts them favorably with those of his host, a Pharisee, and finally says, "Her sins, many as they are, are forgiven because she has loved much" (7:47). This does not tell us what Jesus preferred prostitutes to do, but it does suggest that he did not make grace conditional on a prostitute's escaping her place in society.

10. This remains the most satisfactory interpretation of this passage; see Best, "Mark iii," 309–19.

to that of Matthew, but the redefinition of adultery that goes with it is somewhat different. Matthew's version contemplates only the husband's divorcing of the wife and its consequences. It is, after all, a discussion of the correct interpretation of Torah between Jesus and the Pharisees, and Torah provided for no other possibility. Mark, however, is less interested in the legal niceties of the issue and presents a more comprehensive version of the saying that would cover more of the eventualities of current practice: "Whoever divorces his wife and marries another commits adultery against her; and if she divorces her husband and marries another, she is committing adultery" (10:11–12).[11]

The fundamental principles behind Mark's version, however, are similar to those implied by Matthew's: marriage establishes a unity of flesh, that is, a familial relationship, between two persons who are equals in terms of their sexual ownership of one another. Their equality of ownership means that each can commit adultery against the other. Their unity of flesh means that neither husband nor wife is free to dispose of the other as a possession. Mark's version differs, however, in that it places the whole question of adultery on the partner who initiated divorce and remarriage and says nothing to prohibit the remarriage of one who has been the object of divorce.

Since most scholars believe that Mark's Gospel was the first such work to be written, it is worth noting the context in which he chose to place this material about divorce and remarriage. He created a distinct geographic unit in his narrative, beginning with Jesus' entry into "the territory of Judaea across the Jordan" (10:1) and concluding with his moving, by way of Jericho, up to Jerusalem (10:46–52). The contents of this unit, however, have long seemed miscellaneous. They include prohibition of divorce; reception of the children; the rich man's question; a discussion about possessions and salvation; Jesus' third prediction of his passion, death, and resurrection; a competition over precedence among the disciples; and the healing of blind Bartimaeus. Our own recognition that wives and children are a kind of property, however, and that hierarchy in the family was an expression of property relationships makes the continuity in Mark's arrangement easier to detect, for all the units gathered together here are really dealing with property ethics.

11. Mark may also have adapted the formula for his largely Gentile Christian audience, since among Gentiles the woman, too, commonly had the right to divorce her spouse. Brooten (*"Konnten Frauen,"* 78–80) suggests, however, that Mark was following widespread Jewish practice, which sometimes gave the wife the power of divorce, as distinct from the more limited provisions of the Torah.

The prohibition of divorce and redefinition of adultery took the wife out of the realm of disposable property and made her equal to her husband. So, too, Jesus' welcoming of the children takes them from the bottom of the family hierarchy and makes them persons in their own right (10:13–16). When Jesus invites the rich man to become a disciple, he demands that he separate himself from property and family (10:21). The man fails, and Jesus says to his disciples that it would be easier to put a camel through the eye of a needle than for a rich man to be saved. The disciples, assuming that riches are a sign of divine favor and also, through almsgiving, a means to it, are shocked (10:23–27). Peter notes that the disciples have left all, both family and other possessions, to follow Jesus; and Jesus assures them that they will be rewarded, "but many who are first will be last and the last first" (10:28–31). James and John (rather than their mother, as in Matthew) ignore both this saying and Jesus' reminder that he is on his way to his own death (10:32–34) and ask for the positions of highest honor in Jesus' reign; but Jesus tells them that honor, among his disciples, must be sought through service (10:35–45). Finally, as Jesus leaves Jericho on the road up to Jerusalem, a blind beggar, an utterly marginal and unimportant person, calls for him. The title he uses is a royal one, "Son of David," emphasizing Jesus' place at the peak of the same hierarchy which relegates the beggar to its lowest stratum. As in the earlier episode of the children, those around Jesus try to keep the lowly person away, but Jesus summons the man and places himself at his service in illustration of his own teaching (10:46–52).

The entire chapter thus forms a unified treatment of the family and related issues of property and hierarchy. Its message is that full disciples must give them all up: wealth, family, and their dominant place in the hierarchy. Even the more distant follower who retains spouse and family must give up the rights of ownership and domination over them. The family is stripped of its unquestioned centrality in the culture and in the lives of its members, while the adult males who follow Jesus are deprived of the status they had enjoyed as heads of such families. All this is done "for my sake and the sake of the gospel" (10:29).[12]

LUKE-ACTS

Luke confirms the picture we have found in Matthew and Mark, though he sometimes does it in a more pointed way. For instance, where

12. For a searching analysis of the relationship of this ethic to Mark's narrative about Jesus and his understanding of the reign of God, see Via, *Ethics of Mark's Gospel*, 67–168.

Matthew has Jesus say that "he who loves father or mother more than me is not worthy of me" (Matt. 10:37), Luke has this version: "If anyone comes to me and does not hate his own father and mother and wife and children and brothers and sisters, yes, and even his own life, he cannot be my disciple" (Luke 14:26). In this case, Luke's version is likely to be closer to Jesus' own words, for it is easier to understand how such provocative language could have been softened in the tradition than how it could have been newly introduced. Similarly, where Matthew has Jesus tell a would-be disciple that he must leave "the dead to bury their own dead" (8:22), Luke adds a further saying: "Yet another person said to him, 'I will follow you, sir, but first give me leave to say farewell to the people at home.' But Jesus said, 'No one who has once put hand to plow and then looks back is fit for God's reign'" (9:61–62). Jesus himself left his family to begin his wandering ministry as teacher and healer; and even before that, Luke tells us, as a child of twelve, he once renounced his parents' authority in order to pursue his true father's business in the temple (2:41–52).

Luke's treatment of the dispute with the Sadducees about levirate marriage, an episode that he shares with both Matthew and Mark, is also distinctive. All three Synoptic evangelists agree that there is to be no marrying or giving in marriage[13] in the life of the resurrection. The other two explain this simply as a result of the fact that the resurrected will be "like the angels in heaven" (Matt. 22:30; Mark 12:25). Later Christian interpreters shared with Neoplatonic philosophy the presupposition that angels (or their Greek equivalent, the *daimones*) were purely spiritual beings without any sexual component in their nature. To be like the angels, then, was to be nonsexual, with the consequent understanding that, whatever the precise language of the passage might say, Jesus really meant that there would be no sex in heaven. This, however, is in potential conflict with the scriptural tradition about angels. As we have seen, both Genesis and Jude (and also *1 Enoch*, which Jude regarded as scriptural) regarded some angels at least (commonly called the Watchers) as sexual beings capable of having intercourse with human women and even of begetting children with them.[14] What Jesus may have

13. Women could not "marry" in the ancient sense, but only be "given in marriage."
14. See above, chapter 7. Note also the evidence of *Testament of Reuben* 5, though it blames the whole incident on human women who seduced the Watchers and it is a little unclear whether the author thought that actual sexual intercourse took place. *Jubilees* tells us that the angels of the presence and of sanctification (the highest angelic ranks) were created circumcised (15.27) and that acts of fornication, impurity, and injustice committed by the Watchers brought on the Flood (7.21–25).

thought about the presence or absence of sexual activity in the life of the resurrection must remain unknown; there is no clue in the saying itself. The presumed asexuality of angelic beings, however, is unlikely to be the point of his comparison, for there is no reason to suppose that he or his audience knew of it.

Luke, fortunately, is more specific in his version of Jesus' saying, enabling us to say precisely what Luke, at least, understood to be the point of comparison. Angels are immortal beings and therefore entirely exempt from the need for legitimate offspring to carry the life and wealth of a family across the generations. The disappearance of marriage at the resurrection is therefore simply a result of the disappearance of death and, with it, of the whole family structure characteristic of earthly society. "The children of this age," says Jesus, "marry and are given in marriage, but those found worthy to attain to that age and the resurrection of the dead neither marry nor are given in marriage. For they are no longer capable of dying, for they are equal to angels and are children (or sons)[15] of God inasmuch as they are children of the resurrection" (20:34–36).

Luke's most extreme break with the family and its normative hierarchy appears in a tradition unique to his Gospel, the parable of the prodigal son (15:11–32). The behavior of the prodigal is a complete betrayal of his family. What belonged to him only as an offshoot of his "father's house" (the elder brother, of course, would continue the direct line) he wasted on private pleasures. Having come to no good, he acknowledged what anyone in Jesus' world would surely have agreed to—that he was no longer worthy of the title "son." He returned to his father only to beg for the position of a hired hand. Even this perhaps stretched the claims of family loyalty, but his present state was so wretched that he had nothing to lose. The truly outrageous element in the parable, however, was the father's behavior. Having seen his failed son approaching, he ran to meet him, rather than waiting with patriarchal dignity to receive him as a suppliant. He embraced and kissed him without waiting for any explanation or speech of repentance, and he received him back with the kind of rejoicing that marked him as the long-lost child returned, quite without reference to the way he had failed his family. He reaffirmed the elder son's right of succession, yet treated this as a reason for him to rejoice at his brother's return instead of

15. The phrase "sons of God" may be a reminder of the story of the Watchers, for that is the title given them in Gen. 6:2.

excluding him. This, says the Jesus of Luke's Gospel, in a stunning reversal of the hierarchical relationships that gave families their structure, is the way God acts.

Luke stood, then, in the same tradition as Matthew and Mark on the issue of the family—though he was perhaps willing to press that tradition a bit more vigorously at certain points. A curious and unique feature of his Gospel, however, is the way in which he led his reader from the existing presuppositions about family, embedded as they were in the religion of Israel, to the radically new situation envisioned by Jesus' teaching. Luke's Gospel begins in an atmosphere redolent of the world of ancient Israel, the era of patriarchs, judges, and kings. An elderly priest and his wife are childless. Through an angel, the priest learns that his wife will conceive, though she is barren and past the age of childbearing. The prophecy proves true, and she rejoices that God has removed the reproach of her barrenness (1:5–25). The son born to them in due course is John the Baptist. Reminiscences of the stories of Abraham and Sarah, of Jacob and Rachel, of Hannah and Elkanah, identify this as the narrative of yet another family in Israel that has received the Lord's blessing of fertility and offered the fruit of that blessing to God in faith and service.

Near the end of his Gospel, however, Luke has Jesus say to the women of Jerusalem: "Behold, days are coming when they will say, 'Blessed are the barren and the wombs that have not given birth and breasts that have not nursed'" (23:29). In time to come, blessing and curse will be reversed. The family will be a hindrance, and those who are free of it will be counted fortunate. The shift between the era of the family and this new and changed world comes to a focus in John the Baptist, as the series of sayings in Luke 16 shows. At first sight, they seem miscellaneous and even chaotic. Jesus insists that, like the unrighteous steward, one must sacrifice one's household for one's own well-being. Everyone must make a choice between God and mammon, which includes not only property and money, but also the family which is their possessor. One cannot serve both, and the wise person will make use of the goods of this world to secure a place in the world to come (16:1–13). The Pharisees, whom Luke characterizes here as "fond of money," object, and Jesus responds, "What is exalted among human beings is an abomination before God" (16:14–15). In what at first seems a non sequitur, he continues, "The law and the prophets as far as John! From then on, the reign of God is being proclaimed as good news and everyone is forcing a way into it. And it is easier for heaven and earth to pass away than for a single serif to drop from the law. Everyone who divorces his wife and marries another is committing adultery, and the one who marries a woman divorced from her husband is committing adultery" (16:16–18). Then comes the parable of the rich man and Lazarus, which teaches that one's fortune in the world to come will be a reversal of what one enjoyed in this (16:19–31).

The theme that holds these seemingly disparate materials together is the change of worlds and the sacrifice of family and other property which it demands. It is easier to change worlds than to drop even the smallest stroke from a letter of the law. Yet, Jesus has changed the law. What was permitted by the law he treats as sin. The life of wealth and ease in one's family—which the law exalted, the Pharisees esteemed, and the rich man of the parable enjoyed—he undermines. The distance between these worlds is "a great gulf fixed." John, the joy of his parents' old age, was the culmination and the conclusion of the former era; but in the new era the patriarchal family, however sanctified by the law and the prophets, ceases to be. This is not, for Luke, a repudiation of the law in its own place and time, but it is a decisive step beyond it into another world altogether.

Luke's second volume, the Acts of the Apostles, has less to say about the family. This is as one would expect in light of his treatment of the subject in his Gospel. The family was surely still tolerated, since Luke tells us enthusiastically of the conversion of whole households (e.g., that of Cornelius, 10:44–48, or Lydia, 16:15) and makes a good deal of the role of Priscilla and Aquila, who were wife and husband (18:2–3, 18, 24–26). Yet, the first story he tells of an individual as distinct from a mass conversion concerns a eunuch (8:26–39). And one would never know, from what he tells us, that Christians continued to marry and set up new family units. Indeed, he presents the Jerusalem church, in its early days, as taking its meals together and sharing all its possessions freely (4:32–37), implying that it regarded itself as a single family and had obliterated the boundaries of the traditional family, at least within its own ranks. Luke also shows the church treating women as fully responsible human beings, as in the case of Ananias and Sapphira (5:1–11); and he stresses the importance of women such as the daughters of Philip, who prophesied (21:9); Priscilla, whose importance as a teacher appears to have outshone that of her husband (her name usually precedes his, as in 18:26); and Lydia, who was the first European convert (16:14–15).

Luke's account of the earliest Christian churches, then, implies that, being attentive to the principles Jesus had established with regard to the family, they had allowed its importance to decline among them. Women, as a result, were free to participate in the life of the community in an active way. The leadership of the churches, however, seems to have remained mainly in the hands of men. Luke says nothing, for example, about women as traveling missionaries in the manner of Paul, even though they appear as prophets, teachers, and patrons of local churches. In this way, we can see in Acts the foundations of future problems and uncertainties. The early Christians wished to honor Jesus' teaching with regard to the family; yet, they were not prepared, as a whole, to implement the far-reaching changes in traditional social life that it called for. Perhaps Luke's own emphasis on the importance of women was in part an effort to correct this reluctance.[16]

JOHN

The subject of family and sexual property does not form a very large concern of the Gospel of John—certainly not to the extent that one could glean from it a "position" on the subject. The most one can say is that John is not at odds with what we have read in the three Synoptic Gospels. Jesus is closer to his mother in this Gospel than in the others. She even appears in the role of exemplary believer in the story of the wedding at Cana, where she appeals to Jesus with regard to the lack of wine and perseveres in faith that he can and will act (2:1–11).[17] Even here, however, he rebuffs her in a way that seems disrespectful; and, in the long run, Jesus makes the church the true family of every believer by giving Mary and the beloved disciple to each other as mother and son at the cross (19:25–27). The essential thing about believers is that they are children of God (1:12–13), having been born from above (or again) of water and spirit (3:1–13).[18]

John's Jesus feels no difficulty about talking with a lone Samaritan

---

16. Alternatively, Luke may be seen as having suppressed information about a time of much richer female participation and leadership in the church; cf. Schüssler Fiorenza, *In Memory of Her,* 160–62. In any case, later transmitters of the text of Acts found Luke's book too favorable to women and revised it accordingly; see Witherington, "Anti-Feminist Tendencies," 82–84.

17. Countryman, *Mystical Way,* 24–26.

18. Ibid., 16–17, 29–31, 118–19.

woman, though both the woman and Jesus' disciples sense an awkwardness in the situation (4:9, 27). Even when the woman turns out to be oft-divorced[19] and living with a man to whom she is not married, he shows no evidence of concern (4:16–18). In fact, she becomes a missionary to the people of her own city (4:28–30, 39–42). Another apparently unmarried woman, Mary of Magdala, holds a particularly important place in this Gospel, being one of the few followers who stood by the cross (19:25) and the first witness both of the empty tomb and of the Risen Lord (20:1–18). Finally, Jesus had a close association with two unmarried sisters, Mary and Martha of Bethany, who seem to be, as persons, more important and better known to the Johannine community than their brother Lazarus (11:1–2).

John's Jesus, like the Jesus of the Synoptics, also reverses hierarchy as a key to his ministry. At the last supper, he strips and assumes the role of a slave by washing his disciples' feet (13:1–10). This is despite the fact that he is not only their teacher and master, but actually, as John has told his readers from the very beginning, the creative power of God, the eternal Logos from whom all creation comes (1:1–18). He then tells his disciples that this is the example they are to follow in their relationship with one another (13:12–17). "If you know these things, blessed are you—if you do them!"

Finally, we may note Jesus' encounter with a woman about to be stoned for adultery (7:53—8:11). This is not, properly speaking, a part of John's Gospel at all; but most of the manuscripts that preserve it place it here.[20] It is undoubtedly an early tradition. In this story, Jesus does not question the existing definition of adultery or overtly alter the character of the family. Yet, what he does is as devastating to the status quo as any of the teachings preserved in the Synoptics. By inviting whoever was sinless to cast the first stone, he forces the crowd to reevaluate the cheap sense of virtue that we get from committing violence in the defense of familiar social institutions. The eldest, which is to say the wisest, leave first. When all have gone and Jesus is left alone with the woman, he, too, refuses to condemn her and sends her away. He says to her, "Sin no more." Adultery has not, then, ceased to be a sin; but Jesus has made the social sanctions against it unenforceable, once again drastically undermining the social institution of the family.

---

19. This is more likely than that she had been five times widowed.
20. For a summary of the textual questions, see Metzger, *Textual Commentary*, 219–22.

SUMMARY

Although the Gospel of John is less interested in the question of family and sexual property than the three Synoptics, there is nonetheless a broad agreement manifest in all four New Testament Gospels with regard to Jesus' teaching on these issues. I shall attempt to summarize it here.

Jesus was not friendly toward the family as an institution. Although he was not understood to have abolished it entirely among his followers, he came close to it among his immediate disciples. Of them, he demanded a drastic separation from family. His other followers, he insisted, must cease to treat it as central to their world. The demands of the reign of God are supreme, and no this-worldly obligation may rival them for the allegiance of those who are already being drawn into the life of the world to come. One cannot serve God and mammon—any kind of mammon.

More specifically, Jesus demanded that the wife no longer be regarded as disposable (i.e., divorceable) property. Instead, husband and wife were to be understood as human equals who now constitute one flesh. This deprived the patriarch of one important sanction for his control of the household, and Jesus' rejection of the usual penalty for adultery deprived him of another. It is not surprising, then, that the early Christian movement was marked by the active and independent involvement in it of women, both married and single. In addition to changing the status of the wife, Jesus also altered that of the children. By making the child and not the father the model for entry into the reign of God, Jesus again negated the family structures of the society and reversed the hierarchical assumptions that governed all of life.[21]

As to specific offenses against sexual property, as defined in the Scriptures of Israel, Jesus retained the prohibition against adultery, though not its punishment. He redefined adultery, however, so that the principal form of it now came to be the divorcing of one spouse and marrying of another—a perfectly respectable and legal undertaking by most other contemporary standards. The result was that adultery was no longer the exceptional behavior of the vicious few, but the normal behavior of society at large. At the same time that he reshaped the

---

21. Riches has drawn a valuable connection between this tendency and Jesus' disregard of purity; both represent the deliberate breaking down of boundaries. See his *Jesus and the Transformation of Judaism*, 132–33. On the general importance of the reign of God for Jesus' ethics of the family, see Schrage, *Ethics of the New Testament*, 18–40, 91–98.

formal definition of adulterous acts, Jesus also redirected attention from the act itself to the intention involved in committing it. The essence of adultery was seen to lie either in the indiscriminate character of the sexual desire itself, which ignores the marital status of the desired, or else in covetousness, that is, in the intent to possess what belongs to another.

The Gospels have little to say about incest, though they seem to agree with John the Baptist's denunciation of Herod Antipas. With regard to prostitution, too, the Gospels have little to say. Since Jesus, however, does not seem to have been anxious about unattached women and since he even held up contemporary prostitutes as a religious example at one point, we may guess that, insofar as he took prostitution to be ethically wrong, he followed the example of Proverbs in apportioning blame to the man who visited the prostitute more than to the prostitute herself. Jesus still allowed a marriage to be annulled on grounds of *porneia*, but this, as we have seen, was probably limited to the situation where a bride who was claimed to be a virgin turned out not to be.

In short, the property ethic was maintained—but in a way that threatened the family more than it supported it. Since Jesus saw in the family a rival claimant for the commitment and loyalty of his followers, it is not surprising that he should undermine it. The thing that demands explanation is rather why he should have wished to retain any ethic of sexual property at all. The answer lies with his emphasis on purity of the heart, which prohibited one from robbing or defrauding others (Mark 7:21–22). While Jesus had little interest in the goals of the family—the bearing of legitimate heirs or the acquisition, accumulation, and passing on of wealth—he saw sexual access in itself as a fundamental good of the created order. Since sexual access is an important possession, he forbade his followers to rob others.

In the existing state of affairs, however, sexual access belonged only to males. In order to restore the created equality of women, Jesus had to arrange for it to belong equally to them. Hence, the abolition of divorce and, with it, the collapse of intrafamily hierarchy. This situation, in turn, called for a new explanation of how a family, or any community, was to live. The old way had been for one person to enjoy the status of patriarch and demand obedience of others. Jesus' new way was for all to assume the position of children or slaves. In the absence of competition among those advancing themselves for leadership, those who were last would become first. Even God, he taught, has given up standing on his dignity as Father of the Universe and is running out to greet returning prodigals.

10

Paul and Sexual Property

We have seen that Jesus, according to the traditions preserved in the Synoptic Gospels, insisted on the subordination of the family to the reign of God. In the apocalyptic teaching current in Jesus' day, the reign of God could come into full command of the creation only through the end (*eschaton*, in Greek) of the world as we know it; this is what is technically called a "future eschatology." The tradition of Jesus' teachings depicts him as having spoken in just this way, using the traditional imagery of cosmic catastrophe (e.g., Mark 13). At the same time, he also speaks as though the reign of God were already present and available in his own ministry and that of his disciples—what is technically called a "realized eschatology." In some sense, this made his ministry the true end of the familiar world, regardless of whether the actual date of the eschaton were near or far off. Thus, Jesus himself embodies God's reign, so that he could legitimately call disciples away from their parents, spouses, and children; yet, Christians continued to expect it in its fullness only in the future.

Paul's teaching about the family and sexual expression involves a similar insistence on both the priority of God's reign and the dual character of its manifestation, present and future. The language he uses to convey this teaching, however, is not always the same as that of the Synoptic Gospels. In fact, the actual phrase "reign of God" is not particularly common in his writings; but he gets at the same fundamental ideas with different terms, some of them very closely related to the day-to-day realities of the family itself. Paul addresses the present reality of

God's reign (realized eschatology) in terms of *belonging to Christ* and its expected fulfillment (future eschatology) in terms of *awaiting his return.* We shall need to explore each of these motifs in order to understand how Paul made use of them in relation to sexual ethics. He was not, after all, a philosopher who could speak about property, sexual or other, in an abstract way. His interest in it was determined by the relationship he saw between the gospel he preached and the ongoing life of this world.

BELONGING TO CHRIST AND
AWAITING HIS RETURN

In contemporary American society, the image of "belonging to Christ," though not without power, is essentially a dead metaphor, since human beings no longer own other human beings in the sense that was normal in antiquity. Such metaphors become spiritually and intellectually dangerous, for it is all too easy to cut them loose from their anchorage in familiar realities and make them mean anything we like. In other words, they may cease to teach us anything and become mere code words for whatever notions happen already to be precious to us. Thus, "belonging to Christ," in our contemporary milieu, may mean anything from "feeling a strong commitment to the Christian faith" to "feeling assured that Jesus will take care of me" to "feeling confident of my superiority over others." In a world immediately familiar with the phenomenon of slavery, Paul's own usage is likely to have been more concrete and focused.

Paul, in fact, was willing to describe himself as Christ's slave, servant, or agent *(apostolos);* some variant of these expressions is found in the salutation at the beginning of virtually every letter in the Pauline corpus. Belonging to Christ, however, was not something unique to apostles. As Paul was "Christ Jesus' slave, a called *apostolos,"* his addressees, too, were "Jesus Christ's called ones" (Rom. 1:1, 6). Or again, defending the doctrine of the general resurrection against its detractors at Corinth, he explained that Jesus' resurrection implied that of all believers in an appropriate order: "Christ the firstfruits, then, at his coming, those who belong to Christ, then the end . . ." (1 Cor. 15:23–24).

This could be, to be sure, merely the language of partisanship. At Corinth, Paul knew of parties whose members claimed, "I belong to Paul"—or to Apollos or to Cephas or to Christ (1 Cor. 1:12). Even though he had founded the congregation there himself, he may have had to defend his claims to authority in it against the pretensions of a

"Christ party," for in a subsequent letter he wrote, "If anyone is personally confident that he belongs to Christ, let him do the reckoning over again on himself, because just as he belongs to Christ, so, too, do we" (2 Cor. 10:7). Paul was not prepared, at Corinth or anywhere else, to acknowledge any authority in conflict with the gospel that he believed had been entrusted to him. Such a language of partisanship, however, by no means exhausts the significance of what Paul means by "belonging to Christ."

To the Galatians, he wrote of Christ's ownership as originating in a kind of purchase. The purpose of the letter was both to defend Paul's own teaching and to dissuade the Galatian Christians from adopting a fuller observance of the Torah, including circumcision of Gentile males. Paul wanted to assert the incompatibility of the gospel with such a use of Torah and found the metaphor of ownership useful in making his point. He turned specifically to the normal ancient practice of enslaving prisoners of war—not only captured soldiers, but also the civilian populations of conquered cities. In some cases, such prisoners could be ransomed—either by payment of money or by substitution of another person of equal value. The law, he argued, takes us prisoner by placing us under a curse when we do not fulfill it completely, but "Christ has ransomed us from the curse of the law by becoming a curse on our behalf (because it is written, 'Cursed be everyone that hangs on a tree'), so that the blessing of Abraham might be extended to the Gentiles in Christ Jesus, so that we might receive the promise of the Spirit through faith" (Gal. 3:13–14). Before Christ, according to Paul's metaphor, the Jewish people were, so to speak, property of the law, while the Gentiles were excluded from God's elect. Jesus, by substituting himself for those imprisoned under the curse, liberated Jewish believers and, at the same time, freed God's promise from its association with the law, thus allowing the Gentiles new access to God. "You are all one in Christ Jesus. And if you belong to Christ, then you are seed of Abraham" (3:28–29).

The ransoming of prisoners, however, did not simply restore the ransomed to their previous station. They may not have become slaves of their ransomer, but they remained, at the very least, heavily indebted and were never again free to act apart from or against their benefactor. Thus, Paul could hail the gospel as both granting freedom and placing limits on it: "You have been called for freedom, brothers and sisters—only not freedom as an opportunity for the flesh. Rather, act as slaves to one another through love" (5:13). After offering a list of vices to be avoided and virtues which are the "fruit of the Spirit," Paul continued, "Those who belong to Christ have crucified the flesh with its passions and desires. If we are living by Spirit, let us also conduct ourselves according to Spirit" (5:24–25). The crucifixion by which Christ took our place and ransomed us has made a decisive division between the old part of our lives when we lived according to the principle of selfishness and the new part when we are to live by a principle that accords with our benefactor's death and life.[1]

When Paul speaks of the Christian as Christ's slave, he is using a household illustration to show what it means to belong to the reign of God. Inevitably, the illustration introduces the whole question of hierarchy, whether in terms of owner to slave or parent to child. If the church is a household, who is father or master? Who is mother? Who is child or slave? Thus Paul referred to himself, under God, as the father of the Corinthian church and its members as his children: "It is not to shame you that I am writing these things, but to instruct you as my beloved children. Even if you have many tutors in Christ, you do not have many fathers, for in Christ Jesus through the gospel, I begot you" (1 Cor. 4:14–15).[2] This language assumes what all of Paul's correspondence assumes—that he had a certain right to define the gospel and give authoritative rulings in churches he had founded, much like a patriarch in his own family. While Paul was no tyrant, seeking to impose his will on every detail of church life, neither was he shy about intervening where he thought anything of importance was at stake.

At the same time, Paul recognized that the distance between the faithful as owned and the Ransomer as the owner relativized most distinctions within the church to some degree or other. In the same letter where he asserted his paternal status in relation to the Corinthians, he also discouraged them from forming parties around their teachers: "Let no one boast of human beings; for all things belong to you, whether Paul or Apollos or Cephas, whether the world or life or death, whether things present or things to come—all belong to you and you to Christ and Christ to God" (1 Cor. 3:21–23). While this does not obliterate the hierarchy within the church (Paul still expected to be heard and obeyed), it does relativize it sharply by acknowledging that, as Jesus had said, "The one who wants to be first among you must be servant of all."

---

1. On "flesh" in Paul, see above, chapter 6.
2. Paul also described his behavior toward the Thessalonians as paternal (1 Thess. 2:11).

The Christians, then, are God's slaves and God's children, and only in some lesser sense are they the children of Paul or of any other apostle.

Paul could also speak of the believers as Christ's bride, another way of expressing the same subordination: "I am jealous of you with a jealousy on God's behalf. For I had betrothed you to a single husband, to bring you as a chaste virgin to Christ, but I am afraid that somehow, just as the snake deceived Eve with its craftiness, your minds might be corrupted from their simplicity and dedication to Christ" (2 Cor. 11:2–3). Paul spoke here in the persona, once again, of the church's father, anxious that his daughter should not prove to be less than he has claimed. As the betrothed virgin must not let herself be seduced by other lovers, the church must resist teachers and spirits and gospels at variance with what Paul taught them (11:4). One of Paul's followers, the author of the Epistle to the Ephesians, later elaborated the image of church as bride of Christ and reapplied it to ordinary marriage with an effect that we must consider later in this chapter.

The images of the Christian as God's slave and the church as God's household were not the only means Paul had of directing attention to the uniqueness of life lived according to the gospel. He also spoke of the Christian community, in a way somewhat reminiscent of Qumran, as God's temple, with the rest of the world, Jewish and Gentile together, lying outside the sacred precincts. Baptism was the transition into this sacred status and the fact that one could receive it only once meant that, unlike other sacral washings, it was an irreversible as well as an unrepeatable act. The threshold of this temple could be crossed only in one direction. Those who transgressed after baptism, even though they must expect some kind of suffering in punishment for it, would not finally be abandoned by God (1 Cor. 3:10–15)—though Paul made at least an apparent exception to this rule for those whose ambitions and jealousies disrupted the peace of the community (3:16–17).

Yet another image important to Paul was that of the body of Christ, with the Christians as various limbs and organs of the body. He could use this, when he wished to emphasize the equality of believers, to suggest that Christ is to the church what the whole is to its parts (1 Cor. 12:12–27). Again, when he wished to emphasize Christ's domination over the church and to exclude that of angels or "elements" of the cosmos, he could treat Christ as the "head"—the first principle and ruling part—which alone gives the church its unity (Col. 1:15–20; 2:8–10, 16–19). Plato, many centuries before, had taken the head to be the original, essential, and dominant portion of the human body;[3] Paul was speaking out of the same kind of cultural background which typically treated the head as the most honored part of the body and the feet as the least. Thus, the image conveyed a strong sense of hierarchy.

Yet another way Paul had of speaking about the Christian's relationship with Christ was his distinctive use of the phrase "in Christ," in which he incorporated a rich and complex set of meanings that remains difficult to interpret and impossible to exhaust. There is no need here to attempt even a listing of the possible interpretations. It will be enough to note the substantial overlap between "being in Christ" and "belonging to Christ." Those who are in Christ are free of condemnation (Rom. 8:1); those who have fallen asleep in Christ have a hope of resurrection with him (1 Cor. 15:17–22); for them, the old things have passed away and become new (2 Cor. 5:17); all are one in Christ (Gal. 3:28). One could cite more examples, but these should suffice to show that the phrase could be used synonymously with "belonging to Christ." Christians, for Paul, are sharply distinguished from the world at large by their unique relationship to God through Jesus.

This relationship is certain in the present world, but not complete. It will reach fulfillment only in the life of the world to come, and Paul considered the inbreaking of that world to be close at hand. He expected, during at least the earlier part of his ministry, that it would come before he himself died (1 Thess. 4:17; 1 Cor. 15:51–52). Thus, it was not a part of some remote or incalculable future, but an imminent reality that one must take into account in the present. One great object of Christian behavior was to conduct oneself "in a way worthy of the God who *is calling* you into his own reign and glory" (1 Thess. 2:12; emphasis added), for this great transition was at most a few years distant—something to be spoken of in present, not future tense. Thus, the Christian who belonged to Christ already, who was a member of Christ's body, a building block of God's temple, who lived "in Christ"—this person must frame the conduct of day-to-day life in the expectation that it would soon give way to a world that would make utterly different demands. Under the circumstances, one must avoid crediting the life of this world, through one's actions, with a permanency that it cannot possibly enjoy; and one must live instead by the values of the world to come—most of all by that love which, alone of this world's goods,

3. Plato *Timaeus* 44d–e.

continues into it unchanged (1 Corinthians 13). These are the ways in which the reign of God makes itself felt here and now. Paul, like Jesus, insisted that every aspect of human life, including sex and the family, must yield to them.

SEX AT CORINTH (1 COR. 5—7)

The only sustained discussion of sexual ethics in Paul's writings (or, indeed, in the whole of the New Testament) is found in 1 Corinthians. It owes its existence, it seems, not to Paul's own interest in the subject, but to that of the Corinthian Christians. They produced highly divergent interpretations of what the gospel demanded in the way of sexual ethics, ranging from libertinism to a complete rejection of both marriage and sexual intercourse. These divergences may well have resulted from a failure on Paul's part to address the issue specifically when he was founding the congregation. Some Corinthians, having absorbed Paul's conviction that the gospel supersedes the law, may have separated this principle from its context and supposed that it meant the end of all moral constraints. Others observed that Paul was on friendly terms with traditional households, like that of Stephanas, whom he described as the "firstfruits of the province of Achaia" (1 Cor. 1:16; 16:15); and they assumed that Christians were to continue that kind of family life. Still others, noting Paul's own celibate state and his negative use of the term "flesh," concluded that the gospel demanded (or at least encouraged) a complete separation from sexuality.

These differences within the congregation produced tensions which could not but come to Paul's attention, since, at the time of writing 1 Corinthians, he was just across the Aegean at Ephesus—a relatively short distance by the standards of the Roman Empire. Some in the congregation informally reported to him about the activities of the libertines, and the congregation sent him an official enquiry about the teachings of the ascetics. The difference of these two modes of enquiry suggests that the congregation as a whole was less perturbed by the libertines than by the ascetics—that their basic assumption, in other words, was that sexual ethics was not a matter of high importance in the Christian community. Paul's understanding of purity, as outlined above in chapter 6, could easily convey that impression, especially if it was combined with hostile language about the Torah.

We have already seen (above, pp. 105–6) that Paul had to write his Thessalonian converts to remind them that adultery was inconsistent with Christian behavior. He had been at Thessalonica, however, only briefly. At Corinth, his mission lasted, according to Luke, a year and a half (Acts 18:11). During that time, it seems likely that he not only argued the case for his own particular understanding of the gospel, but also communicated, both personally and through the work of his companions, traditions about Jesus' life and teaching. In discussing the Lord's Supper or the resurrection of the dead, he could remind the Corinthians of such traditions that he himself had imparted to them (1 Cor. 11:23–25; 15:1–8). In his discussion of divorce, too, he cites such a tradition (7:10–11), but he does not claim to have handed it on to them previously. This might mean that the Corinthians had never heard of it at all; but, at the very least, it suggests that it formed no significant part of Paul's own teaching. In writing 1 Corinthians, Paul could not simply "remind" the congregation of what he had already told them, but had to begin at the beginning to instruct them about sexual ethics.

Incest

Paul began with a reported case of incest: "It is actually reported that there is harlotry among you—a kind of harlotry not [found][4] even among the Gentiles, namely that someone has his father's wife" (5:1). The verb "has" suggests something more than casual intercourse, perhaps the creation of a full household. The woman in question could be the man's mother, but there seems no reason for Paul to have avoided saying so if that were in fact the case. More likely, she was a subsequent wife of his father, now either divorced or widowed. According to Leviticus, this would be incest just as much as intercourse with his own mother; in specifying punishments for incest, the Holiness Code made no distinction as to whether the father's wife were the son's own mother or not (20:11).

Since this was basically an offense against the patriarch's majesty, it is not surprising to find that Greco-Roman law, working with a very similar family structure, agreed with that of Israel in forbidding it. This is the significance of Paul's exclamation about "a kind of harlotry not [found] even among the Gentiles." There is at least a hint of Jewish prejudice against dirty Gentiles in the manner of Paul's exclamation, but

---

4. Some manuscripts have an expressed verb in the clause *(onomazetai),* which gives the reading "is not even named among the Gentiles." This is probably an effort by a later scribe to fill in the apostle's elliptical style of writing. My own "found" is a similar effort, made necessary by the narrower scope of English grammar.

there is a serious argument here, too—namely, that one cannot excuse this case of incest on the grounds that, where Jewish and Gentile laws differed, Gentiles were not compelled to abide by Jewish practices. The abolition of purity requirements, from Paul's point of view, was not an end in itself, but a necessary means to the end of including outsiders within the Christian community. There was no need for the church to terminate a purity rule which was equally at home in both Jewish and Gentile society, which did not, in other words, act to divide the two.

Yet, Paul's language shows that he thinks of the offense primarily in terms of family hierarchy, not purity.[5] He did not use purity language from Leviticus by speaking of "lying with" the father's wife or "uncovering the father's nakedness." He wrote rather of "having" the father's wife, of possessing one who belonged properly to another. We do not know, to be sure, whether the man's father was still alive or whether the relationship was clandestine. Paul's language suggests that it was open. Even if the father were dead, however, the subordination of the individual to the family in ancient society meant that such a union, by setting the son on a par with his father, constituted an act of disrespect for the family that gave the son his identity and place in the world. Whether a living father was in fact being insulted was not germane.

Many Christians at Corinth seem to have accepted this relationship as permissible under the gospel. Some may even have seen it as a laudable example of the abrogation of the Torah purity code, for Paul continued, "You people are puffed up and have not turned instead to mourning, so that the man who has committed this act might be removed from among you!" (5:2). It seems unlikely that the whole congregation was proud of the man. We know that the "strong" and the "weak" at Corinth were deeply divided over the question of eating foods sacrificed to idols. There were, then, people in the congregation who believed that some purity rules still held. It is possible, however, that even the Weak took this case of incest less seriously. It did not, after all, affect the community in its assembling together for meals, for Torah does not treat the uncleanness of incest as something that can be communicated to foods.

In the community as a whole, then, some may have been proud of the incest while others ignored the problem, seeing it as insignificant and

---

5. Neyrey ("Body Language," 138–42) has interpreted most of 1 Corinthians as an application of purity concerns. I think he is mistaken, however, in assuming that all control asserted over the sexual orifices necessarily springs from purity considerations and in ignoring Paul's failure to apply the purity language available to him to the subject.

priding themselves on their devotion to the gospel. Paul wrote, with regard to them, "Your boasting is not good. Do you not know that a little leaven leavens the whole batch of dough? Clear out the old leaven so that you may be a new batch of dough—as, indeed, you are unleavened. For, in fact, our Passover offering, Christ, has been sacrificed. Let us, then, observe the festival not with old leaven or with leaven of wickedness and evil, but with unleavened loaves of sincerity and truth" (5:6–8). Some may read this passage as a return to purity language, on the assumption that leaven was unclean. The vocabulary, however, does not support such a reading.[6]

The reference to the Passover here is rather a way of speaking about the new and strange "end time" in which the Christians stood. The Messiah has come as sacrifice and will shortly return to reign. In the meantime, Christians are living in a festival of liberation, like that which celebrated the deliverance from Egypt. As people who live permanently in the Passover festival, feeding on the flesh of the Passover offering, they must forswear things which might be overlooked during ordinary time. The leaven must be cleared out, not because it is impure, but because it is inappropriate to the new and sacred time. The violation of the majesty of a father was a kind of theft, depriving another of legitimate property. The Corinthian church, in its self-confidence, was mishandling the problem as if it were of little importance. Yet, living as it was on the verge of the world to come and even belonging already to that world by virtue of its relationship to Christ, the church must not tolerate behavior unsuited to the new time.

Paul, then, considered the case of incest to be a serious offense. This was not because of the purity element involved, for he reinforced his argument by appealing not to purity, but to an eschatological theme— the advent of the end times, the time of liberation, here symbolized by

---

6. There are two objections to seeing this as a purity issue. One is that leaven was not forbidden as unclean by the purity system of Israel. Though in some sense its prohibition during Passover seems like a purity rule, it does not seem to have been perceived in that light. Cf. McCombie, "Jesus and the Leaven of Salvation," 450–62. The second objection is that the verb *ekkathairō*, though etymologically linked to the purity vocabulary, was not used as part of that set of technical terms—at least, not in the LXX, where it and the related *ekkatharizō* refer to the clearing of land (Deut. 32:43; Josh. 17:15, 18), the sorting out of soldiers (Judges 7:4, B text), the cleaning of wounds (Isa. 4:4), and even the removal of what is holy (tithe) from one's house (Deut. 26:13). It once has the metaphorical meaning of "purging evil" (Judges 20:13). In the New Testament, it appears only here and in 2 Tim. 2:21, where it refers to separating oneself from false teachers. The Passover image in 1 Cor. 5:7, then, should not be read in terms of the purity code.

the special qualities of the Passover festival. It was not a new, specifically eschatological ethic, however, that he sought to enforce through this appeal; rather, it was the familiar ethic of the existing family structure, committed to keeping the son in subordination to the father. Paul did not argue for the retention of that structure or its accompanying ethic, but assumed it. His appeal to the distinctive time in which Christians live served to reinforce not the gravity of incest, but the necessity of regarding every ethical issue as serious.

Paul issued instructions for separating the offender: "As for me, absent in body but present in spirit, I have already judged as though present the man who has so acted: with all of you gathered together in the name of the Lord Jesus and with my spirit [present] with the power of our Lord Jesus, to hand such a person over to Satan for destruction of the flesh, so that the spirit may be saved in the day of the Lord" (5:3–5). The exact nature of the scene which Paul envisaged or the punishment which would ensue is not clear. The effect, however, seems to be one of putting the offender back outside the pale of the church, insofar as Paul could conceive of such a reversal of baptism. It was not a final doom, but an interim action which would lead, through destruction of all that is resistant to God (the "flesh"), to eventual salvation.

Along with it went a kind of shunning, a deliberate avoidance of the offender by the rest of the congregation. Paul had suggested shunning, in general terms in an earlier letter, and now applied it specifically:

> I wrote you in the letter not to mingle with people given to harlotry, not at all [meaning] those of this world, or its greedy folk *(pleonektēs)* and graspers or idolators, since you would then have to leave the world. But as things are, I wrote you not to mingle if anyone called a brother is given to harlotry or greedy or an idolator or slanderer or drunkard or grasper—not even to eat with such a person. (5:9–11)

This passage is particularly revealing as to the nature of the sin, according to Paul. There is no purity language here, but a good deal to do with taking what properly belongs to another. Even the habitually drunken person is one who takes from the family and gives nothing back; and "idolatry" here (as in Col. 3:5) is a synonym for greed. Paul saw the case of incest at Corinth as belonging to the same class of offenses as theft.[7]

This helps to explain why the following verses, which seem out of

---

7. Zaas ("Cast Out the Evil Man," 259–61) has noted that Paul invokes the common excommunication formula found in Deuteronomy, but less as a technical procedure than for the sake of its traditional resonances.

place to the modern reader, seemed to Paul to belong in this location. He was not finished with the topic of sexual ethics; yet, he launched into an excursus on Christians and the public courts (5:12—6:11). The gist of this passage is that, since the saints will eventually, along with God, judge the universe, they should certainly be able to handle their own internal disciplinary needs. Even the least distinguished of them should be capable enough for worldly cases (6:4). This includes cases like that of the man who committed incest (5:12–13), but it also includes every kind of civil dispute among Christians: "It is already a loss to you that you have suits against one another. Why do you not rather suffer injustice? Why do you not rather suffer deprivation? But you are actually committing injustice and depriving others—and brothers and sisters at that" (6:7–8). What seems to the modern reader to be an abrupt shift of subject matter will not have seemed so to Paul. The case of incest was part of a larger picture in which Christians were wronging one another in a variety of property matters.

Paul had not forgotten that sexual ethics was his principal topic here, for he returned to them at once, deliberately placing them in the context of a broader property ethic. This passage is framed in his "indicative-imperative" style: this is who you *are,* and therefore this is how you *must* (or, in this case, must not) behave.[8]

> Or do you not know that unjust people will not inherit God's reign? Do not be deceived. Neither those given to harlotry nor idolators nor adulterers nor *malakoi* nor *arsenokoitai* nor thieves nor greedy people *(pleonektēs)*—not drunkards, not slanderers, not snatchers—will inherit God's reign. And these things some of you were; but you have been washed, but you have been hallowed, but you have been set right by the name of the Lord Jesus Christ and by the Spirit of our God. (6:9–11)

This list combines the terminology Paul applied to the case of incest *(porneia;* 5:1) with the other categories of people he directed the church to shun (5:9–11) and a few new ones as well: adulterers, thieves, and the difficult *malakoi* and *arsenokoitai* whom we discussed above (pp. 117–20). Since this list reinforces Paul's admonition to suffer injustice

---

8. Unless Paul meant to contradict his other assurances that those who belong to Christ cannot be lost, he presumably did not mean that the baptized person who reverted to behavior inconsistent with the gospel would be damned. Indeed, the exclusion of the man who was committing incest looked forward to his eventual salvation (1 Cor. 5:5; cf. 3:10–15). Paul's ethics are subtle and were open to misunderstanding already in his own time. It appears, however, that for him the ultimate sanction of ethics was not the threat of damnation, but the danger of being found incoherent with the salvation one has already been given by grace.

and deprivation rather than make use of the public courts, the passage can only make sense if all the sexual offenders listed in it are to be understood as offenders against property, whether that of their own family or that of others.[9]

What was not acceptable was sexual activity that was entirely self-regarding (i.e., without regard for one's place in and duty to one's family) or that which preyed on the sexual property of others. Given this context, it is natural to understand *malakos*, as in widespread early Christian usage, as meaning "masturbator."[10] It need not define every act of masturbation as sinful; that would be more in the character of a purity rule. Like the colloquial English "jerk-off," however, it could define the person so devoted to the pursuit of private pleasure as to be devoid of responsibility. *Arsenokoitēs*, as suggested above (pp. 127–28) in our discussion of 1 Timothy, could refer to the male, slave or free, who used his sexual attractiveness to ingratiate himself with a rich and elderly lover in the hope of receiving a substantial legacy, thus replacing more legitimate heirs. These suggestions about the meaning of the two terms are, I fear, as speculative as any others, but they have the merit of fitting particularly well the present context.

Prostitution

The term *malakos*, in particular, looks forward to the next topic—males in the Christian community who make use of prostitutes. We have seen that Proverbs condemned this practice as a waste of family resources. Paul's approach to the subject was related but more complex. Very likely, the libertine party at Corinth had adopted some slogans of the Cynic

9. Ariès ("St. Paul and the Flesh," 36–39) combines this list with the one found in 1 Tim. 1:9–10 and produces a more complex analysis. This approach is dubious in light of the probable difference in authorship and occasion of the two passages. For the Corinthians passage, he seems to suggest a division into four diminishing categories: sins against God (idolatry), sins against the flesh (harlotry, adultery, and whatever the *malakoi* and *arsenokoitai* do), sins against property (theft, greed, drunkenness, "snatching") and sins of the tongue (slander). It will be seen, however, that this requires a substantial rearrangement of the list. If one wishes to analyze the exact order of terms, the Ten Commandments offer a better model. Harlotry and idolatry are sins against the commandments to have only one God and to eschew images. Paul then jumps to the area of his immediate concern, the commandments against adultery and theft, which are closely related to each other; and he concludes with two or three elements related to the commandments against false witness and covetousness.

10. Cf. Boswell, *Christianity, Social Tolerance, and Homosexuality,* 363–64. For a good summary of the ancient notion of "softness," sometimes mistakenly translated into English as "effeminacy," see Veyne's *History of Private Life,* 178–79; it was compounded of indolence and a propensity toward sensuality.

moralists such as "All things are permitted" and "Food is for the belly and the belly for food" (with the additional implication that sexual intercourse is as uncomplicated an expression of natural desires as eating is).[11] Paul recognized that these slogans bore a certain resemblance, on the surface, to his own teaching, which held that, before God, the Torah no longer governed human existence and that there was nothing intrinsically wrong with eating food sacrificed to idols. That may, indeed, have encouraged the Corinthian libertines to adopt them.

Paul could not, however, accept them in an unqualified way, and he began his discussion by quoting them and modifying them:

> "All things are permitted me"—but not all are profitable. "All things are permitted me"—but I for one will not be made free with by any of them. "Foods are for the belly and the belly for foods"—and God will destroy both the one and the others. The body, however, is not for harlotry but for the Lord, and the Lord for the body; and God has raised the Lord and will raise us, too, through his power. (6:12–14)

At first sight, it might appear that "body" here is a euphemism for "genitals," since it is in opposition to "belly;" but that cannot be true. Not only would it be quite different from Paul's usual use of the term "body," but there is no reason for him to contrast one part of the body (the stomach) with another in terms of destruction and resurrection. The whole of the existing body will die and, in that sense, be destroyed; and the resurrection body, as Paul will say later in this letter (15:35–44), is in some sense radically different from the body that goes into the grave.

The term "body," for Paul, normally refers to the unity and wholeness of the human being.[12] The distinction here, then, must be between foods as something relatively peripheral to the person as a whole—something which does not involve one's full humanity—and sex which is more nearly central. What belongs to Christ now and what God will raise from death is the whole person:

> Do you not know that your bodies are members of Christ? So then, am I to take Christ's members and make them members of a harlot? May it not happen! Do you not know that the person who cleaves to a harlot is one body [with her]? "For the two," it says, "will become one flesh." But the person who cleaves to the Lord is one spirit [with him]. (6:15–17)

The Christian's body already belongs to Christ, whether this is sym-

---

11. Cf. Conzelmann, *1 Corinthians*, 108–10.
12. Cf. Robinson, *The Body*, 26–33.

bolized as the unity of Christ's body or as a kind of marital union with Christ. All sexual expression, then, must take Christ's ownership into account.

Sex with a prostitute might seem to establish no relationship at all beyond the brief one required for the satisfaction of desire. Paul, however, in a daring interpretation of Gen. 2:24, claimed that every sexual act between a man and woman established a union of flesh like that of marriage, though not, apparently, indissoluble. In other words, the prostitute and the man who has used her actually belong to each other for the duration of their sexual intercourse, though not beyond. The man who rented the prostitute no doubt thought of this "ownership" as being entirely on his side. Not so, according to Paul; for he also becomes her property and makes his body members of her. In Paul's own terminology, the relationship thus established is "one body"; but in the terminology of Genesis, it is a relationship of "one flesh." Since, for Paul, "flesh" referred not to the whole person but to that in us which resists God, Paul could also argue that the union created by an isolated sexual act is animated by "flesh" and therefore pulls one away from God. The believer's bodily union with Christ, on the other hand, is not "one flesh," but "one spirit." That is to say, it is animated by the principle which draws one toward God.

Paul was insisting that the man who had intercourse with a prostitute was not unchanged by that act. While the act was not strictly unlawful (at least, for the man), it was destructive of one's spirit, that is, one's relation to Christ and to God:

> Flee from harlotry. Every sin that a person commits is outside the body, but the man who uses harlots is sinning against his own body. Or do you not know that your body is temple of the Holy Spirit that is in you, which you have from God, and you do not belong to yourselves? For you were bought at a price; so glorify God with your body. (6:18–20)

Where Proverbs discouraged a man from using prostitutes because he belonged to his family, Paul discouraged it because he belongs to God. The body, the person as a whole, is the Spirit's temple, into which other forms of worship must not be introduced. One might well ask, then, whether the implication of this line of reasoning is not, finally, to forbid sexual intercourse altogether. The answer, as we shall see, was more complicated than that.

Marriage

There were people in the Corinthian church who would have been happy with a complete rejection of sexual intercourse—who, indeed, were advocating it already, though we do not know on what grounds. The church had sent Paul a letter with enquiries about several matters of outstanding concern. The first of these, it seems, was exactly this question. Paul began his answer by agreeing with abstinence in principle,[13] but discouraging most people from putting it into practice:

> Now, concerning the things about which you wrote—it is a good thing for a man not to touch a woman, but on account of the harlotries let each man have his own wife and each woman have her own husband. Let the husband give to the wife what is due, and in the same way the wife to the husband. The wife does not have authority over her own body, but the husband; in the same way, too, the husband does not have authority over his own body, but the wife. Do not deprive each other, unless perhaps by agreement for a fixed time, to have leisure for prayer—and then come back together so that Satan will not put you to the test on account of your lack of self-control. I am saying this by way of permission, not command. I want all people to be as I am myself, but each person has his own gift *(charisma)* from God, one this and another that. (7:1–7)

Paul will make his reasons for prizing celibacy explicit later. For the moment, the important point was that there was nothing intrinsically wrong with sexual intercourse. If Paul regarded celibacy as in some sense preferable, he also regarded it as a *charisma* (gift) from God, given only to certain individuals. Paul taught that such gifts were given the individual for the benefit of the church, not as a sign of one's own moral superiority (1 Corinthians 12). If a person's sexual drive, then, is too strong to permit celibacy, that only means that his or her gifts lie elsewhere.[14]

For those who had not received the gift of celibacy, Paul had to specify circumstances for sexual intercourse that would not be in conflict with Christ's ownership of the Christian's body. He found them in Christian

13. "It is a good thing for a man not to touch a woman" is so absolute a formula that it may be the teaching of the Corinthian ascetics rather than of Paul himself. Cf. Phipps, "Paul's Attitude," 127–29. Whatever its origin, however, he cites it as if he agreed with it before he begins his modification of it—a reasonable rhetorical approach to a volatile situation.

14. A subsidiary point in this passage is worthy of mention: the allowance for sexual abstinence is to give *leisure* for prayer, not to purify the couple for it. In other words, it is a deliberate simplification of life, not a disguised purity observance.

marriage. The distinctively Christian thing in Paul's description of marriage was his careful balancing of the husband's sexual ownership of the wife with an equivalent ownership of the husband by the wife. Paul's standards are related to those set by Jesus when he prohibited divorce and expanded the definition of adultery, but they differ in emphasizing the sexual element in marriage. Sexual desire, according to Paul, is a fact of human life that must be reckoned with intelligently and faithfully; it is not to be ignored or rejected. Marriage exists for the sake of mutual sexual satisfaction; and neither partner can pursue a sexual course that does not involve the other, whether celibacy or the use of prostitutes, since each is property of the other.

Having set forth this conception of marriage, Paul proceeds to apply it to three distinct groups: those without any marital attachments, those already married, and those who are betrothed. Paul begins, then, by encouraging the unmarried and widowed to remain as he is; "but," he says, "if they do not possess self-control, let them marry, for it is better to marry than to be on fire" (7:9). While this may seem a poor recommendation of marriage, it is significant that Paul recognized the satisfaction of sexual desire as a legitimate and sufficient reason for entering into it.[15] The reason for such a position is not immediately clear, but we shall see that it had to do with Paul's convictions about the nearness of the eschaton. Continuation of one's family could no longer be the prime reason for marriage, and he was actually constructing a new justification for it in terms of sexual desire and the reign of God.

The second group Paul addressed were the married. To them, his advice was basically, "Stay as you are." He enunciated the general principle behind this advice only at the end of the section he devoted to them:

> Only let each person proceed just as the Lord has apportioned, as the Lord called. And this is how I arrange things in all the churches. Was someone circumcised when called? Let him not be surgically altered to restore a foreskin. Was someone called in the uncircumcised state? Let him not get circumcised. Circumcision is nothing and uncircumcision is nothing, but keeping God's commandments [is what is important]. Let every person stay in the calling in which he or she was called. Were you a slave when called? Let it be no concern to you; but even if you can become free, rather make use. For the slave called in the Lord is the Lord's freedperson; likewise, the

---

15. Yarbrough (*Not Like the Gentiles*, 22–23) notes that some rabbis taught that marriage was necessary because of the male passions; but even they presented it only as the alternative to impurity. Paul makes it the proper response to sexual frustration.

free person called is Christ's slave. You were bought at a price; do not become slaves of human beings. Let each person stay by God, brothers and sisters, in the state in which he or she was called. (7:17–24)

That there is no overt reference to marital status in this passage occasions no difficulty, for the analogy between slaves and other family members was familiar. Paul is emphasizing that sexual and other property matters should be left as much as possible exactly as they were at the point when one became a Christian.

Paul's point—an important one for him, as it is how he arranges matters in all the churches—is that, even though one status may be "better" than another, either in terms of the Torah or in social terms or even (as is the case of celibacy) in his own reckoning, one cannot recommend oneself to God by changing one's status. Just as the change from uncircumcision to circumcision implied a doubt of the sufficiency of grace (see above, p. 100), so any change in manner of life, such as a change from marriage to celibacy, could easily be an unnecessary and unfaithful attempt to make oneself more acceptable in God's sight. We might object that the slave was probably seeking only a more dignified and secure future; but, as we shall see, Paul assumed that there was no true future this side of the eschaton, only a brief, transitional present.[16]

It is possible that Paul allowed exceptions to this principle in cases where they might serve the good of the church or the proclamation of the gospel. He suggested in his letter to Philemon that he would like him to forgive his runaway slave Onesimus, now a convert of Paul's, and send him back to help Paul in his work; and it has long been argued that he was even hinting that Philemon should emancipate Onesimus for this purpose.[17] Again, Luke tells us that Paul had circumcised Timothy, whose mother was Jewish, so as to make him a more acceptable member of his entourage when he was working in Jewish communities (Acts 16:1–3). The principle held, however, wherever it was not overridden by missionary needs. Given that the initial subject of the whole of chapter 7 was sexual abstinence, Paul was asserting his principle of

16. This remains the simplest reading of the passage. I suspect that the effort to interpret "rather make use" as meaning "grasp the opportunity of freedom" rather than the more obvious "remain a slave" is prompted by embarrassment that the great apostle should have dismissed the legitimate grievances of slaves so lightly. *Mallon* ("rather"), of course, creates a contrast with something preceding it; and the *ei kai* ("even if") of the immediately preceding clause underlines it so emphatically as to make almost inescapable that this is the source of the contrast.

17. E.g., Moule, *Colossians and Philemon*, 177.

stability here in order to undercut any idea that married believers might "do better," either spiritually or socially, by separating from their spouses.

For Christians married to other Christians, the tradition of Jesus' teaching was already clear: "For those who are married, I direct—not I, but the Lord—that a wife not be separated from her husband (and even if she is, let her remain unmarried or be reconciled to the husband) and that husband not divorce wife" (7:10–11). Although Paul did not cite the exact words of the tradition here, we can see that he knew its substance in a form closely related to the one found in the Sermon on the Mount: "Every man who divorces his wife except for reason of *porneia* makes her commit adultery, and whoever marries a divorced woman is committing adultery" (Matt. 5:32).[18] This version of Jesus' dictum says that remarriage on the part of the divorced woman constitutes adultery, but, like Paul, says nothing about remarriage on the part of the man who has divorced her. Paul probably alluded with some precision to the formula as he knew it, for elsewhere in this discussion, he himself observed an exact balance between the rights of husband and wife. Accordingly, the imbalance here is unlikely to be of his own creating. Paul's interest in the tradition, however, was somewhat different from that of the Synoptic evangelists. They used it to assert the inherent indissolubility of marriage and so deprived the husband of full property rights in the wife. Paul used it rather to discourage all changes of status after conversion. What is at issue for him is not so much the institution of marriage itself as how one ought to live in the last days.

In Paul's churches, however, a good many of his converts were married to non-Christians, who would scarcely have acknowledged a saying of Jesus as authoritative. What is more, Paul had himself drawn a sufficiently trenchant distinction between those inside the church and those outside that his converts might be tempted to think that they had a duty to withdraw from intimate association with outsiders. In this case, too, however, Paul was convinced that people should remain, if possible, as they were:

18. Paul's passive verb, "be separated," implies that the husband would be the initiator of any divorce; and only remarriage of the divorced woman occasions adultery. Murphy-O'Connor ("The Divorced Woman," 601–6) has argued that Paul did not, in fact, feel bound consistently by Jesus' dictum, but applied it pastorally according to principles that Murphy-O'Connor does not make explicit. Paul may indeed have been inconsistent, but perhaps one should not move to that conclusion without exhausting alternative explanations.

And to the others say I, not the Lord: if any brother has a nonbelieving wife and she consents to live with him, let him not divorce her; and if any woman has a nonbelieving husband and he consents to live with her, let her not divorce her husband. For the nonbelieving husband is hallowed in the wife and the nonbelieving wife in the brother—since otherwise your children would be unclean, but as it is they are holy. If, however, the nonbeliever separates, so be it. The brother or sister is not enslaved in such cases, but God has called you in peace. For how do you know, wife, whether you will save your husband? Or how do you know, husband, whether you will save your wife? (7:12–16)

Paul's principal concern was that the Christian partner in such a relationship should not directly terminate it. While admitting that Jesus' own prohibition of divorce and remarriage could not apply in so unequal a situation, Paul argued that there was a benefit to the children and to the nonbelieving spouse which made the marriage worth preserving.

The nature of the benefit Paul had in mind is not immediately obvious. He describes it, in part, in language borrowed from the purity ethic. The children of a mixed marriage are "holy," but in the event of a divorce they would become "unclean." It is impossible to give any meaning to this statement on the level of the Levitical purity codes, since the Christian spouse might as easily be Gentile as Jewish and, in that case, unclean herself or himself.[19] The language must be metaphorical; it seems to presume that the children were not themselves Christians and would remain with the nonbelieving parent after a divorce. Since the church at Corinth was still only a few years old at this time, one may guess that the marriages in question were not recent matches between Christian and non-Christian partners, but existing marriages in which only one spouse had been converted. The nonbelieving partner, then, would have reason to claim that the other's conversion had supervened upon their prior contract for a normal Jewish or Gentile marriage. But

19. For a similar usage, see 2 Cor. 6:14—7:1. Paul tells his audience not to be "crossyoked with nonbelievers"; that is, he uses the image of different species of animals being crossbred (something forbidden in Lev. 19:19, with the same unusual vocabulary in the LXX that Paul uses here) to admonish Christians against inappropriate association with nonbelievers. Such associations could include intermarriage; but if the passage is genuinely Pauline and is in its correct context, then it must be an exhortation to the Corinthians to withdraw from rival teachers, for it is preceded and followed by appeals to "make room for" Paul in their affections (6:11–13; 7:2). In a similar vein, Yarbrough (*Not Like the Gentiles*, 88–93) understands Paul, in 1 Corinthians 5—6, to be stressing the purity of the Christian community. This would refer metaphorically, however, to the distinctiveness of the community and not to a renewed law of physical purity.

what would be missing for the children after a divorce? Some edifying influence the Christian parent might be presumed to have on them? Perhaps. A more concrete explanation, however, can be offered by comparison with what Paul had to say about the matter of prostitution.

Paul objected to Christians visiting prostitutes because the body that belonged to the Lord could not also belong to a prostitute. That objection might seem to be equally valid as against mixed marriages; and Paul did, in fact, say later that widows might remarry "only in the Lord" (7:39). (Consistency would demand that he also forbid the contracting of mixed marriages for the young, but the subject never comes up). The existing marriage, however, which became a mixed marriage only by conversion of one spouse, was another matter. The Christian spouse "belonged" both to Christ and to a nonbeliever. This created an impossible tension, which Paul apparently resolved by declaring that, actually, in these cases, Christ's ownership extended through the believing partner to the whole family. Thus, the children are "holy," because they are, at one remove, part of that community that is the Spirit's temple (6:19). Paul even applied the same principle, though more hesitantly, to the nonbelieving spouse: "How do you know whether you will save your husband or wife?"

If the Christian allegiance of the believer, however, became intolerable for the nonbelieving spouse, that was another matter. The Christian was not "enslaved" and could accept a divorce initiated by the other party. Paul was not explicit as to whether the Christian was then free to remarry, but the likelihood is that that is what he intended. After all, if the other partner were determined on a divorce, the Christian might not be able to refuse it. If there was any point in saying that the believer was not "enslaved," it has to have meant that such a one was free both to consent to the divorce and to continue a normal life after it. While this may seem to fly in the face of the demands of Jesus cited earlier, it was in tune with the emphasis found in the Gospels that laws exist to enhance a faithful human life, not to place burdens on it: "The Sabbath was made for humanity, not humanity for the Sabbath."

For Paul, then, the unmarried were free to marry, though he advocated celibacy, and the married were not to seek any change in their status. There remained, however, an uncomfortable middle zone between these two groups—the betrothed. These would have been younger people whose families had contracted marriages for them, but who were just reaching the age when it would be normal for the marriage to be consummated. Though they were not married, they were obligated to one another—and to one another's families—in a way that was only just short of marriage. Were they, like the unmarried, to be encouraged to remain celibate? Or were they, like the married, to be admonished to stick by their existing obligations? Either way, they must inevitably make some change, since betrothal was never intended to be a permanent status.

Paul seems to have regarded this as a thoroughly awkward situation, but sought to resolve it by discouraging further betrothals and by permitting those already betrothed either to proceed with the marriage or to prolong the betrothal indefinitely:

> Now, concerning the virgins, I have no command of the Lord, but I give a considered opinion as one who has received mercy from the Lord to be faithful. I consider, then, that what really is good in light of the imminent distress—that it is good for one to be as one is. Are you bound to a wife? Do not seek dissolution of the relationship. Are you unattached? Do not seek a wife. But even if you do marry, you have not sinned, and if the virgin marries, she has not sinned. But such will have tribulation for the flesh, and I [am trying to] spare you. . . . But if anyone considers that he is behaving in a disgraceful way toward his virgin, if he is a person of strong passions and this is how it needs to be, let him do what he wishes; he is not sinning; let them get married. The man who has taken a firm stand in his heart, however, being under no compulsion, and has authority over his own will and has come in his own heart to a determination to keep his virgin, he will do well. Thus, the man who marries his virgin does well and the one who does not will do better. (7:25–28, 36–38)

Throughout this long and awkward passage, Paul assumed that the man alone would make the final decision to proceed with the marriage or not—a breech of his usual insistence on mutuality, but perhaps an acknowledgment of existing social practice. He offered the man the option of "keeping his virgin," which apparently meant that he would continue the betrothal indefinitely. One may guess this would mean taking on a husband's responsibilities in most respects, for the bride's family would scarcely have smiled on the prospect of her living a cloistered existence under their wing for the rest of her life. The other choice was to proceed with the marriage. Paul expected the man to decide on the basis of his own sexual needs.[20] If he was in an unforced

---

20. So my translation above. It is also possible to translate, in v. 36, "if she is getting beyond marriageable age and this is how it needs to be." No certainty seems possible, but the passage otherwise shows no particular concern for the woman's desires in the matter.

control in the matter, he could do what Paul most approved—remain celibate. But if not, Paul was at pains to insist that sexual intercourse was not sinful and that marriage was its appropriate context.

Since Paul was abrogating existing agreements when he allowed an indefinitely continued betrothal, it was necessary for him to state very clearly why he thought celibacy a good thing. He did not base his positive evaluation of it on a rejection of sexual desire or sexual intercourse as such. On what did he base it, then? On the nearness of the reign of God, whose advent was expected to be preceded by a time of tribulation for the righteous. Celibacy was to give those who practiced it a kind of single-mindedness that would make this period easier to get through:

> [The married] will have tribulation for the flesh, and I [am trying to] spare you. This is what I mean, brothers: the allotted time is limited from now on, so that even those who have wives are to be as if they did not and those who mourn as if they did not and those who rejoice as if they did not and those who buy as if they did not take possession and those who use the world as if they did not use it up. For the form of this world is passing away. And I want you to be free from care. The unmarried man cares about the Lord's business, how to please the Lord; but the married man cares about the world's business, how to please his wife—and he is divided. And the unmarried woman and the virgin cares about the Lord's business, to be holy both in body and in spirit; but the married woman cares about the world's business, how to please her husband. I am saying this for your own good, not to throw a noose over you, but with a view to [your being] presentable and constant toward the Lord without distraction. (7:28–35)

For Paul, the value of celibacy was directly related to the chaotic and troubling times which had already begun and would lead shortly to the end of this world and the inbreaking of the reign of God. Those who were divided, being still entangled in the world's business, would have much trouble. The ideal was to be able to wait on the Lord without further distraction. Paul did not therefore advocate an abandonment of existing marriages or of one's livelihood; yet, even in these, one must be alert not to treat them as of ultimate importance. Hence, Paul was reluctant to see believers change their existing state, whether in terms of marriage or personal freedom or ethnic identity, since such changes implied too great a concern for the world's business. The one exception was for those whose sexual desires were too strong to permit a choice of celibacy. Since resort to prostitutes was not consistent with Christ's ownership of the believer, Paul encouraged these people to marry and affirmed that to do so, though not the best choice in a perilous time, was entirely innocent.[21]

Summary

First Corinthians 5—7 shows Paul working out the implications of a limited number of basic principles related to sexual property. Paul began with the existing sense of sexual property. He took the existing definitions of incest (at least, where Jewish and Gentile definitions agreed) for granted. He freely used the language of possessions in speaking about the relation of husband and wife. He condemned adultery as a property offense, and he strongly opposed resorting to prostitutes. In all this, his teaching is not materially different from that of the ancient Israelite tradition. Still, what was centrally important for Paul was not that tradition, but another kind of property relationship which took precedence over it.

All Christians belonged to Christ, and all other forms of ownership must be made to accommodate this overarching reality. This theme was not entirely new with Paul. His habit of speaking about women as the equals of men in the matter of sexual property is comparable to the tradition of Jesus' teaching as found in the Synoptic Gospels; and his insistence on the priority of "the Lord's business" is comparable to the demands Jesus made in terms of discipleship. Still, Paul presents these ideas in terms of his own coherent framework, which begins with the principle that Christ owns the believer and insists that sexual life acknowledge that. Sex with prostitutes will not afford such an acknowledgment, but sex with a believing spouse will and is therefore a good thing. Even if the spouse is unconverted, the stability of the married relationship means that Christ's ownership can be thought of as extending, at one remove, to the nonbelievers in the family. New marriages, however, are to be contracted only "in the Lord." Finally, belonging to Christ means that the Christian will soon be passing through a period of

21. Balch ("1 Cor 7:32–35," 398–435) has illuminated the Stoic background of Paul's language about marriage. Yet, he is in error, I think, in proceeding as if the eschatological context in which Paul uses this language were not the primary determinant of its meaning. In seeking to maintain that Paul did not prefer celibacy to marriage, he, with others, ignores the plain sense of v. 38:". . . the man who does not marry will do better." The chief desideratum for Paul, however, is that one should remain as one is, whether married or not. On the eschatological element in Paul's ethics, see Schrage, *Ethics of the New Testament*, 181–86, 222–29.

trials which will conclude the timespan of this world and usher in the reign of God. Insofar as marriage means attachment to family and therefore to the values of this world, it is—like circumcision, social status, or business—a distraction from the Christian's true loyalties. Accordingly, Paul reckoned it inferior to celibacy, not as being sinful, but as representing a danger to single-mindedness in the eschaton.

WOMEN AND FAMILY LIFE

Despite all that has been said, Paul, in some ways, was quite conservative—perhaps uncritically so—in his appraisal and acceptance of contemporary family life, particularly as regards the status of slaves and women. When he was speaking most self-consciously, he asserted the equality of women, as we have seen. In 1 Corinthians 7, we have found him balancing virtually every statement of the husband's authority over the wife with an equivalent acknowledgment of the wife's authority over the husband. This had its foundation not only in the tradition of Jesus' sayings about divorce, but also in the early Christian conviction that women were capable of praying and learning as well as men. Thus, Paul allowed a married couple to refrain from sexual intercourse temporarily because it would allow *both* of them leisure for prayer (7:5).

Paul expressed the principle involved with uncompromising clarity when he was combating the pressure on his Gentile churches in Galatia to accept circumcision: "All of you that have been baptized into Christ have put on Christ. There is neither Jew nor Greek; there is neither slave nor free person; there is no male and female. For you are all one person in Christ Jesus; and if you belong to Christ, then you are seed of Abraham, heirs by promise" (Gal. 3:27–29).[22] When Paul used this formula elsewhere, however, he omitted the reference to "male and female" (1 Cor. 12:12–13; Col. 3:11), and his attitude toward women in the church was not always so egalitarian as in the matter of marriage. Later in 1 Corinthians, for example, he forbade women to speak in the assemblies, "for they are not permitted to speak, but let them be subordinate, just as the law also says. And if they want to learn something, let them ask their own husbands at home, for it is shameful for a woman to speak in an assembly" (14:34–35).[23]

22. Since this formula was probably pre-Pauline, it may represent a period in the Gentile mission more radical than Paul. Cf. Schüssler Fiorenza, *In Memory of Her,* 208–12.

23. These verses are located after 14:40 in some manuscripts of 1 Corinthians, leading some to question their authenticity. They may, indeed, be a later interpolation, which would make Paul somewhat less inconsistent with the principles of baptism that he inherited. The evidence for rejecting them, however, is not strong.

Paul made an exception in the case of women who were "praying and prophesying" (1 Cor. 11:3–16)—if, indeed, he was not referring to purely private behavior in this passage, which does not mention the assembly. Yet, he insisted that, in doing so, they must wear a veil (or perhaps wear their hair in a certain way) as sign of their subordinate status. On behalf of this rule, he used arguments that are in sharp contrast to the Galatian formula and even to his treatment of marriage. For example, in the opening words of the passage, he says: "I want you to know that every man's head is Christ, but a woman's head is the man, and Christ's head is God" (11:3). Or again: "It is not man from woman, but woman from man; for in fact man was not created for woman's sake, but woman for man's sake" (11:8–9). Paul must have sensed that this argument was in conflict with what he held elsewhere, for, having advanced it, he at once pulled back: "Except that there is no woman without man nor man without woman in the Lord; for just as the woman is from the man, so also the man is through the woman—and all things are from God" (11:11–12). The true point of conflict perhaps comes to expression only in Paul's concluding statement: "If anyone chooses to be quarrelsome, *we* have no such custom, nor do the assemblies of God" (11:16). Paul found the existing Corinthian practice peculiar and wished to bring them into line with churches elsewhere.[24]

The freedom which the women of the Corinthian church enjoyed was unexampled in Paul's experience, however much it might seem to be implicit in his own teaching. He could not very well forbid them to prophesy. That would seem to be resisting the Spirit, forbidden by Paul elsewhere (1 Thess. 5:19–20). In any case, prophesying by women had a venerable history in Israel and, according to Luke, had been a part of Christian practice from the beginning (Acts 2:1–21). Paul was convinced, however, that women in the church were still, as it were, metaphysically dependent on men. He could therefore forbid them to function in their own right in the assemblies and could demand that, when the Spirit chose a woman to prophesy, she do so in garb that expressed her subordinate status.

I have suggested elsewhere that this inconsistency reflects the sacral nature of equality in the early Christian church.[25] Women and men were fully equal as recipients of baptism and the Lord's Supper but seldom

24. For a more positive reading of this passage in relation to the equality of women, see Schüssler Fiorenza, *In Memory of Her,* 228–30.
25. Countryman, "Christian Equality," 116–27.

outside that context. Paul's "no male and female" was part of a formula that defined the meaning of baptism; the presence of women at the assemblies in Corinth shows that they were participating in the Lord's Supper, which took place there (11:18). In prophesying, women were exercising a gift of the Spirit which could not be denied. Yet, as Paul argued in another context, prophetic spirits were subject to the prophets (14:32–33), and this allowed the churches to specify when, where, and in what garments women might prophesy. Thus, even in the matter of prophecy, Paul was able to justify treating women as less than fully equal.

Why, then, was Paul so careful to formulate his teaching on marriage in a way that emphasized the equal and inviolable ownership of both spouses? We must note that he did so only in the case of believers who were already married to one another. In the case of mixed marriages, Christ's ownership of the believing spouse reached out through her or him to the rest of the household, but not in any permanent way, since divorce could take place. In the case of Christians who were betrothed, Paul acknowledged no rights on the part of the female; the male alone was to make the decision about whether to proceed with the marriage— and he was to make it on the basis of his own sexual needs. It appears, then, that equality in marriage was rather narrowly circumscribed, referring only to sexual rights in the most limited sense in marriages already consummated between believers. One begins to suspect that even this much egalitarianism, outside the strictly sacral sphere of the sacraments, was actually foreign to Paul's personal outlook. It may have owed its presence in his teaching entirely to the influence of the traditions of Jesus' words about divorce. To be sure, Paul referred to them (1 Cor. 7:10–11) only in their least egalitarian form; but, even in that form, the prohibition of divorce was sufficient to bring the man's unique ownership of his wife to an end.

Paul, however careful about defending these limited areas of equality, marital and sacral, and however insistent that family goals must yield to the imminence of God's reign, did not draw the conclusion that the family itself had to be reshaped. Perhaps his conviction that the eschaton was very close made projects of social reform seem pointless; or perhaps his own celibacy, in response to the eschaton, meant that family structures held no existential importance for him in any case. Whatever may be the reason, he said little or nothing about them in those of his letters that are of unquestioned authenticity. He broke this silence only in

Colossians, which, if it is truly his own and not the product of one of his followers, is unusual in several respects. For one thing, it is addressed to a church that Paul himself had neither founded nor visited personally, though it emerged from his mission through the work of Epaphras. For another, its language and theology are full of a kind of cosmic concern otherwise atypical of Paul, but which may reflect the interests of various heretical teachers who were at work at Colossae.

The Colossian heretics were probably ascetics. They told people, "Do not handle, do not taste, do not touch all the things that perish with use" (Col. 2:21–22).[26] Paul granted that such rigorism had "a rationale of wisdom in the form of will-worship and humility—severity toward the body"; but he also insisted that it was "of no value in relation to gratification of the flesh" (2:23). "Will-worship," apparently Paul's term here for asceticism, might even serve to gratify the "flesh," in Paul's sense of the word; for the flesh, being that in us which resists God, can actually seek refuge from grace in the cultivation of a righteousness of works. Paul rejected not only the works-righteousness implicit in such asceticism, but also its negative assessment of the material world—"all the things that perish with use." He considered foods, in and of themselves, to be irrelevant to salvation and sexual desire, if it were insistent, as something to be satisfied in an appropriate way.

In responding to this asceticism, Paul sought to lead the Colossian congregation back toward an ethic more consistent with his own teaching. As a good rhetorician, he started with language that appealed to their existing ascetical concerns, warning them against "harlotry, impurity, passion, lust [literally, evil desire]"; but he concluded the list, ". . . and greed (*pleonexia*), which is idolatry," thus pulling it into the orbit of "purity of the heart" (Col. 3:5). He followed this with another list of vices, this time of a more social nature ("anger, fury, wickedness, blasphemy, shameful speech"), and then concluded, "Do not lie to one another" (3:8–9). Finally, he introduced a list of contrary virtues to be cultivated: "compassionate feelings, goodness, humility, gentleness, long-suffering," forbearance, forgiveness, "and, above all, love" (3:12–14).

26. Though uncommon, this is the simplest translation of the passage. It is usually avoided because it appears to be nonsense; but it is fully intelligible as a deliberate exaggeration, on Paul's part, of ascetic rules designed to keep one separate from selected or representative elements of the material world. "Perishable," here, is being equated with "evil." The first prohibition of the series ("Do not handle") could refer to sexual intercourse; cf. Schweizer, *Colossians*, 166–67.

This effort to lead the congregation away from asceticism and toward a more social understanding of virtue formed the context for Paul's treatment of family life. Asceticism would have undercut the family even more completely than the teaching of Jesus and Paul, since it wanted not just to subordinate sex to the reign of God but to reject it as intrinsically evil. Paul responded by reaffirming traditional Greco-Roman household mores.[27]

> Wives, be subject to your husbands, as is appropriate in the Lord.
> Husbands, love your wives and do not grow bitter toward them.
> Children, obey your parents in all respects, for this is well-pleasing in the Lord.
> Parents, do not goad your children, so that they will not grow dispirited.
> Slaves, obey in all respects your lords according to flesh, not in outward appearance as if you were pleasing human beings, but fearing the Lord in simplicity of heart. Whatever you do, work from the heart as for the Lord and not for human beings, knowing that from the Lord you will receive the inheritance as your reward. Be slaves of the Lord Christ, for the unjust person will get back the injustice committed and there is no favoritism.
> Lords, practice justice and equity toward your slaves, knowing that you, too, have a Lord in heaven. (Col. 3:18—4:1)

Nothing in this passage would have seemed new or unusual, except perhaps for the reassurance offered slaves of an eventual righting of the imbalance. Note that nothing comparable is offered to wives.

The great question is why Paul should have bothered to say it at all, since he did not think it necessary to do so in other letters. The principal answer offered in the letter is the one already suggested—that Paul was combating an antimaterial asceticism by reaffirming the traditional household. There may have been another reason as well. Having urged the Colossians to pray for themselves and for him, Paul continued: "Conduct yourselves with wisdom toward the outsiders, buying up what time there is. Let your speech always be gracious, seasoned with salt, so that you will know how you must answer each person individually" (Col. 4:5–6). The concern manifested here for public opinion would not have been without some cause. Ascetic teaching that forbade sexual intercourse could create, by its disruption of family life, serious public antagonisms, such as those which occasioned the near-fatal misadventures of Thecla in the second-century romance called *Acts of Paul*. Paul's reinforcement of traditional family life and his concern for prudence in

---

27. For the background of this and similar New Testament lists of household duties, see Balch, *Let Wives Be Submissive,* 21–62.

relationships with outsiders were parallel ways of protecting a community that was already emerging into an unwelcome notoriety.

The associate of Paul who drafted Ephesians appears to have used Colossians as a model. Since Ephesians is of a more general character— perhaps originally a circular letter, not addressed to any single church— it does not speak to the specific problems of asceticism and public opinion that were so prominent at Colossae; and partly for this reason, it has the effect of making the conservatism of its borrowed family ethic seem more a matter of principle and less one of temporary needs. The author enlarged on the relatively brief formulas of Colossians. In the matter of the wife's subordination to the husband, he added a theological justification related to those Paul used in 1 Corinthians 11 to justify his insistence that women wear veils when prophesying: "The husband is the wife's head, as Christ in turn is the church's head, being savior of the body" (Eph. 5:23). This is a doctrine of "one flesh," but without any egalitarian implications. The author also adapted Paul's image of the church as Christ's bride to provide a model for relations between spouses, returning to the "one flesh" pronouncement in Genesis to support this interpretation. He treated the Genesis passage, however, not as a direct statement about human marriage, but as a "mystery" to be understood allegorically of Christ's relationship to the church and which then, in turn, becomes a model for human marriages. The point of this exercise is not, as in Jesus' teaching, to affirm the indissolubility of marriage or the equality of the wife, but to construct a hierarchical analogy: as Christ is to church, husband is to wife. In the process, it would seem that even the degree of equality that Paul had defended in 1 Corinthians 7 has been lost.

CONCLUSIONS

Paul regarded sexual desire as a natural appetite, though one too central to human identity to be treated as casually as hunger. Christians were to restrict the satisfaction of this appetite to forms consistent with the fact that they are the property of Christ. This demanded a respect for the property of others, and Paul retained major features of the existing property code for sexuality. Adultery continued to be a serious ethical violation, and Paul was capable of becoming quite angry about a case of incest. He strongly opposed the use of prostitutes, though he did not treat it as on a par with adultery or incest. His objection to *arsenokoitai* also had a basis in respect for property. More positively, he regarded marriage "in the Lord" as normal for those Christians who did not have the gift, or *charisma*, of celibacy, but he tolerated existing mixed marriages and even found some value in them. He believed that, because of the imminence of the eschaton, celibacy was a better choice for Christians than marriage; but he was careful to avoid any implication that marriage or sexual intercourse were at all wrong in themselves.

Paul regarded women as equal to men in the receiving of baptism and the Lord's Supper and also, in a somewhat more limited way, in terms of sexual ownership. He was careful to assert that, with regard to sexual intercourse, the wife owned the husband in the same way as the husband owned the wife; and he adhered to the Christian tradition forbidding divorce, though he adapted it somewhat in dealing with betrothals and mixed marriages. Outside these rather narrow confines, he believed that women must show subordination to men, even in their exercise of the gifts of the Spirit. He thus manifested a continuing acceptance, on the whole, of the family mores common to both Jews and Gentiles of the time.

Paul's tendency to leave things as they were took on the character of a principle insofar as the imminence of the eschaton implied that working for major change, either in society or in the status of individuals, was only misplaced effort. In his earlier letters, however, he did not much trouble himself to reinforce the traditional family ethic; only in Colossians did he explicitly confirm the validity of the patriarchal household. The ascetic nature of the heresy at Colossae—its negation of the material world as such—provided the occasion for this shift in emphasis. Paul wanted to reassert the value of the material world and also to distinguish those who adhered to his teaching from those who would disrupt the family for ascetic reasons. By confirming traditional Greco-Roman family mores, he accomplished both purposes at once. The disciple of Paul who wrote Ephesians, however, converted this teaching, with the help of other Pauline motifs, into something like a principled acceptance of the very family structures which Jesus had undercut so sharply in his ministry and which the earlier Paul had apparently regarded as peripheral.

The New Testament on Sexual Property

Compared with the Gospels and the core works of the Pauline corpus, the remaining books of the New Testament have less to say about sexual ethics. As regards specific sexual acts, they share, at most, a general opposition to adultery. These works are important, however, for their ways of dealing with family life and the sexual and other hierarchies implicit in it. In this area, they reveal tensions like those we have already seen in the writings of Paul and his associates—tensions between the tradition of Jesus' egalitarianism and rejection of the family and the developing Christian acceptance of and adaptation to existing social structures. Some fall nearer to the one pole of these tensions, some to the other.

THE CHURCH AS REPLACING
THE FAMILY

1 John, 2 John, 3 John

The three letters that bear the name of John never refer unambiguously to family life; yet they are full of language expressing family relationships: fathers, brothers, and children, all of whom are "beloved." By itself, this language might not seem significant; but in a context that entirely ignores the literal family structure from which the author and his community borrowed it, it suggests that, for Johannine Christianity, the church had replaced the family, at least in theory. This shift could occasionally give rise to a peculiar way of speaking. The author, for example, wrote to Gaius: "Beloved, you are performing a faithful act in whatever you do for the brothers—and strangers at that!—who have testified to your love in the presence of the church" (3 John 5–6). The church now constituted the Christian's family, with the odd result that complete strangers might be able to claim the most intimate relationship.

The masculine gender of much of this language is notable, but need not signify any retreat from the equality of women. Since the masculine was also the common gender in the language of the day, "fathers" could serve as the equivalent of "parents," and "brothers" would be the normal way of saying "brothers and sisters." For "children," the author used terms *(teknon, teknion)* that were neuter. At the same time, he addressed one of his letters to "the elect lady and her children" (2 John 1). One cannot be sure whether he was addressing an individual Christian woman and her dependents (perhaps the church that met in her home) or whether he was personifying a church in the feminine.[1] In either case, however, he did not treat the feminine gender as intrinsically less worthy than the masculine.

James

The Epistle of James implies a similar set of attitudes. Like the Johannine letters, it makes use of the expression "brothers" with a frequency that is quite out of proportion to its length, at least by usual New Testament standards. Its author insists on a lively and practical concern for such (2:15–16) and particularly designates the care of the "unfamilied" as a central expression of religion: "Religion pure and undefiled in the presence of the God and Father is this: to take responsibility for orphans and widows in their tribulation, to keep oneself unblemished from the world" (1:27). As we have seen above (pp. 131–33), "to keep oneself unblemished" in this context probably meant to refrain from participating in angry contests for church leadership. The contrast, then, is between a man's struggle to confirm his own (and therefore his family's) standing in the Christian community and a willingness to devote himself instead to the benefit of those without influence or authority—and quite without any claim on his energies.[2]

1. The most literal interpretation is that he was addressing a woman who was patron and leader of her local Christian community. Cf. Schüssler Fiorenza, *In Memory of Her,* 248–49.
2. Cf. *Letter of Aristeas* 228, where King Ptolemy asks a Jewish sage, "To whom should one show favor?" The sage replies, "To parents, by all means, for God has in fact established a commandment of the highest importance on the matter of honor shown to par-

In the teaching of Jesus, we found that this kind of negation of family was associated with a positive view of women. That the same was true for James is evident in his habit of using female imagery or language alongside male. Even in referring to the individual Christian, where "brother" by itself would have been sufficiently clear in Greek as referring to either sex, James specified "brother or sister" (2:15). He also balanced male with female imagery in referring to God: "Every good and every perfect gift is from above, coming down from the Father of the [heavenly] lights, with whom there is no shifting or shadow of change, [who] of free will has given birth[3] to us by word of truth so that we would be a kind of firstfruits of his creatures" (1:17–18). Again, in arguing for the necessary complementarity of works and faith, James employed both a male example (Abraham's sacrifice of Isaac) and a female one: "And in the same way, too, was not Rahab the harlot justified by works when she received the messengers and hurried them off by another route?" (2:25). Except for the Gospel of Luke, such balancing of male and female is unique to James in the New Testament.

James reaffirmed the commandment against adultery. In context, however, he seems to have been less interested in the commandment for its own sake than in its rhetorical usefulness. He assumed that his audience would not have committed it, but observed that the keeping of one commandment was not the keeping of the whole law: "For the one who said, 'Do not commit adultery,' also said, 'Do not commit murder.' Now, if you do not commit adultery but you do commit murder, you have become a transgressor of law" (2:11). In the immediate context of the passage, this serves to underline James's point that showing partiality to the rich is as grave an offense as any other (2:1–10). In the larger scheme of the work, it prepares for the moment when James will call his audience "adulterers" because of the strife they perpetrate within the church (4:1–12). In due course, he will even intimate that they are, in some sense, murderers, by associating them with the rich who killed Jesus (5:1–6). Thus, for James, adultery and murder, partiality toward the rich in the church, and the crucifixion of Jesus are all on a single

---

ents. And, next, he reckons the treatment shown to friends, having described the friend as 'equal to the self.' But as for you, you do well in bringing all people into friendship with yourself." It is the unique and supererogatory goodness of a king to treat all as his friends; ordinary mortals need attend only to family and friends in the usual, more restricted sense.

3. The verb *apokyeō* is used overwhelmingly of the mother's role in procreation, not the father's.

continuum of transgression, so that the person who is guilty of one is, by extension, guilty of all. This need not mean that James regarded them all as equally grave offenses; we cannot know his teaching on that aspect of the matter. It does mean that he regarded them all equally as offenses and indications of grave deficiencies in the character of their per-petrators. James, accordingly, defends the rights of sexual property, but otherwise undermines the foundations of the ancient family by the attention he pays to the poor, the widow and orphan, and women generally.

THE CHURCH AS INCORPORATING
THE FAMILY

1 Peter

If the letters of John and James represent the antifamily end of the spectrum, 1 Peter and the Pastorals stand at the profamily end—and do so largely without benefit of the careful nuances which we found in Paul's writings. The author of 1 Peter strongly affirmed hierarchy in society at large and in the household.[4] Christians were to obey the imperial government strictly, even though they might in some sense claim to be free of it by virtue of their relationship with the one God (2:13–17). As an extension or application of this general social duty, Christian servants were to obey their owners (2:18–25). If this involved unfair hardships at the hands of a harsh master, they might take comfort in the fact that, like them, Jesus too had suffered unjustly. "In the same way, wives," the author continued, were to be subject to their husbands. Even men who were not believers might yet be converted by their wives' modest, plain, and unassuming behavior; and the women would have the benefit of knowing that they were imitating "the holy women" of old, specifically Sarah, who called Abraham her "lord" (3:1–6).

Unlike Colossians and Ephesians, 1 Peter has no directions about suitable behavior for the Christian slaveowner. This could indicate either that the author's presumed audience did not include any such or that he trusted them to behave properly without special directions. He did give directions to Christian husbands. These are less demanding than those

---

4. He did not therefore completely reject the idea of church as household; cf. Elliott, *Home for the Homeless*, 200–208. Despite Elliott's arguments, however, 1 Peter still seems to me to represent a retreat from an earlier Christian position that was less friendly to the family.

in Colossians and Ephesians but do call to mind the fact that their wives are members of the Christian community in their own right: "You husbands in the same way—live together with the female sex according to knowledge, as with a weaker vessel, apportioning honor as to those who are also co-heirs of life's grace, so as not to impede your prayers" (3:7). The "knowledge" that is to govern the husband's dealings with his wife is a double one: knowledge of her intrinsic weakness and knowledge of her status in the grace that gives life. The wife, consequently, is to be understood as a composite being, partly inferior to the husband and partly equal. Under the circumstances, he is to remain in charge, dealing with her variously as her composite character demands.[5] The goal of all his dealings with her is to keep prayer unhindered—but whose prayers? His or those of the married couple? The language does not permit of an assured answer; and one cannot be sure to what extent the Christian woman was still an active participant in the church's worship and to what extent she was now only a passive recipient of salvation.

The conservatism of these family ethics was not incidental for the author of 1 Peter, but served as part of a larger purpose to render the Christian communities as respectable as possible. "Keep your conduct good among the Gentiles, so that when they slander you as evildoers, they may see some of your good works and glorify God on the day of visitation" (2:12). Perhaps the author was partly concerned with paving the way for conversions (as in the case of Christian women with non-believing husbands), but he was also aiming to reduce the public hostility toward Christians that was threatening to break out into serious persecution (4:12–19). The first line of defense was to make it hard for outsiders to find a complaint against Christians: "And who will do you harm if you have become zealous for what is good?" (3:13). A conservative family life was one essential bulwark of respectability.[6]

The Pastoral Epistles

First Peter is not entirely without a sense of the church as replacing the family. "Love of the brothers" was still an important virtue (3:8). Yet, this was a minor theme; the main thing was to approximate the public

5. The tone of these directions is closely related to that of *Letter of Aristeas* 250–51, which gives advice about women's nature (bold, but irrational and weak) and affirms that the man must always be the "pilot."

6. Balch (*Let Wives Be Submissive*, 61–109) has shown how the passage in question is responding to specific charges typically brought against eastern religious sects and minority groups at the time.

virtues of the environing society. The Pastoral Epistles take up a somewhat more central position in the overall spectrum. Their author was still aware of the importance of women in the church's early development. He noted that Timothy had first learned his faith from his mother and grandmother (2 Tim. 1:5), and he still named Prisca (or Priscilla) before her husband (2 Tim. 4:19). He retained enough sense of the church as family to admonish Timothy that he should treat the older members as if they were his parents and the younger ones like brothers and sisters. In practical terms, however, the church was to function as family mostly for those who had no alternative, especially childless widows.

The author of 1 Timothy wished to regulate and restrict the status of "widow," which must have carried a certain prestige in the church. Officially registered widows, it seems, pledged not to remarry (5:11–12). Paul had not regarded celibacy as a virtue in and of itself, but only as a means of leaving oneself free for the Lord's business. In the Pauline tradition, then, it seems likely that the widows would have served some special role in the church's life, and this, in turn, may have attracted to their order women of influence within the community, regardless of their need for support. It is even possible that virgins were being enrolled as "widows" in this sense. The author's anxiety about the misbehavior of younger widows, whom he thought likely to become lazy gadabouts and busybodies (5:13), suggests that they were, in effect, the church's principal pastors to and among women. The author's effort to tighten regulations about the enrollment of widows was likely to diminish their numbers and convert them from an order of ministers into a class of indigents within the church.

On the whole, one must reckon this author as one unfriendly to equality between the sexes. It is not surprising, then, that he was also an advocate of traditional family life within the church. Although he did not provide a detailed listing of obligations like those in Colossians, Ephesians, and 1 Peter, he urged the same kind of household morality. Slaves were to be obedient to their owners (Titus 2:9–10), particularly if the owners were Christians (1 Tim. 6:1–2). The older women of the church[7] were to teach the younger ones to be domestic and submissive

---

7. These, in fact, may have been female "presbyters," in the official sense; but it is impossible to be sure, since the Greek expression could mean either thing. The opposition of "older" to "younger women" in the text, however, suggests a distinction purely of age, since *neōteros* was not elsewhere in the New Testament a title of office. For the opposite interpretation, see Schüssler Fiorenza, *In Memory of Her,* 289–91.

to their husbands (Titus 2:4–5). The author said nothing at all to slaveowners or to husbands about their obligations to their subordinates. Since it is clear that both categories were represented within the communities he addressed, his silence probably reflects a certain identification with them and assumption that it was the other groups who were the "problems." He saw husbands and masters as stable, moral, respectable folk, slaves and women as tending to be unruly elements.

In the case of women, at least, the author demanded their subordination not only in the household, but also in the life of the church as a whole, and he justified this demand theologically. It was the business of the men of the congregation to pray, of the women to be modest and to adorn themselves with good works (1 Tim. 2:8–10). "Let a woman learn in silence in all submission; and I do not permit a woman to teach or to have authority over a man, but to be in silence. For Adam was made first, then Eve; and Adam was not tricked, but the woman was tricked and wound up in transgression. She will be saved, however, through childbearing—if they remain in faith and hope and sanctification with moderation. This is a reliable saying" (1 Tim. 2:11—3:1). It is difficult in the extreme to coordinate this "reliable saying" with another from the same author which insists that God has saved us "not as a result of works of righteousness which we ourselves have done, but according to his own mercy through a washing of rebirth and renewal of Holy Spirit" (Titus 3:4–8). One may wonder whether he regarded Paul's doctrine of justification by grace alone through faith alone as applying only to males, while females were to be saved through bearing children with faith, hope, sanctification, and moderation. However this may be, our author has brought us a long way from Paul—not in his demand for subordination or in his appeal to the order of creation, both of which are found in Paul, but in his astonishing and unprecedented theology of childbearing.

The emphasis in the Pastoral Epistles on hierarchy was not confined to the household or to relationships between the sexes. On a world level, the author emphasized the duty of Christians to pray for the emperors and others in power (1 Tim. 2:1–4) and to be obedient to them (Titus 3:1–3). Within the church itself, there was also a clear chain of authority descending from above. Speaking in Paul's persona, the author wrote, "For God is one, and one also the mediator between God and human beings, the human being Christ Jesus, who has given himself as a ransom for many, the testimony for our own times, for which reason I have been appointed herald and apostle—I am telling the truth, I am not lying—teacher of Gentiles in faith and truth" (1 Tim. 2:5–7). Thus, God's sovereignty is manifest in the role of the emperor and his subordinates (2:1–3), in the work of Christ and the ministry of his agent Paul (2:4–7), in the priority of men over women in the ministry of the church (2:8–15), and not least in the ordering or reordering of the church's formal structure which the author of the Pastorals aimed to achieve (3:1–13).

Without question, one of the major desiderata of the author of these letters was the establishment of a regularized local ministry based on holders of office *(episkopoi, presbyteroi, diakonoi)* as opposed to charismatic figures such as apostles, prophets, and teachers. To that end, the author wrote in the person of Paul himself, addressing associates of Paul whom he represented as apostolic delegates, responsible for the regularization of ministry in specific provinces (Timothy in Asia, Titus in Crete). Qualifications for the offices in question, if summed up, amount to a description of the prosperous male householder who is respected both in the larger community and in the church and who can be counted on to administer the church's hospitality appropriately and not to misappropriate the church's funds for his own use or pleasure (1 Tim. 3:1–13; Titus 1:5–9). The job of such an officer was to keep order within the church, particularly by correcting or silencing false teachers (1 Tim. 4:1–7; Titus 1:10–11). It is possible that women as well as men were admitted to the diaconate (1 Tim. 3:11). (It is unclear whether the passage in question refers to female deacons or to the wives of men in that office.) Even if they were, however, men clearly dominated the author's scheme for the reordering of the church.

The emphasis in the Pastorals on traditional Mediterranean family life represents a thoroughgoing identification on the part of the author with the typical male householder; the hierarchy at whose peak he stood; and, indeed, the hierarchical principle as such, whether applied to family, empire, or church. Under these circumstances, of course, it would be necessary for the author also to insist on the inviolability of sexual property, and we have already seen that he did so (see above, pp. 127–28). In this regard, he was consistent with the Pauline tradition that he was developing. On the whole, however, his development of the sexual property ethic stood in marked contrast to that of Paul. His subordination of women, while anticipated to a degree in 1 Corinthians 11 and 14, lacked the balancing influence of an acknowledgment of their religious equality, as in 1 Corinthians 7. What is more, the subordination of the family as such to the reign of God disappeared altogether from this author's thought.

Hebrews

The Epistle to Hebrews evinces very little interest in sexual ethics. In relation to the family, however, it expresses an interesting ambivalence that is integral to its author's overall theological stance. On the one hand, the author of this work valued what one can only call, using Platonic terminology, the world of "being" over that of "becoming." He praised the priesthood and sacrifice of Christ because, unlike those of the Israelite cultus, they were once-for-all, singular, and eternal. In comparison, the family signified all that is temporary—subject to decay and incapable of any final achievement. It was evidence of insufficiency that the Aaronide priesthood had to be passed down from father to son in order to circumvent the reality of death (7:23–24). The scriptural model of authentic priesthood was Melchizedek, who was "without father, without mother, without genealogy, having neither beginning of days nor end of life" (7:3). Such arguments suggest a low view of the family as an institution of this passing age, already hastening to its end (1:2).

At the same time, the phenomena of this world may afford shadowy hints of the realities of the world above, which is also the age to come. Thus, the author distinguished Moses from Christ by the household analogy of servant and son (3:5–6). He explained persecution as a kind of disciplinary beating, analogous to the way a father would train his sons—indeed as proof of the Christians' legitimacy, since even an earthly father would not waste a beating on bastards (12:5–11). And he treated Esau, the *pornos* who sold his birthright, as an image of the failed Christian (12:16). It is not surprising, then, that he advocated continued respect for marriage: "Let marriage be held in honor among all of you and the marriage bed be undefiled, for God will judge *pornoi* and adulterers" (13:4). *Pornoi*, here, may mean men who use prostitutes— the literal sense of the term. On the other hand, the term may be a general one for anyone who holds family property in contempt—the sense in which the author used it in referring to Esau (12:16). In any case, the connection with property is evident from what follows immediately: "Let your manner of life not be addicted to money; be satisfied with what you have" (13:5). The author's emphasis on the imminence of the eschaton (e.g., 3:1—4:13) seems to have contributed, like that of

Paul, to a sense that one ought to leave the institutions of this world more or less untouched.

Such a tendency may have contributed to the relatively low importance of women in this epistle. In his recital of the heroes of the faith, the author mentioned Sarah, but only in passing; the most probable translation of the verse in question is "By faith, even though Sarah was barren, he [Abraham] received power for depositing seed even at [his] time of life" (11:11). In the same list, Rahab the harlot appears; but, unlike James, this author treats her as a passive recipient of rescue rather than an active participant in salvation history (11:31). He also noted that there were women who "received their dead by resurrection" (11:35). The reference is probably to the widow of Zarephath (1 Kings 17:17–24) and the Shunammite woman (2 Kings 4:18–37), but again the language treats them purely as recipients—consumers, as it were—of miracles, without acknowledging their active roles in occasioning them. The Epistle to Hebrews, then, while it is not entirely averse to the prominence of women in the Christian community nor entirely committed to family, remains more traditional in this respect than any other New Testament writings except for 1 Peter and the Pastorals.

LICENSE AND SELF-CONTROL (2 PETER)

I have noted above (p. 135) that the author of 2 Peter regarded licentiousness as a particularly serious problem in his time and as a characteristic of the false prophets and false teachers that he attacked. He predicted that "many people will follow them in their licentious acts, on account of whom the way of truth will be blasphemed; and with greed they will make you a source of profit for themselves by means of fabricated sayings" (2:2–3). Accordingly, self-control, as the opposite of license, was a fundamental Christian virtue, founded upon faith, virtue, and knowledge, and leading to patience, piety, brotherly affection, and love (1:5–7). The placement of self-control in this list suggests that the author thought of it less as an end in its own right and more as a means by which one moved from one's basic commitment to the gospel and knowledge of it toward the quasi-familial life of affection and concord in the church. Completely unbridled behavior was bound to be destructive in the church as in any other community.

While the author of 2 Peter drew this motif from Jude (2 Peter 2:2–3 being based on Jude 4), he expanded and underlined it in a way that suggests it was of particular importance to him. He not only included self-control in his list of Christian virtues; he also interpreted the sin of Sodom as license (2:7) and used the concept of license effectively in a summary indictment of his opponents: "Uttering words of empty bombast, they lure with the desires of the flesh, with acts of license, those who have barely escaped, who are still living in error, promising them freedom, though they themselves are slaves of decay; for whatever one is worsted by, to that one is a slave" (2:18–19). Since he also described these teachers as "having eyes full of adultery and indefatigable at sin, enticing unstable souls, having a heart practiced at greed *(pleonexia)*" (2:14) and claimed that they were shamelessly sybaritic (2:13), it is safe to say that he regarded the complete rejection of limitations on their personal conduct as one of their outstanding characteristics. What he called "license," they, as he acknowledged, called "freedom."

The author of 2 Peter, as his linking of adultery and greed shows, assumed that a property ethic should govern sexual acts, but he did not choose to explore that ethic in any detail. Since his was probably the last of the New Testament books to be written, the mainstream of orthodox Christianity was probably fairly clear about its definition of sexual morality, and he could assume that his hearers knew that definition. Teachers who taught otherwise were being excluded on both doctrinal and ethical grounds and categorized as "gnostics."[8] The challenge, then, for this author was no longer one of defining a Christian sexual ethic, but of insisting that Christians practice it, insisting, in other words, on the need to accept some limitations on the fulfillment of one's desires in order to make life in an ongoing community possible.

THE REVELATION TO JOHN

The final work in the New Testament canon stands apart from the others in its treatment of the family and sexual property. It is easier, however, to say that its position is distinctive than to say exactly what that position is. There is little reference to or interest in family life as such. The sense of extreme urgency about the nearness of the eschaton perhaps made it irrelevant. Celebrating the fall of "Babylon," the seer wrote, "The voice of bridegroom and bride will never be heard in you again" (18:23). This seems to be the only reference to literal family life in the book. In addition, there is a condemnation of the adultery and *porneia* associated with "Jezebel" (2:20–24), but we have already seen that it is difficult to

8. E.g., see Countryman, "Tertullian and the Regula Fidei," 214–26.

know exactly how to interpret these (see above, p. 136). By way of contrast, John's celebration of the one hundred forty-four thousand male virgins suggests a highly negative attitude toward family life (14:4), which, in turn, may help to explain this author's comparative reluctance to use family metaphors in dealing with God and Christ. In this work, Jesus is called "Son of God" only once (2:18),[9] and his Davidic descent is alluded to only twice (5:5; 22:16). God has the title "Father" and John refers to Christians as "brothers" only five times each.

Sexual language was very important for John, however, as a way to speak metaphorically about larger realities. All that is most deeply wrong in the present age is summed up in the figure of the "great harlot, seated beside many waters," clothed in purple and scarlet and riding on the scarlet beast. She is "Babylon," that is, Rome, the persecutor of God's saints (17:1–6). By contrast, the powers of the age to come first descend to earth in the figure of another woman, pregnant, "garbed with the sun, the moon under her feet, and a wreath of twelve stars on her head" (12:1–2). She gives birth to a male child, "who is going to shepherd the Gentiles with an iron rod" (12:5), and also to all the faithful (12:17). This same new age is consummated with the arrival of the New Jerusalem, the Bride of the Lamb (21:9—22:5). Finally, it is the Spirit and the Bride who invite the reader into the new world (22:17).

In the Revelation, sexual and family motifs have a positive value only insofar as they are connected with the world to come. The most appropriate way for the Christian to live in the present appears to be virginity. The bridegrooms and brides of this age are doomed to end in sterility in any case. Only the new age can be portrayed as a fertile woman, giving birth to the Messiah and his witnesses. Only the new age affords a fit time and place for the celebration of a marriage feast. While John the Seer was never explicit enough for us to be sure, one suspects that he regarded all sexual activity in this age as inappropriate, if not sinful, for Christians.

THE NEW TESTAMENT ON
SEXUAL PROPERTY

According to the Gospels, Jesus' teaching sharply diminished the role, importance, and internal stability of the family. By treating women as equals in sexual ownership and by taking children as symbols of citizen-

---

9. The title "son of God" is extended to the individual martyr in 21:7.

ship in the reign of God, Jesus undercut the rule of the patriarch, which was the generative principle of family life among both Jews and Gentiles in his time. Also, by setting the call to discipleship in opposition to the family and its obligations, he radically subordinated family as such to the same reign of God. He did not do so out of some kind of sexual asceticism such as one encounters, later on, in Gnosticism. Though he was himself apparently unmarried, there is no suggestion of an antisexual bent in the Gospels themselves; even in his discussion with the Sadducees, it was marriage that he ruled out of the world to come, not sexuality. Jesus also did not reject the concept of sexual property, but he changed the content of it by making husbands the property of their wives as well as wives of their husbands. Perhaps the most immediate consequence of this shift was to broaden the definition of adultery to include sexual intercourse outside their marriage on the part of husband as well as of wife. Matthew, however, depicted the disciples' awareness that this shift also destroyed the family as they had known it.

With Paul, if not before, a process of adapting this radical teaching to existing family patterns began. Although Paul was careful to acknowledge the wife's ownership of the husband in matters strictly internal to their personal relationship, he demanded that in other respects the usual subordination of wife to husband be retained. Under most circumstances, he excluded women from leadership in the assembly. Though he could not refuse inspired women the right to prophesy, he prescribed clothing that would express their subordination. In the household, he reasserted a conventional morality for women, children, and slaves.

This does not mean that Paul was reestablishing the primacy of the family. He believed, in fact, that celibacy was the form of life most appropriate to the eschatological crisis in which Christians found themselves. In this, the author of the Revelation may well have joined him. His conservatism in matters of the family was rather an expression of his conviction that this was not the time for Christians to make sweeping changes in the life of this world—the same conviction which led him to advise all Christians to remain in the state of life in which they had first been called by God. He recognized, however, that the *charisma* of celibacy was not given to all. He discouraged the married from denying each other's conjugal rights. And since many single Christians, if he refused them permission to marry, would resort to forms of sexual expression of which he disapproved on other grounds, he approved of marriage as a way to satisfy male sexual needs. In the process, he became the only New Testament author to acknowledge sexual satisfaction as a legitimate and sufficient reason for marriage.

Paul maintained the prohibition of adultery. It is not surprising that, as the accidents of history in the church at Corinth have allowed us to see, he also regarded the prohibition of incest, in the ancient Israelite sense, as of continuing validity. Since he also believed that Christ's relationship with the Christian constituted a kind of ownership analogous to the father's ownership of the rest of the family, he drew some further ethical conclusions from this principle. Paul's conservatism with regard to day-to-day family life, then, should be understood primarily as an incidental adaptation to the end time. In ethical theory, he was not materially less radical than Jesus.

The other New Testament books, however, show a more mixed picture. While the authors of James and the Johannine Epistles retain a sense of the church as replacing the family, and James gives clear expression to the equality of women in that context, most of the other authors lean more to the reaffirmation of traditional family life. This is particularly true in 1 Peter and the Pastoral Epistles, where the impetus of Jesus' and Paul's radicalism has very nearly spent its force, at least on this matter. Their authors were dealing with threats to the church, both external and internal, which they felt required the church to present an unexceptionable face to the public and exert clearer control within its own community. In the process, they converted Paul's eschatologically based approval of traditional family mores into a principled insistence on them. Whatever their needs and intentions were at the time, however, this had the subsequent effect of nullifying most of the fundamental egalitarianism and the rejection of family found in Jesus' gospel. First Peter and the Pastorals, on the whole, have dominated later Christian thought on the subjects of marriage and women.

Once this traditionalist ethic was widely agreed upon, the only remaining question was whether the average Christian would live up to it. Thus, the author of 2 Peter no longer had to define a sexual ethic, but only to stress the importance of restraint in social environments. He agrees with the other New Testament writers (with the possible exception of John the Seer) in accepting the reality and legitimacy of sexual property and an ethic based on it. This agreement, however, masks for us the real difference between the radical ethic of Jesus and that of 1 Peter or the Pastorals, which is barely distinguishable from that of the environing culture, Jewish or Gentile.

3

Dirt
Greed
SEX

12   New Testament Sexual Ethics and Today's World

A close reading of the New Testament, as we have discovered, shows how alien its sexual ethics are to the world of today. They are framed in terms of purity and property systems that no longer prevail among us. Although we have grown accustomed to reading the Bible as if it pertained directly to our own experience, such a reading ignores much that is important in the texts themselves and is, for the most part, incapable of dealing with them literally—that is, in terms of their simplest, least adapted sense. The reader may therefore be tempted to conclude that the sexual ethics of the New Testament are now irrelevant, even for Christians, and that we must begin from the beginning to construct some kind of sexual ethic suitable to our own era. I believe this conclusion would be mistaken.

As I have argued elsewhere, one of the primary contributions which Scripture makes to the work of the Spirit in the life of the Christian community is that it stands outside our present and therefore prevents us from treating our contemporary world as an inevitability. The antiquity of the biblical writings means that they give Christians other models of social life to stand alongside those we know directly. These models come from the past and are therefore in some sense irretrievable. Every culture, including that of the first-century Mediterranean world, is a whole and not recoverable in isolated pieces; even when isolated pieces survive or are consciously revived, they will no longer mean the same thing in their new contexts. The first-century Mediterranean world—or its sexual ethics or any other single aspect of its culture—is not, then, of

237

the substance of the gospel. To suggest that it is would be to place the gospel forever beyond our reach. The spiritual function of the Bible's antiquity is rather to relativize the present, to rule out in advance the notion that things can be only as they are. We cannot return to the past, and we do not know what shape the future will take. What we can do is seek, with the help of the past, to understand the present in its own terms and proclaim the gospel in ways pertinent to it.[1]

In sexual matters, as elsewhere, this is the goal of Christian theology. The dominance of dogmatic or systematic theology in Western Christianity since the Scholastic period has created the unfortunate illusion that the gospel is a system of ideas which can be fully comprehended by any person of adequate intelligence quite apart from any necessity of personal transformation. Nothing could be further from the teaching of Jesus, as presented in the New Testament Gospels. This teaching is unsystematic in form; but, what is more important, it is devoted to the transformation (*metanoia*, conversion) of the hearer rather than to the creation of a theological system. In the earlier eras of Christianity, the "theologian" was preeminently one whose encounter with God shaped the person with such power that he or she could speak of God with the authority of grace.

Such speech was more often "occasional" than systematic; that is to say, it responded to occasions of immediate concern, seeking to explicate them in terms of grace and making no pretense to a complete or exhaustive knowledge of God. Thus, Paul wrote to the Corinthians in order to speak to conflicts and problems raised in the life of their congregation, not to explicate the whole of his gospel. Dogmatic theology has sometimes pretended to a complete and perfect knowledge of things sacred, and it has suggested such pretensions to the unreflective even when it has known better than to take them seriously itself. The idea that an ordinary human being could, through a form of intellectual endeavor, be fully in command of the mysteries of the gospel or that anyone could progress toward knowledge of God faster than one was in fact being transformed by that knowledge is fundamentally alien to early Christianity.

Theology, in the older, presystematic sense, assumes that we live in our own moment, our own historical and cultural context. We meet, in that context, God's grace as definitively made known through the minis-

1. Countryman, *Biblical Authority*, 77–93.

try, death, and resurrection of Jesus. We experience grace as transforming our life; and we proclaim the power of grace as we have known it. This is not to say that all theology must always take the form of personal testimony. In most cases, this would prove boring—for the very good reason that one person's experience becomes relevant to another only insofar as the one can show the other how they belong to the same world and share the reality or possibility of intimately comparable experience. What this means, rather, is that all theology must be true to the speaker's living, not spun out as the logical consequence of an objectivized intellectual system, but cohering with an experience of grace in the world we actively share. If this theology is to be, moreover, Christian theology, then it must meet the further criterion of continuity with the experience of grace expressed in the New Testament.

This brings us to the other side of the New Testament's relevance today. If Scripture is important partly because it is alien to and therefore relativizes our own historical-cultural situation, it is even more important in that it can show, by reference to the way the grace of God broke into the self-sufficiency of another culture, how it breaks into our own as well. The New Testament writers did not try to construct a new sexual ethic from the ground up. They took over the existing cultural patterns and refocused them, pushing some elements from the center to the periphery, altering the balance of powers allotted to various members of society, and, most important, relativizing the familiar life of this world by subordinating it to the reign of God. The result was that Christians could, in many ways, continue to conform to familiar cultural mores while, at the same time, understanding these familiar institutions in ways which undermined their absolute claims.

This suggests a pattern worth applying to the present situation. Ideally, it would invite us to comprehend the nature of sexual institutions in our own time and culture, and then to subject them to the same kind of critique on behalf of the gospel of God's grace. This will prove difficult. The difficulties arise both from the side of the modern world and from that of the gospel. Our world has been (and perhaps still is) passing through an era of great changes, making it difficult for us to know what in fact our social structure provides in the way of sexual institutions. The world of the first century was probably more fixed and settled in this regard. At the same time, the demands of the gospel of grace are being constantly renewed and fitted to new situations by the Spirit who animates the church. There is no simple list of them that can be lifted out of Scripture or the church's past experience and reflection and applied without further ado to the present.

This is not a task for one theologian, but for the church. It will require insights from many perspectives, both on the modern world and on the Bible, brought together in what I suspect will be a long conversation. I am not so foolish as to propose, in one chapter, to resolve all the relevant questions or even to raise them. I hope rather to show that the major emphases of the New Testament, if applied with appropriate sensitivity to our cultural and historical distance from the first-century Mediterranean world, will yield the outlines of a sexual ethic that is both intelligible and practicable in our world and also coherent with the gospel of grace. It goes without saying that the following discussion in no way stands on its own, but is intelligible only in terms of the preceding chapters. If any wandering reader has turned directly to this part of the book, may I respectfully suggest here that this chapter will make better sense if you go back to resume where you left off?

In the following pages, I shall first put forward a series of principles drawn from the preceding study. I call these principles "generative" because I believe that, when applied, they will give rise to explicit ethical guidelines, such as I have sketched in the latter part of this chapter. These, in turn, I present not as invariable rules, but as a kind of alarm system whose violation signals a very high probability (amounting in some cases to a practical certainty) that the principles behind them are being violated. Throughout the present chapter, I am writing as a Christian for Christians. In the present confused state of our culture, I presume that any coherent statement of a sexual ethic will hold some interest for a larger public, but I do not propose what follows as a universally applicable ethic, for it is directly dependent on the message of the gospel.

GENERATIVE PRINCIPLES

The preceding historical study of the New Testament has provided a basis for defining six principles that must enter into the formation of any Christian sexual ethic today. Most of them are drawn directly from the New Testament; one of them (the third) speaks rather of the distance of the first-century world from our own time. These are not "first principles," for they are themselves dependent on more fundamental assertions about God, God's grace, and humanity under God's grace. The oneness of God, which implies a oneness of this created world and of humanity in it; the absolute priority of God's action over our own, both in creation and in subsequent acts of grace; the sinfulness of humanity, which becomes most destructive in the form of claims to righteousness; God's presence in flesh through the incarnation; the call to *metanoia* (repentance, conversion, transformation) and the demands made on us in this world by our citizenship in the age to come; the equality of all human beings under grace and the priority of love over all other virtues—all these are prior to the principles enunciated here. The links which lead from the ones to the others can, in fact, be made explicit, but this is not the place to do so. At present, it is enough to have shown that these generative principles are those which the New Testament itself lays down for dealing with the questions of sexual ethics or which the change of cultures compels us to take into account.

1. *Membership in the Christian community is in no way limited by purity codes.* Individual Christians may continue to observe the purity code of their culture, but they may not demand that other Christians do so. If one wishes to assert that any given proscription is a part of Christian sexual ethics, one must justify that claim by showing that the act in question infringes some principle other than purity. Any claim that a given sexual act is wrong in and of itself will be found ultimately to represent either a lack of ethical analysis or a hidden purity claim.

2. *Christians must respect the sexual property of others and practice detachment from their own.* There are two points to be made here. The first is that the New Testament interests itself in property not so much in order to defend me against my neighbor as to defend my neighbor against me. Paul, for example, wrote to the Corinthians that it would be preferable for them to suffer injustice and deprivation at one another's hands rather than take their cases to the public courts where they would themselves probably be seeking to commit injustice (1 Cor. 6:7–8). The second is that property also had value, for the New Testament writers, as an extension of the self; in this respect, the essential question was not "How shall I maintain what is mine?" but "How shall I dispose it in obedience to the reign of God?" The self is not something to be preserved and enhanced at all costs, but rather a means by which we become compatible with and enter the world to come.

3. *Where, in late antiquity, sexual property belonged to the family through the agency of the male householder, in our own era it belongs to the individual.* The difference between the ancient and modern worlds in this respect is one of focus. The ancient householder could say "mine"; the modern

individual is usually still implicated, to some degree, in the restrictions and pressures of a family. "Family" and "individuality" are the poles of a continuum, with life taking place in the area of tension between. Nonetheless, the brief treatment of family-oriented society provided in the preceding chapters should be enough to show the distance between a world in which the individual is the primary arbiter of his or her sexual acts and one in which these were functions of the life of a family. If the New Testament's critique of sexual property is to be illuminative in our present world, we must take into account that the type of "owner" has changed; and such a change in ownership will always imply a change in the character and understanding of what is owned.

4. *The gospel can discern no inequality between men and women as they stand before God's grace.* The New Testament writers came to accept a good deal of inequality between the sexes in day-to-day life; but this represented an accommodation to existing patterns, not the working out of the gospel principle. Perhaps this principle could never have been worked out very effectively in a family-oriented society, since it implied the destruction of the existing family order. The early Christians, in general, found it achievable only in the context of celibacy. It remained, however, a principle of basic importance.

5. *Marriage creates a union of flesh, normally indissoluble except by death.* This principle brought sexual union into the family in a new way which rivaled the existing family structure; indeed, had not Paul and some later New Testament writers reaffirmed the subordination of women, it would have dissolved the ancient family. In a society which defines the individual as the basic social unit rather than the family, the meaning of "one flesh" must necessarily go through some redefinition if this principle is still to be challenging, intelligible, and useful.

6. *The Christian's sexual life and property are always subordinate to the reign of God.* This is not a rejection of the values of sexual life, but rather a focus on God's calling of each person under particular circumstances, which may demand sacrifice of lesser to greater good. Since Christ "owns" all believers, their lives must cohere with this reality—not by some show of pietism, transforming each aspect of life into a kind of religious show, but by the clear linking of what is more peripheral to what is more central.

To say how these principles give rise to a sexual morality in our own time calls for an exercise of judgment in relating them to the facts of our sexual life. Grace calls us not to leave this world, but to live in it, wherever God calls us to be, as citizens of God's reign. This calls for ethical discernment of the problems and possibilities implicit in our milieu in order to see what God asks us to do in this context.

DERIVED GUIDELINES

Rejection of the Requirements of Physical Purity

When the New Testament rejected the imposition of the purity codes of the Torah on Gentile Christians, it was not in order that a new, distinctively Christian purity code might take their place. Except for hints of such developments in Jude and Revelation, the New Testament did not justify any sexual rule by appeal to physical purity. Indeed, it exhibited a strong concern that purity, as a distinction dividing human societies from one another, should give way before a massive awareness of the grace of God, extended impartially to all human beings. The creation of its own purity code has been one of several ways in which the church has at times allowed itself to become a barrier to the gospel of God's grace. A Christian sexual ethic that remains true to its New Testament roots will have to discard its insistence on physical purity.

The great difficulty of this demand is that it excises what has become, at least for many Americans, the very heart of Christian sexual morality. It therefore places the churches under a great test—essentially the same test as that which confronted the pious among the Jewish people during Jesus' own ministry and the circumcision party within the earliest Christian church at the time of Paul's Gentile mission. Will the churches hang onto their own self-defined purity and so hold themselves aloof from those excluded by it, or will they proclaim the grace of God which plays no favorites? Will they make their existing purity codes conditions of salvation, or will they acknowledge that they have no right to limit what God gives?

To be specific, the gospel allows no rule against the following, in and of themselves: masturbation, nonvaginal heterosexual intercourse, bestiality,[2] polygamy, homosexual acts, or erotic art and literature. The Christian is free to be repelled by any or all of these and may continue to practice her or his own purity code in relation to them. What we are not

---

2. I use this term in its common sense of intercourse with an animal, not the technical psychological sense in which it designates a distinctive complex of attractions and behaviors.

free to do is impose our codes on others. Like all sexual acts, these may be genuinely wrong where they also involve an offense against the property of another, denial of the equality of women and men, or an idolatrous substitution of sex for the reign of God as the goal of human existence.

Christians have increasingly accepted that masturbation or even non-vaginal heterosexual intercourse, in and of themselves, are not wrong. Bestiality, where it is the casual recourse of the young or of people isolated over long periods of time from other humans, should occasion little concern. It is probably too isolated a phenomenon to justify strong feelings. More difficulty may attach to the other issues in the list. They therefore call for a somewhat more detailed discussion.

Polygamy is more likely to be a serious issue in the Third World than in the modern West. Nowhere, however, does the Bible make monogamy a clear and explicit standard for all Christian marriage. Our usage in this matter must derive from the Greco-Roman milieu in which the church spent its formative early centuries. This does not mean that the modern church should seek to reinstitute polygamy where there is no cultural demand for it; but it does mean that, in cultures which have hitherto been polygamous, monogamy as such should not be made a condition of grace. The church, however, should concern itself with the question of the equality of women and men, particularly with regard to the way marital patterns affect the status of women. Monogamy offers no guarantee of equality; but the relative benefits of monogamy and polygamy in this respect should be the principal point at issue wherever the church must make such decisions.

Homosexual orientation has been increasingly recognized in our time as a given of human sexuality. While most people feel some sexual attraction to members of both the same and the opposite sex and, in the majority of these, attraction to the opposite sex dominates, there is a sizeable minority for whom sexual attraction to persons of the same sex is a decisive shaping factor of their sexual lives. It appears that this orientation is normally inalterable and that there is no strong internal reason for the homosexual person to wish to alter it. To deny an entire class of human beings the right peaceably and without harming others to pursue the kind of sexuality that corresponds to their nature is a perversion of the gospel. Like the insistence of some on the circumcising of Gentile converts, it makes the keeping of purity rules a condition of grace. It is sometimes suggested that homosexual persons be told to become celibate. While celibacy is a venerable Christian tradition and may even, as Paul suggested, be called for under certain circumstances, it is also a *charisma* (gift) and can never be demanded of those to whom such a gift has not been given. Paul indicated that the presence of this gift is known by the ability of the celibate person to deal with ungratified sexual desires without being dominated by them. For those without this gift, Paul considered the satisfaction of their desires, so long as it was within the boundaries of the property ethic, entirely appropriate. Any insistence on celibacy for homosexuals as such is, accordingly, contrary to the New Testament witness.

Erotic literature and art (commonly called "pornography")[3] form a widespread and diverse phenomenon which may at times be contrary to Christian ethics, particularly when they set up idolatrous ethical standards which treat the self and its sexual gratification as the final goal of all existence or when they present as acceptable the degradation of adults (usually women, in our society) or abuse of children. Explicit verbal and pictorial representations of sexual acts are not forbidden by the gospel— apart from such considerations which may render one or another particular item ethically obnoxious. By the traditional standards of Western Christianity, however, whatever is sexually explicit is impure. Although we tend to think of the issue of pornography as limited to newsstands, so-called "adult" bookstores, and theaters, actually it permeates our whole society, as attested, for example, by our lack of an ordinary vocabulary in English (as distinct from a medical or an obscene one) for the discussion of sexuality. Anxiety about the erotic is, most importantly, the thing which prevents the clear and open sexual education of our young. We are currently reaping the consequences of this purity rule in the form of widespread pregnancies among teenagers who are neither capable of nor very interested in the rearing of children. And we shall be very lucky indeed if we do not promote the rapid spread of AIDS by our unwillingness to speak explicitly to children in the educational process. The pleasure attached to explicit sexual portrayals, in words or pictures, should be accepted as the powerful ally of any effort to teach the responsible use of so beautiful a thing. We cannot, however, expect to forbid sexually explicit representations in most respects and still make good use of them in one narrowly permitted area, namely, education.

3. Some reserve the term "pornography" specifically for those erotic materials involving degradation of women. These, I think, are contrary to Christian sexual ethics, but not because of their erotic element.

Children will not usually trust claims on which they have no independent controls whatever.

The New Testament, of course, does not demand that those Christians whose consciences are committed to some purity law give up the practice of it. No one should be required to take an interest in erotica or to indulge in sexual practices which, however permissible, seem to that person a violation of conscience. For that person, they would indeed be wrong actions. Conscience, of course, is not fixed in its final form, and one must expect that it will mature along with our comprehension of other aspects of God, the world, and the gospel. It remains true, however, that every Christian is responsible to his or her own present understanding. Those whose confidence in grace is great enough to free them from purity codes (the "strong," as Paul called them) may not force their position on others; but neither may those who observe such codes (the "weak") refuse the strong the right to follow their consciences. Since neither group has any right to deprive others of what properly belongs to them, it follows that the weak should not attempt to prevent open sexual education, outlaw erotic art and literature, or keep homosexual persons out of the church and ministry. The strong, on the other hand, must not make their standard of conduct a prerequisite of grace any more than the purity rules are. Paul urged the strong to avoid occasions of public offense to the weak. This is good, so long as the weak also commit themselves to a clear recognition that the strong have a part in the church; it would be a betrayal of the gospel, however, if the needs of the weak were made an excuse for the reinstitution of purity law as a condition of grace.

There has been a tendency, over the past century or so, to reinstitute purity law under the guise of mental health, by claiming that deviations from it are a kind of sickness. Our society, having made a religion of medicine and a priesthood of physicians, is tempted to invoke the word "sickness" as a mere synonym of "impurity" without imparting any definite meaning to it. This sham was long used to threaten children who masturbated with such dire consequences as insanity; but the most obvious and shameful use of it has been against homosexuals, who have been labeled as sick merely because they differed from the majority. Even though intelligent and truly comparable studies have now shown that there was never any foundation for such claims, there are those who, on dogmatic grounds (nothing else being available), still make them.

The identification of sickness and impurity has become even more apparent in the irrational anxieties focused recently on people with AIDS. These anxieties have induced many to seek a radical separation from carriers and potential carriers of the virus, even though competent authorities have repeatedly assured the public that the virus is communicated only in quite specific ways. The irrationality and intensity of such responses testify to the enormous power that the purity ethic can still have for us. It is not death which is the primary source of these fears, for the advocate of quarantines may well be willing to take much greater risks, day by day, in driving metropolitan freeways. The great fear is of contracting a disease as "dirty" to many in the modern world as leprosy was in antiquity.

Those who wish to rescue our society's purity rules by designating everyone who deviates from them as "sick" are merely renaming purity; they are not telling us anything new or illuminating. In many cases, they have even been uttering falsehoods; and, in the process, they have harmed many generations of the young who were forced to fear that masturbation or homosexual attractions were signs of insanity.

Respect for the Property of Others

Where statutory law concerns itself with property mainly in order to conserve what already belongs to me from seizure by another, the great Jewish religious teachers of antiquity were concerned primarily to protect my neighbor from me. This was not unique to the Christian tradition, but is found also in the Mishnah's well-known definition of the four types of human beings: the "type of Sodom," who says, "What is mine is mine and what is yours is yours"; the evil person, who says, "What is yours is mine, and what is mine is mine"; the ignorant person, who says, "What is mine is yours, and what is yours is mine"; and the saintly person, who says, "What is mine is yours and what is yours is yours."[4] We have already examined the way adultery or incest infringed on the property of others in the ancient family system. These were so intimately involved, however, in that family system that we shall have to reevaluate their meaning, below, in the context of the shift to the individual as the basic social unit.

Under the present heading, I should like to do something simpler, but equally important—suggest what property meant, in a positive vein, for

---

4. *Aboth* 5.14. Need one observe that this is yet another piece of evidence to show that the ancients did not typically identify the sin of Sodom as homosexual intercourse?

the New Testament writers and relate this to what I believe to be its most significant violation in our era. For the New Testament, property represents a certain personal realm in which one can act in obedience to the reign of God; it is, as in the etymology of our English term, all that pertains or "is proper to" each person. As such, it is something which may be trusted in and hoarded to the soul's detriment, or something to be given in alms or even surrendered entirely, if the claims of discipleship require it. It generates claims and counterclaims; but it is better to suffer loss than to take one's brother or sister to court. In every case, including sexual property, one must administer and care for one's property with a view to sanctification, that is, one's transformation into a citizen of the reign of God. Property, in other words, is the wherewithal of being human in this age—which can also become, by grace, the wherewithal of becoming a fit citizen of the age to come.

The wherewithal of being human must include, at the very minimum, sustenance, space, the means to grow, the community of other humans, and some freedom of choice. Theft of sustenance or space is the most obvious kind of violation of property; yet, violations of that trust which is the foundation of human community or of the freedom of choice are at least as grave. If in antiquity, given the existing concept of family, adultery was the characteristic violation of sexual property, in our own age, it has become rape.[5] When committed by a stranger, it violates the victim's freedom of choice; when committed by a family member or presumed friend, it violates the bonds of human community as well. The metaphorical space which surrounds each of us and which we characterize as "mine" is of the essence of our being human. It offers some protection for the freedom to develop and become what God is calling us to be, which is the principal goal of being human. When it is opened voluntarily to another, it is also a means of community. But when it is broken into by violence, the very possibility of being human is at least momentarily being denied to us. As there is nothing more precious to us than our humanness, there is no sexual sin more serious than rape.

Rape, as property violation, includes not only the use of physical violence to gain sexual access to another, but also the use of social,

---

5. The difference between the cultures in this respect is vividly apparent in Philo, who argued that the law of Moses specified no punishment for the forcible violation of a widow or divorced woman because that was, in effect, only half the crime that adultery was (*Special Laws* 3.64). So, too, in ancient Athens, rape was considered a less grave offense than seduction (Pomeroy, *Goddesses*, 86–87).

emotional, and psychological violence. This takes the form of sexual harassment in workplaces, of sexual impositions by trusted authorities upon their clients, and of manipulative pressures in intimate relationships. Our contemporary culture, with its constant glorification of sex, largely for commercial ends, creates a climate in which this sort of violence flourishes. It offers leverage for the unscrupulous to press inexperienced or unwilling persons into acts which they have not freely chosen. Even within marriage or other established sexual relationships, both physical violence and these other forms of rape are by no means unknown.

An ethic consistent with the gospel will condemn not only individual acts of rape, but also those in which whole groups attack other groups to deny them the property necessary to their humanness. Assaults on women or homosexual people, whether as individual attacks or as political and legal campaigns to deny them equality as citizens and human beings, are the most obvious cases in point. This kind of communal violence may also be based on differences other than sexual, especially on racial, ethnic, and economic ones. Even here, however, sexual elements are often entangled in the violence. For example, in the United States, white men have often justified their violence against black men by accusing them of having sexual designs on white women, while reserving to themselves the right to make sometimes violent use of black women. What is more, violence may be done to others' freedom not only through direct assault, but also through patronizing the less powerful, making them dependencies and therefore properties of the more powerful. Both kinds of violence have been characteristic of the relations of men with women and of rich with poor in our culture.

All these kinds of violence have sunk their roots deep in our culture, and it is difficult to imagine their complete eradication. The Christian, however, has an obligation to name them and struggle against them inwardly, in personal relationships, and in the larger society. In this respect, it is disturbing that some Christian denominations seem to have taken the side of violence themselves. Their condemnations of homosexual people, for example, are accompanied, at the very best, by only the mildest of rebukes to those who persecute them; some denominations, such as the Roman Catholic and Southern Baptist, even encourage denial of their legal rights. Some who call themselves "Evangelical," "Charismatic," or "Pentecostal" also oppose equal freedom for women and call for complete subservience even on the part of battered wives.

Until this changes, it is unlikely that our society will begin to treat rape of all kinds with the revulsion that it deserves, for to some extent such violence will always appear to be at least a quasi-legitimate reaffirmation of the dominance of men over women, of heterosexuals over homosexuals, and, indeed, of the powerful generally over the weak.

Sexual Property as
Individual Property

When the owner of property changes, the nature of the property changes also. To take a nonsexual example, a piece of farmland that is underlain by coal deposits suitable for surface mining will appear to be various things to various possible owners. If the owner of the coal is a mining company which may not own the surface of the land but has the right to remove it in order to gain access to the coal, the farmland itself will appear to be incidental to the property that matters. In many cases, such a company is not part of the local community and has no bond to either the human or the natural ecosystem in which the farmland participates, but exists only to make a certain profit through the mining of coal. The coal is therefore purely a capital investment, and the company will make decisions about it in the extremely narrow context of profit and loss—unless, of course, the larger community of state or nation forces a greater measure of social responsibility on the company. At the other extreme, if a resident farmer owns both the farmland and the coal under it, the coal is only one aspect of the larger whole to which she relates. It has an economic value, but the owner will balance that value against her self-understanding as farmer rather than miner, against her identity as part of the local community where she lives and farms, against any sense of spiritual connection she may have to the land, and so forth. These do not predetermine her choice whether to mine the coal or not; but they do create a certain distinctive context for the making of that choice. If, to create a third case, the owner is an absentee landlord with at most a remote family connection to the land, both the arable surface and the underlying coal may still be of interest. Yet, with the withdrawal of the landlord from the local human and natural community, the property comes to be identified mainly with its economic value. Such an owner is likely to make decisions based primarily on economic considerations but is not likely to be quite so narrowly focused as a coal company.

Many readers will recognize the above as a sketch of varieties of ownership in parts of the Appalachian region in the United States. The point is that, even if the property remains, physically, the same object, its relationship to various owners can constitute it as, in effect, several different objects. The same is true of sexual property. In the ancient world, where it pertained primarily to the family and secondarily to the male householder as representative of the family, it meant one thing; in the modern world, where it can pertain only to the individual, it means another. It will be useful to say here a few words about the nature of this transition. The individualization of modern American society is a social fact, an aspect of the environment in which we make ethical decisions, not an ethical principle itself. As such, it is neither good nor bad. It represents some losses as against earlier, family-structured eras and also some gains. If the human being now lacks the kind of inevitable links with a social continuum that the earlier society afforded, that loss must be balanced against the fact that individualization has gone hand in hand with—and is probably the condition for—what progress this century has made toward genuine equality of races, nationalities, and the sexes. The ability of modern people to choose for themselves with regard to education, work, living place, life-partner, religion, or politics became conceivable only as the family ceased to be the basic unit of society and was replaced by the individual.

Individuality can become an ethical principle in two ways. Philosophically speaking, it may become so by a recognition that my individuality is intelligible only as an expression of the principle which renders every other human being an individual, too. This principle was already being expressed in late antiquity in the Golden Rule; respect for my individuality implies respect for that of others. As such, it enters into Christian ethics, but it is by no means the crowning element in them. It could not, for example, have generated the sacrifice of Jesus on the cross or the witness of the martyrs, which require the further principles of love, faith, and hope for their understanding. On the other hand, individuality can also become an ethical principle in the form of individualism—an idolatry of the self, which treats the self as its own source and end. Such individualism has been a pervasive ethical influence in the modern West, enshrined in certain forms of capitalist ideology as the image of the "self-made" person—that is, the person who has chosen to forget the role others played in his fashioning and rise and who regards with interest only those people and things that contribute to his own aggrandizement. This individualism, like any other idolatry, is utterly inconsistent with the gospel.

The gospel does, to be sure, call for serious attention to be given to the self. Jesus held up the unjust steward, who threw caution, morality, and household loyalty to the winds in order to ensure his own future, as a model for the Christian (Luke 16:1–13). From the preaching of John the Baptist onward, belonging to the family of Abraham by physical descent no longer counts for anything in the economy of salvation (Matt. 3:9). Yet, the gospel's rejection of the idolatry of family, the social unit of the first century, implies an equally stern rejection of the idolatry of the individual in our own time. The connection between the two was clearly visible at the time of transition between them, the Industrial Revolution, when William Blake declared that the family was simply a grand excuse for selfishness.[6] This was so in several ways. Insofar as the individual is, in a family-structured society, simply an expression of the family, any claim one makes on behalf of one's family is a claim on behalf of one's self. At the same time, the diffusion of the self in the family that is thus achieved will seem to relieve one of the burden of selfishness. As society became more individualized, however, Blake's insight became more literally true; the lesser members of the family (wife, children, slaves, servants) came to be no longer expressions of the family to which they belonged, but extensions of the male individual who owned them. This modern kind of "family" has little to do with the family of late antiquity, is even more repugnant to the gospel than the ancient family, and is probably inherently unstable in its own right.

In the ancient world, the man, on behalf of his natal family, owned one or more women, either as spouses or as concubines or as slaves. The man received sexual satisfaction; the family received as goods the labor of the women involved and, in the case of the spouse, the promise of legitimate heirs. (In very rich households, of course, the number of subordinate women indicated the prominence of the family as well.) The Greco-Roman world limited a man to one wife at a time, and Western Christianity restricted this still further by rejecting the right of divorce. Even then, however, what the man still chiefly sought in marriage was a combination of sexual satisfaction, household labor, and legitimate heirs. Only the first of these was specific to him; the rest benefited the family.

6. At least, I believe it was Blake. The statement stuck in my mind more than twenty years ago, but I have not been able to locate it again.

What goods, by contrast, does the modern individual seek in entering upon a sexual relationship? The goods the ancients sought have not, of course, ceased to be of importance. Apart from the most individual of them (sexual satisfaction), however, they will seldom appear as the primary reasons for marriage or other sexual relationships in the mainstream of modern American society. Why do most of us marry, and how do we choose our partners? We seek things that can benefit an individual. The thrill of romantic love is, of course, enormously important; and we typically hope that this will form the basis for a lasting intimacy, in which our spouse will provide friendship, encouragement, counsel, solace, and a new sense of family to supplement and eventually replace the natal family. These are, of course, interior goods—goods which cannot be given without a genuine delight in and commitment to the other; and in this respect they stand in sharp contrast to the primary goods sought in antiquity. To be sure, there are external goods involved in modern marriage as well: the expectation of security, financial support, and perhaps the desire for children. Yet, we are inclined to look askance at those who marry for money, and child-bearing and rearing have become a vast and still largely unacknowledged problem for our society. For us, the heart of sexual property in marriage and in other lasting sexual liaisons lies in the interior goods.

When the nature of what is owned changes, the nature of theft necessarily changes as well. From the perspective of the Appalachian farmer, the destruction of the farm in order to mine the coal underneath it is a kind of theft; from the perspective of the mining company, refusal to allow the removal of this "overburden" would be a kind of theft. In antiquity, theft, as applied to sexual property, was easily defined, since sexual goods themselves were external and therefore easily defined. Adultery meant a man's taking the womb and family resources which belonged to another man and using them for the nourishment of his own seed. We continue, for the most part, in our society to regard adultery as wrong, but we are forced to find a quite different reason for so regarding it. We usually say that it is wrong because it is a betrayal of trust—that is, theft of an interior good. Insofar as this is in fact the case in a given situation, it gives a good account of adultery in our modern context; but it does not go far enough.

Trust is not the only interior good essential to marriage or to its equivalents, and the outsider is not the only possible thief. Since, in ancient marriage, the man owned the woman, it was not possible for the man to steal from his wife. If he committed adultery he was stealing from another man. Jesus, however, by redefining adultery, altered this internal balance and made both spouses capable of taking from one another. That is still more true under present circumstances, for partners can easily withhold from each other those interior goods which they have contracted, explicitly or implicitly, to provide; and there is in fact no way to gain them from an unwilling partner. An ancient wife need have no deep affection for her husband in order to bear his children and do her part in the running of the household. Neither partner, in the modern world, can fulfill his or her obligations in such an external, "objective" manner.

The form of adultery most characteristic, then, of our own society, is not adultery with another person, but the purely self-regarding adultery which demands of the partner the full range of goods associated with sexual property but gives few or none of them in return. This is not to discard the older understanding of adultery, in which one person takes from another what belongs to a third party; this is certainly not dead. It is rather to stress the prevalence of adultery in the form of profiteering, the use of a sexual relationship for one's own physical, economic, emotional, or psychological satisfaction with minimal regard for that of the partner. In comparison, the technical act of adultery by sexual intercourse with a third person is a relatively trivial matter.

Our transition from a familial to an individual society has been particularly difficult in the matter of children and lies at the root of many modern troubles, ranging from abortion to unwanted infants to child abuse to educational uncertainties and beyond. Not that these are of a single or simple origin! The increase of child abuse, for example, is probably partly a matter of fact and partly a matter of changed perceptions, for kinds of corporal punishment which were normal parental prerogatives a few generations ago now appear to be abusive. In the familial society, after all, children were the property of the family, part of its assets, and the family's self-interest would dictate that it discipline them without harming them in a way that would damage its own investment. In the individual society, however, children have become an obligation rather than an investment.

This has brought with it the permission for—and even the necessity of—conscious decision making about the conception of children. Agricultural societies, before the advent of modern medicine, might afford the luxury of producing as many children as they could; now, more urbanized societies with lowered birthrates and greater longevity must make deliberate decisions, with the cooperation of those of childbearing age. Since both Jesus and Paul seem to have encouraged celibacy, one cannot imagine that the conceiving of children is any sort of intrinsic Christian virtue. Since it is now also the incurring of a substantial burden which can be borne successfully only out of love, no one should undertake it without due consideration. In most areas of the modern world, the use of birth control should be the norm and the conception of children should represent a deliberate and considered departure from it. (A significant exception must certainly be made for those human groups that are threatened with disappearance or with diminution to numbers too small to maintain their cultural traditions.) No existing method of birth control is inherently unacceptable, though certain ways of imposing them may certainly be.

Some particular discussion of abortion is called for. The Bible contains nothing helpful on the subject. Other early Christian literature, too, has surprisingly little, given that abortion was not uncommon in the Greco-Roman world. One must distinguish two separate issues: abortion as therapeutic for the physical, mental, or emotional health of the pregnant woman; and abortion as a means of birth control. While the ancient family ethic may have regarded the legitimate offspring as of greater importance than the mother in some cases, there can be no basis in the New Testament itself for such a judgment. To the contrary, in making the wife equal to her husband, Jesus implied that she was no longer merely an instrument of his natal family in their quest for heirs. This implies that her health is at least as important as that of an uncertain offspring.

The question of abortion as a method of birth control is more difficult. Human societies—and different voices within our own society—disagree about when the fetus should be considered a separate human being. The Greeks and Romans, who allowed exposure of the newborn if unwanted by its family, recognized this as occurring some time after birth; others have placed it at conception (a process little understood at the time of the New Testament writers), at quickening, or at the earliest moment when a premature infant might survive outside the womb. The child who has actually passed through the birth channel seems qualitatively different from one still in the womb; even the Greeks and Romans tended to expose unwanted newborns to be collected by anyone who might want them rather than killing them outright. Still, there is no compelling logic to tell us how to choose among the other three options. The principal consideration must be that the choice in relation to childbearing should always be, if at all possible, a choice *for,* not a choice *against.* No one should be obligated to bear children and, given the present threat to the world from its human population, no one should do so unless moved thereto as a specific calling and gift. Christians should not, then, place themselves in the position of having to decide repeatedly not to bear this particular fetus, but rather in the position of deciding when they are called to conceive a child.

Now as in other eras, parents conceive children for a variety of reasons, perhaps including innate biological urges as well as social pressures, sentiment, the desire for some kind of genetic immortality, a sense of social responsibility, pure carelessness, and the rest—perhaps a longer list than any one person can imagine. Yet, once born, the child is, in our age, a quite different matter from what he or she was in the first century. The ancient family had to have legitimate heirs in order to maintain its own existence. But what is the child to a society of individuals? If they are individualists, in the idolatrous sense, the child is, of course, nothing at all except an extension of the parents and insurance against their being left unattended in senility. The individual society, however, is not necessarily committed to individualism of this kind, any more than a familial society is doomed to be torn apart by the grander selfishness of its families. In each, the worst case is a possibility, but not the only possibility. Ultimately, the individual society militates against individualistic megalomania on the part of parents, for the children will learn from the society itself that they, too, are expected to become individuals and will refuse to cooperate with parents who sought to use them purely for their own ends. They may, in turn, adopt the same self-defeating individualism, of course, unless something more rational and loving is offered in its place.

What sort of rational and loving alternative can one suggest? That children should be understood as individuals in preparation. They are, in other words, ultimately their own property, not that of their parents; while the parents have the role not of owners but of educators, those who prepare the child to become the best of herself or himself. The model parent will be one who seeks to discern the child's unique qualities, both good and bad, and help the child form the self-discipline to make the best of his or her resources. This is not a kind of "permissive" project, for the child is not yet a realized individual ready to be in full command; it is, rather, a loving and persistent demand that children become responsible for themselves, their choices, their relationships and community, their work, their world. Parents who understand that the child is not obligated to them to be exactly what they want will be better parents. Children who understand that they cannot evade their responsibilities either by habitually obeying or by habitually reacting against their parents are more likely to become stable, creative, and faithful adults.

Parenting is thus a gift to the child of the child's self; it is the passing on of gifts which the parents received from their own parents and from all the others who contributed to their being who they are. It is more like the work of the educator than any other model—not the educator as a communicator of a single specialized kind of information, but the educator as one who cooperates with the pupil as a kind of critic and guide in the shaping of the educated person. This must of necessity be a somewhat disinterested task. The parent who wants only an athlete for a child will be an incompetent parent to a painter. The parent who wants a substitute for adult companionship from the child, making the child a quasi spouse, will confuse the child into thinking that adulthood is a kind of mannerism and so make true adulthood, which is an inner certainty, the more difficult to identify or to achieve. Above all, the parent or other senior family member who uses the trust which that position bestows in order to make the child his or her lover thereby makes demands on the child totally inconsistent with the disinterested love of one who seeks only the other's good.

While in the familial society of antiquity it was the violation of the patriarch's status which characterized incest, in our own, individual society it is the violation of the child's individuality. The inequality between adult and child (and, to a lesser degree, between older and younger child) means that, in a sexual relationship, the needs of the child will be subordinated to the needs of the adult. What the child loses in the process is, above all, the preparatory space and time when responsible adults encourage and assist children to know themselves before assuming full adult obligations. This, in turn, renders the child's growth into real adulthood extremely difficult, creating an alienation not only from the available adult models, but from the child's very self. Adulthood comes to seem a rejection of the past instead of something that grows out of the experience of childhood.

In addition, incest also carries with it, in our culture, a strong purity taboo, often used by the perpetrator of incest to frighten the child into silence. While Christians do not make this the basis for their own objection to incest, we must recognize that some part of the harm done to the child in such cases arises not from the sexual act itself, but from the revulsion with which the society at large greets it—a revulsion which almost inevitably spills over onto the child and encourages the child in self-loathing. Christians have a responsibility to reduce their own inner involvement in this kind of purity response, so that they can deal more constructively with individuals who have experienced incest and also can, one hopes, better instruct society at large. The hiding away of this topic or its discussion only in hushed tones and ambiguous language can only work harm, not good.

Sexual abuse of children, in the context of modern society, is a kind of generalized incest. For the child, every older person is to some extent a parent. The child's growth into individual adulthood is promoted if the child has a variety of adult models and so does not identify adulthood with the characteristics of a single person. If, on the other hand, the child encounters adults as people whose only interest is to take advantage of the child for their own satisfaction, the model of adulthood that emerges is disastrous. Most abusers of children, it is said, are adult heterosexual males, frequently friends or relatives of the child's family. In their case, the disadvantage the young girl experiences may be compounded by an unexpressed wish on the man's part that all women would remain children. In any case, all such abuse contains in it the implied desire that the sexual object not grow up. Thus, it is akin to incest in the harm it does to children.

Sexually, the child must be considered his or her own property. As the child grows old enough to begin wanting to make active exploration of sexuality, the parent or other adult guide will contribute most effectively by teaching the child frankly about the realities of sex, including its dangers, and by holding the child to the necessity of making clear and responsible decisions. A stonewalling technique of refusing to discuss the issue or of presenting all discussion in the form of prohibitions denies the child's developing responsibility and status as an adult-in-becoming. As a result, it encourages either repression and much future sexual misery on the part of the quieter, more obedient child or rebellious irresponsibility on the part of the more energetic and active one. Most children will probably do well to pass through a period of experimentation, though they should not be pushed into it against their wills. They should be shown how to do this as safely as possible. Certainly, no child—and probably few teenagers—is prepared to enter upon a true marriage of equal adults such as the gospel calls for.

Even among young adults, the first choice of a sexual partner is not likely to be the best, and their initial picture of themselves in a serious sexual relationship is not likely to be fully formed. If marriage is treated in the individual society simply as license to have sex, we can be quite sure that many will choose marriage partners for the most inadequate of reasons and with poor judgment. If the decision is not merely one about first sexual experience but about life partners, it will be easier for people to make it in a realistic way. Christian thinkers as diverse as Margaret Mead and Archbishop Fisher suggested some decades ago that the church should not rush to make the unions of the young permanent; but we have yet to honor the importance of their suggestions by giving them due discussion.

Finally, with regard to sexual property, it is necessary to speak in our era about the value of physical health as the property of each individual and about one's obligation not to deprive another of it. Although Leviticus probably refers to gonorrhea, the author seems not to have understood that it was a communicable disease. In our own century, we have passed from a time when sexually transmitted diseases were a major threat to life and health to a time when antibiotics could combat most of them and back to a time when, first with herpes and then with AIDS, they have once again moved beyond our ability to cure. Knowingly to endanger another person with such a disease is clearly a transgression of that person's property, in the sense in which I am here using the term, and is prohibited by the New Testament's sexual ethic.

Equality of Women and Men

Both Jesus and Paul laid it down as a principle that women and men are basically equal in marriage. Although Paul, in the circumstances of his own times, did not find it necessary or appropriate to carry that principle into practice in all areas of married life, the church today, with the shift from familial to individual society, no longer has any reason to delay in this process. Indeed, society has led the way in this matter, and it is entirely consistent with New Testament practice for the church to accept the emerging marital customs of the modern West as the basis for its own usage. This is not to suggest that the situation has stabilized, however, or that the acceptance of equality will be easy, either for men or for women.

What is called for is something more than the revision of household rules and the alternation of household roles. It involves new understandings of manliness and womanliness that can come about only with some pain and anxiety as well as some sense of liberation and joy. If the husband gives up the image of himself as sole ruler of the household, waited on by wife and children, his whim the family's law, he must also give up its spiritual equivalent—the image of himself as the family's unique sacrificial sustainer, isolated in his moral strength and grandeur. If the wife gives up being the servant of all, with no life of her own except in responding to the needs of others, she must also give up the spiritual vision of herself as the one who gives all for others' good. Men cannot give up their responsibilities as sole wage earner and still claim the benefits of that position by demanding an uneven distribution of labor and services; women cannot claim equality and still reserve the right to be dependent if equality does not yield what they want. None of this will be easy, but the survival of marriage in our society surely depends on it.

Spouses in heterosexual marriages will have much to learn in this process from partners in stable, long-term homosexual relationships. They have long experienced the difficulties of maintaining enduring relationships in a society which is even less supportive of them than of heterosexual couples; and they have had to do it without socially prescribed divisions of roles and labor. If there are useful models to be had, they will probably be found among them. On a deeper level, the re-understanding of womanliness and manliness in our changed circumstances will make headway only if the conversation leading toward it includes both heterosexuals and homosexuals. One interesting feature of recent times is the importance of serious, nonsexual friendships between men and women where the man involved is homosexual; perhaps the absence of a sexual factor facilitates this. If heterosexual men were more open to friendships with women, they might find, for the same reason, that they formed them most readily and deeply with lesbian women. While heterosexual men and women begin with the greater attraction toward each other, it does not always lead to real personal knowledge or respect. In a time when the old definitions are no longer serviceable, we shall need the variety of perspective that male and female, homosexual and heterosexual, can offer on one another in order to reach new models of the properties of either sex.

Marriage as Union of Flesh

When the author of Genesis 2 described marriage as making man and woman "one flesh," he was describing their bond as equivalent in power and importance to that of the natal family. Jesus used the phrase as the foundation of his prohibition of divorce. Paul, however, applied it to every act of sexual intercourse, without thereby suggesting that every such act formed an indissoluble union. The image thus raises a number of questions for us to deal with: When is a marriage a marriage? What can the phrase "one flesh" mean in a nonfamilial society? To what extent is the institution of marriage, as transformed by our very different context, still to be understood as indissoluble? What is the role of the church in relation to marriages? To what degree is nonmarital or casual sex permitted or forbidden?

These are difficult questions, but reference to the property aspects of marriage as discussed above may help illuminate them. To begin with, the nature of the property desired in modern marriage, being largely interior and therefore more complex and more difficult to convey successfully, implies that marriage is in itself more difficult to consummate. In the familial world, the first act of sexual intercourse, with its accompanying proof of the bride's virginity, was sufficient, since it showed that the new wife was indeed the property which the husband's family had intended to acquire. Jesus, at least according to Matthew, acknowledged that some marriages were not real marriages, and I have suggested above that he was probably referring to those where the bride was found not to be a virgin.

Is there any sensible way to apply a measure of this kind to contemporary marriages, where the purity of the family line is no longer the primary desideratum? The virginity of either spouse is no longer a primary issue, for the goods sought in connection with marriage in an individual society are goods which can best be offered only by a mature person and such a person will more often than not have acquired some sexual experience. What is still more difficult, the goods are not simply brought to the marriage, but must be developed within it in the form of the relationship between the spouses. Thus, it is very difficult to specify a date, even in the most successful of marriages, when it became clear that the property transactions involved were indeed in good order. Certainly, it could not be known at once. Once the initial romantic enthusiasm wears thin, it may become apparent that one or both spouses is unable or unwilling to give anything of importance to the other. Clearly, one should not and seldom would enter upon marriage knowing that to be the case; but the transition from romance to the business of marital living will always be a somewhat risky undertaking, if only because the romantic face is but one aspect of the other person and sometimes a misleading one at that.

Paul did not count every act of sexual intercourse as constituting an indissoluble bond of marriage. We should not do so, either. This means that not every external marriage in our own experience constitutes a real marriage in the more interior sense demanded in our society. We must therefore be prepared to consider the possibility that what some divorces—perhaps a large percentage of them—do is not to end an existing marriage but to announce that, despite whatever efforts were made and ceremonies performed, no marriage has in fact taken place. This insistence on the property involved in constituting a marriage may appear crass to some readers. Yet it is precisely analogous to what was assumed by the biblical writers, and I venture to argue that it is a far more realistic approach to the ethical issues. To characterize Christian marriage, as some would do, as an idealistic commitment to eternal loyalty without any regard for what one receives in return is ultimately destructive of the whole institution. It encourages abused spouses, female and male alike, to remain with those who profit from them in various ways and give nothing in return. In the process, not only does the abused person suffer to no end, but the abusive spouse is seldom effectively confronted with any realization of what he or she is doing. A sound marriage is not, of course, a dispassionate business arrangement, but it ought to be based on perception of mutual benefit arising from mutual devotion and affection.

One part of our present difficulty arises from the church's custom of blessing marriages. Marriage, in the milieu of the New Testament, was typically the celebration of a secular contract. Since, under the ancient circumstances, the property aspects of the marriage were readily and efficiently verifiable, there was no appreciable delay in ascertaining that the contract had been fulfilled. Only in the Middle Ages, it seems, did the church begin to take a part in solemnizing the occasion; but it was an intelligible step, since all the necessities of the case could be verified. At present, however, when the great majority of church people are married with church ceremonies, the rites give an impression of definiteness to the marriage which cannot in fact be verified at once and perhaps not for many years to come.

At the present time, the church would perhaps be better advised not to solemnize marriages at the inception of the relationship itself, but to wait a period of some years before adding its blessing. When it does so, it may as easily bless homosexual as heterosexual unions, for the new definition of the goods making up sexual property, which has already come informally to prevail in our society, makes no distinction between the two. Two persons of the same sex cannot engender children and could not therefore have contracted a full-fledged marriage in the familial milieu of the New Testament itself; they are, however, fully capable of giving one another the interior goods demanded by marriage in our time. Even after the blessing of a union, the failure of a marriage and consequent divorce probably cannot be ruled out altogether. The church should, however, discourage it. It can rightly ask its members not to proceed to divorce without having done all that they could do to compromise their differences, and it can also insist on the exercise of a high degree of responsibility in the contracting of a further marriage. For an unblessed union, that is, one that has not progressed to the point of mutual stability that would justify the church's blessing it, the church might reserve judgment.

Since the solution I have suggested blurs the distinction between marriage and nonmarital sexual liaisons—a blurring demanded by the actual nature of marriage in our times—we must also ask whether all sexual activities of however casual a nature and however little personal involvement are to be permitted. Jesus did not speak to the matter, but Paul clearly would have said no. Sexuality, as an essential aspect of the self, cannot be treated as if it were either trivial or peripheral. Every sexual act does constitute some kind of bond with the partner, and that bond must, at the very least, be free of falsehood and violence toward the partner and in some way be compatible with the Christian person's relationship with Christ. Paul reproved men in Corinth who visited prostitutes though they had open to them the options of either celibacy or marriage. He did not, however, have occasion to address the situation of the person for whom neither option existed—the sailor, to create an example, who did not have the gift of celibacy but whose exceedingly mobile occupation also did not permit permanent cohabitation with a wife.

We might also add, in our own age, the examples of the homosexual person, for whom no marital forms are provided in our society, the young person of either sexual orientation for whom marriage would be premature but who does not have the gift of celibacy, the single person of whatever age who has not met the appropriate person to contract marriage with, or the widowed person for whom a new legal marriage would create financial stringency or unnecessary confusions about inheritance. At one extreme, one cannot defend the promiscuous person who desires only personal gratification at whatever expense to others. At the other, two widowed persons who wish to contract a faithful and giving relationship without benefit of legal marriage seem to create a problem of words more than of things. Between these extremes, there lies a large area of difficult individual decisions. People will have to wend their way through such decisions, however, for the gift of celibacy is not given to all and the property demands of modern marriage are such that one cannot, even if one wishes, enter upon it lightly.

Some nonmarital liaisons may in fact prove to be preparatory to marriage in the stricter sense. Others may serve to meet legitimate needs in the absence of genuine alternatives. Still others may be abusive and exploitative. Only the last are to be condemned. Prostitution appears to belong most often in the last of these three categories, though perhaps at times it may belong in the second. I think, for example, of abnormal conditions where there is a vast disproportion of the members of one sex; in such cases, those who have no other access to sexual gratification are not to be condemned for resorting to prostitutes, though I am not willing to encourage them in it. The person who prefers prostitutes, however, to a sexual relationship which would make greater demands on him or her must be asked whether this is not an avoidance of deeper relationships in general and therefore also an effort to treat one's sexuality as peripheral or irrelevant to one's humanity.

The same question must be put to the prostitute, provided that one is such of one's own will. In antiquity many prostitutes were slaves and had no freedom of choice as to the use to which they would be put. Jesus' abolition of purity requirements gave these people renewed access to God which must not be taken away from any legitimate successors they may have. In our own day, this would include at least those street children whose only alternatives are return to an intolerable home situation or starvation. If those prostitutes, however, who are such by choice—whether because they make a good living or because of attachment to another person who is abusing them—should wish to be fully active participants in the church, the church would legitimately urge them to accept some other occupation and, if need be, assist them to do so, so that they may honor themselves as sexual beings under the reign of God.

Sex and the Reign of God

Although we have said a great deal thus far about what the New Testament sexual ethic forbids and not much about what it advocates, that is largely a function of the style in which the Bible speaks about sexual matters. This study has worked throughout with specifically moral texts—that is, texts which define acceptable and, more often, unacceptable behavior. Some might feel it preferable to begin with texts speaking to the nature of sexuality rather than defining its limits. There are several difficulties with that approach, however. One is that such texts are few and far between in Scripture. The Bible takes sex more or less for granted and does not explicitly lay out a theological or philosophical understanding of it. The few pertinent verses in Genesis 1 and 2, for example, are brief and allusive in their language, which leaves them open to a variety of speculative interpretations. In order to form a well-founded understanding of a viewpoint alien to our own, we have had to find and study a corpus of materials sufficiently rich that we can test our speculations and see where they do or do not account for all the details. This quality, which is lacking in the theological materials on sex, is abundantly present in the moral ones.

The resulting negative bias, however, is misleading insofar as it suggests that the New Testament writers were negative toward sexuality as such. The results of the present study confirm that that was by no means the case. We have seen that Jesus, for example, attacked the institutions of the family rather than sexuality itself and that Paul specifically acknowledged the satisfaction of sexual desire as a valid reason for marriage. In order to locate the New Testament's positive ethic of sexuality, however, one must refocus from the boundary lines marked out by negative pronouncements to the area that they enclose and give shape to. The New Testament's positive account of sex is that it is an integral part of the human person, particularly as joining us to one another, and therefore has a right to be included in the spiritual transformation which follows upon our hearing of the gospel.

The gospel, as it permeates every aspect of life, will and must permeate sexuality as well. If Christian teaching appears to flinch from sex as something dirty or suspect, it is falsely Christian. This does not mean that sexuality, for the Christian, is to be saturated in a kind of pietism, that the bedroom should become a chapel, or that sex should be submerged in prayer. It means rather that sexuality, like every other important aspect of human life, should be clearly related to the center and goal of that life, the reign of God. The life of the world to come, characterized by a joyful reverence and love, is already the standard by which our growth in faith and hope is measured in this life. Sex, therefore, is to be received with delight and thankfulness. It is a gift of God in creation which also reflects for us the joy of God's self-giving in grace and the perfect openness of true human life in the age to come.

If the reign of God is central, to be sure, other things can no longer make that claim. Sex, in other words, is *not* central—nor is knowledge, wisdom, money, power, success, security, one's job or family or marriage, even oneself. None of these things is wrong, in and of itself. They become wrong only at the moment when they become ultimate goals for us. As long as we can name something which is, for us, a condition of God's reign—as long as we find that we must say, "I am ready for God's reign only if it includes this or excludes that"—then we are still placing idols at the center and goal of life alongside God. Yet, insofar as we are ready to hand back whatever God asks of us, then it becomes, to that degree, innocent for us.

Sex is one of the rich blessings of creation, to be received with delight and thanksgiving. At the point when one's actions no longer express that truth, they become wrong. If I grab something for myself that belongs rightfully to another, whether through direct violence or through manipulation or any other means, I acknowledge what I have grabbed as a good, but I no longer confess it as a part of the whole richness of creation—a richness which includes all goods, including myself and the neighbor whom I have robbed as well. If I make satisfaction of sexual desire the overarching goal of my life, I have put the part in place of the whole and thereby lost perspective on its real value. These considerations are what make libertinism wrong, for they condemn any pursuit of sexual pleasure which is based on megalomania and idolatry. What is less commonly observed is that they also make prudery, legalism, and addiction to respectability wrong. For just as sex is not the final goal of the creation, neither is works-righteousness, the fulfillment of the law, or the sense of comfort that comes from having fulfilled the expectations of my neighbors. The world begins in God's free act of creation and concludes in God's free act of grace—or rather in the rejoicing to which it gives rise. Prudery, narrowness, self-confident respectability will be no preparation for the life of the age of rejoicing. It is not surprising that Jesus alienated those who practiced such "virtues."

This is not to suggest that the path to the age to come is all one of ease and pleasure. Its difficulties, however, are not self-induced. We do not have to make the Christian life difficult with the constant recitation and amplification of rules, for there are real challenges, arising both from our own selfish idolatry and also from our times. As Paul stressed the need for a certain kind of preparedness in the face of what he believed would be an imminent eschaton, we, too, must undertake to be prepared in terms of the needs of our own time. As marriage and family could not be a final goal for the first-century Christian, sexuality and self cannot be today. The Christian will find it very difficult to live in an intimate relation with one who does not understand or accept the kind of demands which God's calling makes. While it is not impossible to live in such a relationship with a nonbeliever, the partner must at least be one who respects commitments that may seem unworldly and which do not place self or sexual partner first. The Christian must also retain a certain freedom to respond to God's call loyally in critical times. While we cannot make any confident predictions about the timing of the eschaton, we live in times when great demands are being made of us in relation to justice, peace, and the survival of the world. If relations of dependency prevent us from responding to those demands, we shall have something to answer for.

Finally, the gospel, the news of God's grace in Jesus and the inbreaking of God's reign, has not yet finished transforming us—and will not this side of the grave. If we look at the great exemplars of its work, in the New Testament and afterward, from Jesus to Martin Luther King, Jr., we shall find that it does not normally act to make us more respectable—to produce conventional, predictable husbands and wives. devoted to nothing more than one another's happiness. For that matter, Jesus himself excepted, the gospel does not even work to produce perfect people. The gospel works rather to express the power of God's love, which rejects our rejections and breaches our best defenses and draws us out of our fortifications toward a goal that we can as yet barely imagine. The measure of a sexuality that accords with the New Testament is simply this: the degree to which it rejoices in the whole creation, in what is given to others as well as to each of us, while enabling us always to leave the final word to God, who is the Beginning and End of all things.

Abbreviations

Antiquities	Josephus, *Antiquities of the Jews*
ATR	*Anglican Theological Review*
CHab	Qumran *Commentary on Habakkuk* (1QpHab)
CNah	Qumran *Commentary on Nahum* (4QpNah)
CPs37	Qumran *Commentary on Psalm 37* (4QpPs37)
CR	Qumran *Community Rule* (1QS)
DR	Qumran *Damascus Rule*
ET	English translation(s)
H	Qumran *Hymns* (1QH)
ICC	International Critical Commentary
JBL	*Journal of Biblical Literature*
JSNTSup	Journal for the Study of the New Testament—Supplement Series
JSOTSup	Journal for the Study of the Old Testament—Supplement Series
LXX	Septuagint (Old Greek version of the Jewish Scriptures)
MA	Qumran *Messianic Anthology* (4QTest)
MR	Qumran *Messianic Rule* (1QSa)
MT	Massoretic Text (standard Hebrew/Aramaic version of the Jewish Scriptures)
NTS	*New Testament Studies*
RSV	Revised Standard Version
SBL	Society of Biblical Literature
TDNT	*Theological Dictionary of the New Testament*
VC	*Vigiliae Christianae*
WR	Qumran *War Rule* (1QM)

Documents associated with Qumran are cited in accordance with the titles given them in Geza Vermes's English translation; the conventional scholarly sigla (for example, 1QpHab) are given in parentheses.

Bibliography

Alter, Robert. "Sodom as Nexus: The Web of Design in Biblical Narrative." *Tikkun* 1/1 (1986): 30–38.

Ariès, Philippe. "St. Paul and the Flesh." In *Western Sexuality,* edited by Philippe Ariès and André Béjin and translated by Anthony Forster, 36–39. Oxford: Basil Blackwell & Mott, 1985.

Balch, David L. "1 Cor. 7:32–35 and Stoic Debates about Marriage, Anxiety, and Distraction." *JBL* 102 (1983): 428–39.

———. *Let Wives Be Submissive: The Domestic Code in 1 Peter.* SBL Monograph Series 26. Chico, Calif.: Scholars Press, 1981.

Barrett, C. K. *The Second Epistle to the Corinthians.* New York: Harper & Row, 1973.

Best, Ernest. "Mark iii. 20, 21, 31–35." *NTS* 22 (1976): 309–19.

Booth, Roger P. *Jesus and the Laws of Purity: Tradition History and Legal History in Mark 7.* JSNTSup 13. Sheffield: JSOT Press, 1986.

Boswell, John. *Christianity, Social Tolerance, and Homosexuality: Gay People in Western Europe from the Beginning of the Christian Era to the Fourteenth Century.* Chicago: University of Chicago Press, 1980.

Brooten, Bernadette. "Konnten Frauen im alten Judentum die Scheidung betreiben? Uberlegungen zu Mk 10,11–12 und 1 Kor 7,10–11." *Evangelische Theologie* 42 (1982): 65–80.

———. *Women Leaders in the Ancient Synagogue: Inscriptional Evidence and Background Issues.* Chico, Calif.: Scholars Press, 1982.

Brown, Peter. "Late Antiquity." In *From Pagan Rome to Byzantium,* edited by Paul Veyne and translated by Arthur Goldhammer. (Vol. 1 of *A History of Private Life,* edited by Phillippe Ariès and Georges Duby), 235–311. Cambridge: Harvard University Press, Belknap Press, 1987.

Buckley, Jorunn Jacobson. "A Cult-Mystery in *The Gospel of Philip.*" *JBL* 99 (1980): 569–81.

Burkert, Walter. *Greek Religion.* Translated by John Raffan. Cambridge: Harvard University Press, 1985.

Catchpole, David R. "Paul, James, and the Apostolic Decree." *NTS* 23 (1976–77): 428–44.

Charlesworth, James H., ed. *The Old Testament Pseudepigrapha*. 2 vols. New York: Doubleday & Co., 1983–85.

Conzelmann, Hans. *1 Corinthians: A Commentary on the First Epistle to the Corinthians*. Translated by James W. Leitch. Hermeneia. Philadelphia: Fortress Press, 1975.

Countryman, L. William. "The AIDS Crisis: Theological and Ethical Reflections." *ATR* 69 (1987): 125–34.

———. *Biblical Authority or Biblical Tyranny? Scripture and the Christian Pilgrimage*. Philadelphia: Fortress Press, 1981.

———. "Christian Equality and the Early Catholic Episcopate." *ATR* 63 (1981): 115–38.

———. *The Mystical Way in the Fourth Gospel: Crossing Over into God*. Philadelphia: Fortress Press, 1987.

———. *The Rich Christian in the Church of the Early Empire: Contradictions and Accommodations*. Lewiston, N.Y.: Edwin Mellen Press, 1980.

———. "Tertullian and the Regula Fidei." *Second Century* 2 (1982): 208–27.

Cumont, Franz. *The Oriental Religions in Roman Paganism*. 1911, Reprint. New York: Dover Publications, 1956.

Douglas, Mary. *Purity and Danger: An Analysis of Concepts of Pollution and Taboo*. London: Routledge & Kegan Paul, 1966.

Driver, S. R. *A Critical and Exegetical Commentary on Deuteronomy*. 3d ed. ICC. Edinburgh: T. & T. Clark, 1902.

Elliott, John H. *A Home for the Homeless: A Sociological Exegesis of 1 Peter, Its Situation and Strategy*. Philadelphia: Fortress Press, 1981.

Enslin, Morton Scott. *The Ethics of Paul*. Nashville and New York: Abingdon Press, 1957.

Forkman, Göran. *The Limits of Religious Community: Expulsion from the Religious Community within the Qumran Sect, within Rabbinic Judaism, and within Primitive Christianity*. Lund, Swed.: C. W. K. Gleerup, 1972.

Gokhale, Jayashree B. "Castaways of Caste." *Natural History* (October 1986): 33–37.

Goodenough, Erwin R. *An Introduction to Philo Judaeus*. Oxford: Basil Blackwell & Mott, 1962.

Grant, Frederick C. "The Impracticability of the Gospel Ethics." In *Aux sources de la tradition chrétienne: Mélanges offerts à M. Maurice Goguel*, 86–94. Neuchatel: Delachaux et Niestlé Spes, 1950.

Haenchen, Ernst. *The Acts of the Apostles: A Commentary*. Translated by Bernard Noble et al. Philadelphia: Westminster Press, 1971.

Hays, Richard B. "Relations Natural and Unnatural: A Response to John Boswell's Exegesis of Romans 1." *Journal of Religious Ethics* 14 (1986): 184–215.

Hengel, Martin. *Judaism and Hellenism: Studies in Their Encounter in Palestine during the Early Hellenistic Period*. Translated by John Bowden. 2 vols. Philadelphia: Fortress Press, 1974.

Horner, Tom. *Eros in Greece: A Sexual Inquiry.* New York: Aegean Books, 1978.

Houlden, J. L. *Ethics and the New Testament.* New York and Oxford: Oxford University Press, 1977.

Johnson, Luke T. "The Use of Leviticus 19 in the Letter of James." *JBL* 101 (1982): 391–401.

Licht, Hans. *Sexual Life in Ancient Greece.* Translated by J. H. Freese. London: Routledge & Kegan Paul, 1932.

Lohse, Eduard, ed. *Die Texte aus Qumran, hebräisch und deutsch.* Munich: Kosel, 1964.

Maier, Johann. *The Temple Scroll: An Introduction, Translation and Commentary.* Translated by Richard T. White. JSOTSup 34. Sheffield: JSOT Press, 1985.

Malherbe, Abraham J. "Paul: Hellenistic Philosopher or Christian Pastor?" *ATR* 68 (1986): 3–13.

Malina, Bruce J. *The New Testament World: Insights from Cultural Anthropology.* Atlanta: John Knox Press, 1981.

McCombie, F. "Jesus and the Leaven of Salvation." *New Blackfriars* 59 (1978): 450–62.

Meeks, Wayne A. *The Moral World of the First Christians.* Philadelphia: Westminster Press, 1986.

————. "Understanding Early Christian Ethics." *JBL* 105 (1986): 3–11.

Metzger, Bruce M. *A Textual Commentary on the Greek New Testament.* London: United Bible Societies, 1971.

Moule, H. C. G. *The Epistles to the Colossians and to Philemon.* Cambridge: Cambridge University Press, 1902.

Murphy-O'Connor, Jerome. "The Divorced Woman in 1 Cor. 7:10–11." *JBL* 100 (1981): 601–6.

Neusner, Jacob. "First Cleanse the Inside." *NTS* 22 (1975–76): 486–95.

————. *From Politics to Piety: The Emergence of Pharisaic Judaism.* Englewood Cliffs, N.J.: Prentice-Hall, 1973.

————. *A History of the Mishnaic Law of Purities.* Part 22, *The Mishnaic System of Uncleanness: Its Context and History.* Leiden, Neth.: E. J. Brill, 1977.

————. *The Idea of Purity in Ancient Judaism.* Leiden, Neth.: E. J. Brill, 1973.

Newton, Michael. *The Concept of Purity at Qumran and in the Letters of Paul.* Cambridge: Cambridge University Press, 1985.

Neyrey, Jerome H. "Body Language in 1 Corinthians: The Use of Anthropological Models for Understanding Paul and His Opponents." *Semeia* 35 (1986): 129–70.

————. "Idea of Purity in Mark's Gospel." *Semeia* 35 (1986): 91–128.

Noth, Martin. *Leviticus: A Commentary.* Translated by J. E. Anderson. The Old Testament Library. London: SCM Press, 1965.

Pedersen, Johs. *Israel: Its Life and Culture.* 4 vols. bound as 2. London: Geoffrey Cumberlege; Copenhagen: Branner og Korch, 1926–40.

Petersen, William L. "Can ΑΡΣΕΝΟΚΟΙΤΑΙ Be Translated by 'Homosexuals'? (1 Cor. 6.9; 1 Tim. 1:10)." *VC* 40 (1986): 187–91.

Phipps, W. E. "Is Paul's Attitude Towards Sexual Relations Contained in 1 Cor. 7.1?" *NTS* 28 (1982): 125–31.

Pomeroy, Sarah B. *Goddesses, Whores, Wives, and Slaves: Women in Classical Antiquity.* New York: Schocken Books, 1975.

Riches, John. *Jesus and the Transformation of Judaism.* London: Darton, Longman & Todd, 1980.

Rist, J. M. *Stoic Philosophy.* Cambridge: Cambridge University Press, 1969.

Rivkin, Ellis. *A Hidden Revolution.* Nashville: Abingdon Press, 1978.

Robinson, John A. T. *The Body: A Study in Pauline Theology.* Studies in Biblical Theology 5. London: SCM Press, 1952.

Ropes, James Hardy. *The Text of Acts.* Vol. 3 of *The Beginnings of Christianity,* part 1, *The Acts of the Apostles.* Edited by F. J. Foakes Jackson and Kirsopp Lake. Reprint edition. Grand Rapids: Baker Book House, 1979.

Sanday, William, and Arthur C. Headlam. *A Critical and Exegetical Commentary on the Epistle to the Romans.* 5th ed. ICC. Edinburgh: T. & T. Clark, 1902.

Sanders, E. P. *Paul and Palestinian Judaism: A Comparison of Patterns of Religion.* Philadelphia: Fortress Press, 1977.

―――. *Paul, the Law, and the Jewish People.* Philadelphia: Fortress Press, 1983.

Schnackenburg, Rudolf. *The Moral Teaching of the New Testament.* Translated by J. Holland-Smith and W. J. O'Hara. Freiburg: Herder & Herder, 1965.

Schrage, Wolfgang. *The Ethics of the New Testament.* Translated by David E. Green. Philadelphia: Fortress Press, 1988.

Schüssler Fiorenza, Elisabeth. *The Book of Revelation: Justice and Judgment.* Philadelphia: Fortress Press, 1985.

―――. *In Memory of Her: A Feminist Theological Reconstruction of Christian Origins.* New York: Crossroad, 1985.

Schweizer, Eduard. *The Letter to the Colossians: A Commentary.* Translated by Andrew Chester. Minneapolis: Augsburg Publishing House, 1982.

Scroggs, Robin. *The New Testament and Homosexuality: Contextual Background for Contemporary Debate.* Philadelphia: Fortress Press, 1983.

Segal, Alan F. *Rebecca's Children: Judaism and Christianity in the Roman World.* Cambridge: Harvard University Press, 1986.

Selvidge, Marla J. "Mark 5:25–34 and Leviticus 15:19–20." *JBL* 103 (1984): 619–23.

Shipps, Jan. *Mormonism: The Story of a New Religious Tradition.* Urbana: University of Illinois Press, 1985.

Sinclair, Scott Gambrill. "The Christologies of Paul's Undisputed Epistles and the Christology of Paul." Ph.D. diss., Graduate Theological Union, 1986.

Snyder, Graydon F. *Ante Pacem: Archaeological Evidence of Church Life Before Constantine.* Macon, Ga.: Mercer University Press, 1985.

Theissen, Gerd. *Sociology of Early Palestinian Christianity.* Translated by John Bowden. Philadelphia: Fortress Press, 1978.

Trible, Phyllis. *Texts of Terror: Literary-Feminist Readings of Biblical Narratives.* Philadelphia: Fortress Press, 1984.

Verhey, Allen. *The Great Reversal: Ethics and the New Testament.* Grand Rapids: Wm. B. Eerdmans, 1984.

Vermes, Geza. *The Dead Sea Scrolls in English.* Reprint with revisions. Harmondsworth, Eng.: Penguin Books, 1968.

_____. *The Dead Sea Scrolls: Qumran in Perspective.* With Pamela Vermes. Cleveland: William Collins & Co., 1978.

Veyne, Paul, ed. *A History of Private Life.* Vol. 1, *From Pagan Rome to Byzantium.* Translated by Arthur Goldhammer. Cambridge: Harvard University Press, Belknap Press, 1987.

_____. "Homosexuality in Ancient Rome." In *Western Sexuality,* edited by Philippe Ariès and André Béjin and translated by Anthony Forster, 36–39. Oxford: Basil Blackwell & Mott, 1985.

Via, Dan O., Jr. *The Ethics of Mark's Gospel—In the Middle of Time.* Philadelphia: Fortress Press, 1985.

Weil, Simone. *Waiting for God.* Translated by Emma Craufurd. New York: G. P. Putnam's Sons, 1951.

Wenham, Gordon J. *The Book of Leviticus.* New International Commentary on the Old Testament. Grand Rapids: Wm. B. Eerdmans, 1979.

Whittaker, Molly. *Jews and Christians: Graeco-Roman Views.* Cambridge: Cambridge University Press, 1984.

Witherington, Ben. "The Anti-Feminist Tendencies of the 'Western' Text in Acts." *JBL* 103 (1984): 82–84.

Winston, David. *The Wisdom of Solomon.* Anchor Bible 43. New York: Doubleday & Co., 1979.

Wright, David F. "Homosexuals or Prostitutes? The Meaning of ΑΡΣΕΝΟΚΟΙΤΑΙ (1 Cor. 6:9, 1 Tim. 1:10)." *VC* 38 (1984): 124–53.

Yarbrough, O. Larry. *Not Like the Gentiles: Marriage Rules in the Letters of Paul.* SBL Dissertation Series 80. Atlanta: Scholars Press, 1985.

Zaas, Peter S. "As I Teach Everywhere, in Every Church: A Study of the Communication of Morals in Paul." Ph.D. diss., University of Chicago, 1982.

_____. "Cast Out the Evil Man from Your Midst." *JBL* 103 (1984): 259–61.

_____. "Catalogue and Context: The Vice-Lists of 1 Corinthians 5 and 6." *NTS,* forthcoming.

Index of Passages

275

Index of Subjects

Page references to definitions or key explanations of terms appear in **boldface** type.

Index of Modern Authors